Revolutionizing Romance

Revolutionizing Romance

Interracial Couples in Contemporary Cuba

NADINE T. FERNANDEZ

RUTGERS UNIVERSITY PRESS

NEW BRUNSWICK, NEW JERSEY, AND LONDON

LIBRARY OF CONGRESS CATALOGING-IN-PUBLICATION DATA

Fernandez, Nadine T., 1964–
    Revolutionizing romance : interracial couples in contemporary Cuba /
Nadine T. Fernandez.
        p. cm.
    Includes bibliographical references and index.
    ISBN 978–0–8135–4722–0 (hardcover : alk. paper) — ISBN 978–0–8135–4723–7
(pbk. : alk. paper)
    1. Interracial dating—Cuba.   2. Interracial marriage—Cuba.   3. Racially mixed
people—Cuba.   4. Cuba—Race relations.   I. Title.
    HQ1031.F47 2010
    306.84'6097291—dc22   2009021736

A British Cataloging-in-Publication record for this book is available from the
British Library.

Lyrics to "Suave, suave" reprinted by permission of the author, Gerardo Alfonso.

Visit our Web site: http://rutgerspress.rutgers.edu

Manufactured in the United States of America

To Jean Ghiggeri Fernandez and Olegario Fernández García

CONTENTS

ACKNOWLEDGMENTS

In the process of writing this book I have benefited from the support of numerous individuals and institutions. I begin with profound thanks to the people who participated in and facilitated my research in Cuba. I am grateful to the young Cubans who shared their stories and homes with me, and the professors and officials at the institutions who helped to pave the way for this research. I especially wish to thank Guillermo Arias Beaton and other members of the Psychology Faculty at the University of Havana; and Pablo Rodríguez Ruiz, Lourdes Serrano, and colleagues at the Instituto de Antropología for all of their support, help, and friendship. Gisela Arandia, Tomás Fernández Robaina at the José Martí National Library, and María Isabel Domínguez and co-workers at the Centro de Investigaciones Psicologicas y Sociologicas all have been inspirational researchers to me. My Cuban friends, neighbors, and colleagues made me feel welcomed and comfortable when I was so far from home and showed a generosity and hospitality that would have been remarkable under normal circumstances, but was truly extraordinary given the conditions of the special period in the 1990s. Their graciousness and warmth will stay with me always.

For their supportive encouragement over the years I thank Jean Lave, Helen Safa, Alejandro de la Fuente, and Sheryl Lutjens; my fellow Cubanologos, Jill Hamberg, Robin Moore, Paul Ryer, Matthew Hill, and Mona Rosendahl; and my dear friends Shawn Parkhurst, Melissa Cefkin, Mazyar Lotfalian, Heinrich Schwarz, and Rich Yeselson. My colleagues at Florida International University encouraged me through earlier drafts of portions of this book. I am also deeply grateful to Alejandro de la Fuente and Faye V. Harrison, whose careful readings of the manuscript provided insightful feedback and suggestions for improvements, which

I have done my best to incorporate. Laura Helper-Ferris was immeasurably helpful with her keen editorial eye and her sharp vision of the big picture. Adi Hovav and others at Rutgers University Press ensured that the publishing process went smoothly.

The New York State/United University Professions Dr. Nuala McGann Drescher Leave Program and State University of New York/ Empire State College generously afforded me time and support to complete this project. While on leave, my family in Denmark provided me with an orchid-filled room in which to write; warm, sustaining meals; and the most priceless gift for a mother—love-filled child care. My steadfast and unflappable husband, Carsten, carried me through many a rough patch. Our lovely daughters, Eva and Lucia, kept me conscious of the preciousness of the everyday. Finally, this book is dedicated with love to my parents, in appreciation of all they have done for me and with deep pride in all they have accomplished in their lives.

While I have been fortunate to benefit from the involvement of all of the aforementioned people, I take sole responsibility for the final product presented here.

Revolutionizing Romance

Introduction

As a teenager, Tamara, a blue-eyed, blond white Cuban woman, dated a classmate, Alberto, a dark-skinned black man. Near the cathedral in Old Havana, a middle-aged white couple looked at the young interracial couple in horror and commented quite loudly, "Look at that blond with light eyes, and she's with a black!" Recounting the story to me, Tamara said, "That really shook me. It was the first time we were out together—like presenting our relationship to society—and that comment really had an impact on me. I felt ashamed because I thought of what Alberto must have felt. I never asked him about that insulting incident. We never talked about it."

Olga, a dark-skinned mulata, and José Miguel, a white man, both in their mid-twenties, had been together several years when I interviewed them. José Miguel said, "It's very uncomfortable when many well-educated people ask disbelievingly if we are a couple. . . . Once I got so insulted, I turned to this [white] man, and pointing to a black woman in the street, I asked him, 'Is that your girlfriend? No? I knew that because you don't date blacks.'"

Centuries earlier, Juan Millián fell in love and married on the island of Fernandina, as Cuba was first called. Millián was a Spanish conquistador who arrived with Diego Velázquez (1465–1524) in 1510 and added Cuba to the growing list of Spanish possessions in the new world.[1] The woman Millián married and later brought back to Spain was an indigenous Taíno. Their marriage was one of the first interracial couplings documented in Cuba (Pichardo 1992). Legally sanctioned or illicit, some form of interracial coupling, also referred to as miscegenation or *mestizaje* (race mixing), has been taking place in Cuba ever since. Through brutality and disease, the Spanish exterminated most of Cuba's indigenous population within the first fifty years of contact.[2] Subsequently, the racial mixing on the island included enslaved Africans, who first arrived in Cuba in 1523; Chinese indentured laborers, who started arriving around 1848;[3] and indigenous populations from the Yucatan, who came to Cuba in 1855 and 1870 (Moreno Fraginals 1978). Haitians and West Indians came to Cuba throughout the republic (1902–1958), largely to work in sugarcane production on the eastern end of the island. These groups mixed with each other and with white Europeans, predominantly Spaniards (whose immigration to Cuba continued well into the twentieth century), but also French (fleeing the Haitian revolution), Irish laborers (who came in the 1830s and 1840s),[4] and, after 1959, Russians and other citizens of the socialist bloc countries.

Interracial couples, indeed, have populated all periods of Cuban history—the colony, the republic, and the socialist state. They have been legally married, lived in loving, long-term, common-law unions, and endured forced concubinage. Interracial couplings have been violent rapes and fleeting amorous trysts. They have taken place between white men and women of color, and between white women and men of color—coming from all ranges and combinations of the class hierarchy, though some combinations of race, class, and gender have been more common and condoned than others. To walk in Havana today is to witness the centuries of racial mixing, to see an infinite array of combinations of skin color, hair texture, and facial features. The mixing has been as much cultural as it has been physical. Radios blare Cuban music infused with African and Spanish rhythms. Menus boast cuisine simmering with spices from Cuba's long, cosmopolitan history. The devout worship at altars dedicated to the Virgin of Charity (La Virgen de la Caridad del Cobre), who represents both the Catholic mother of Jesus and the Yoruba deity of love, Ochún. Racial mixing through interracial couplings and cultural mestizaje have been perhaps the most enduring features of the Cuban cultural and racial reality since Columbus first landed on the island 1492. Scholars (Benítez-Rojo 1992; Foner 1977; Ortiz 1993a) have long proclaimed mestizaje, both physical and cultural, as the essence of the nation. Today, the revolutionary government promotes socialist equality and national unity, in part, as an extension of the nation's deep tradition of mestizaje.

With racial mixing so embedded in Cuban history and national identity, it is easy to take interracial couples as unremarkable and commonplace. They are, indeed, rather common, particularly in cosmopolitan Havana. Given Cuba's long genealogy of mestizaje, the reactions Tamara, Alberto, Olga, and José Miguel receive on the street at first seem counterintuitive. Why are contemporary interracial couples sometimes the targets of racist commentary and social disapproval if the nation has such a long tradition of mestizaje bolstered by decades of socialist equality? This is the central conundrum that motivates this book.

Whether they encounter objections to their relationships at home or in public, many interracial couples quickly understand that their relationships are somehow transgressive. Their presence rubs against the grain of society in some fundamental way—even in a society supposedly based on racial mixture, even after centuries of racial mixing, even in a modern socialist state. Although mixing is central to national identity, racial discrimination continues, and race is a key feature in Cuban culture, history, and daily interactions. This book explores the continuing significance of race through the everyday lives of young interracial couples. It provides an on-the-ground investigation of both the shifting practices and contested ideologies of mestizaje. I argue that the meanings of interracial couples, like the meanings of race, have not remained the same over the centuries or over the course of the Cuban revolution. The meanings of interracial couples have a history.

In colonial Cuba, the state encouraged certain types of interracial couplings as the engines of mestizaje that would propel the nation to modernity/whiteness. For many nineteenth-century intellectuals and leaders, physically whitening the population was essential to the future progress of the nation. From the colonial period we see interracial unions not just as an inevitable result of the scarcity of white women, but also as the linchpin of nation-building strategies—if properly managed. From the colonial to the republican period, white elites remained doubtful of the virtues of physical racial mixing and fearful of particular patterns of interracial couplings. Mestizaje, like race, held an ambivalent place in Cuba's national identity. Nonetheless, the centrality of ideas of physical and cultural mestizaje sets the stage for understanding interracial unions and race relations in contemporary Cuba.

The revolution's position on race has been complex and contradictory. When Fidel Castro's revolutionary government came to power in 1959, it dismantled many structures of institutionalized racism and racial segregation and implemented transformative social programs that led to a significant increase in racial integration in neighborhoods, schools, and workplaces. However, while the revolution's social and economic programs benefited the country's poorest and largely nonwhite citizens, the government did not specifically target the centuries-old racial inequalities on the island. In fact, despite the structural changes, rigid adherence to Marxist ideology and a dire need for national unity in the face of U.S. hostility caused the revolutionary government to put racial issues on the back burner. The rectification campaign in 1986 recognized that blacks, women, and youth were not equally represented in Cuban leadership and called for affirmative action efforts to increase their participation.[5] However, many white Cubans objected to these measures, and sometimes the efforts backfired (or were deliberately undermined) as the individuals placed in these leadership positions were sometimes not the best qualified for the job—thus affirming and naturalizing blacks' position in the racial hierarchy. In general, the revolution embraced a color-blind approach to race relations, employing class as the idiom of inequalities. In the early years of the revolution, white anxiety over racial integration focused on real and imagined interracial unions. Interracial couples carried a political significance that would be absent from later generations.

Tamara's, Alberto's, Olga's, and José Miguel's experiences attest to the fact that, even now, interracial couples can create social unease. These young couples, products of revolutionary Cuba, met in their racially integrated schools, were attracted to each other, and started dating. Nothing could have been more "natural" or ordinary in their eyes. The structural changes and egalitarian ideologies of the socialist revolution shaped the courtships of their generation in now taken-for-granted ways. The fact that these couples formed across class, racial, and gender divides in patterns and combinations rarely seen in other historical periods is significant and speaks volumes to the level of racial integration on the island.

Yet the stance that the revolution had "solved" the race problem, the subsequent official silence on race, and a continuing nationalist ideology of mestizaje left some interracial couples without a framework in which to discuss the negative comments they encountered at home and on the street. Their contradictory experiences could not be more striking. The revolution's color-blind approach and silence created egalitarian spaces for interracial couples to flourish, but it also created spaces for racism to continue.

The silence on race has provoked a loud and varied response from academics. For some scholars, such as the Cuban Black Nationalist Carlos Moore (1988), the silence is an illustration of the blatant racism of the Castro government—a conscious unwillingness to address the situation and needs of Afrocubans. Some (Pérez Sarduy and Stubbs 1993) argue that the continued marginalization of Afrocubans in social and cultural relations in Cuba cannot be fully understood, principally because of the revolutionary policy of silence and the unavailability of data by race. Even in the early 1980s Cuban social scientists may have started studying racial issues, but the results of these investigations were not publicly available. The Cuban census did collect data by skin color in 1981 and 2002, but much of it was not circulated or widely released in a form that could be used by researchers. The silence, however, is not new. The historians Alejandro de la Fuente (2001) and Ada Ferrer (1999) have documented the long cultural roots of this silence and illustrated how at certain historical conjunctures black Cubans have been able to employ the silence as a tool in their struggle against racism (de la Fuente 2001). The ideological, social, and political contexts surrounding the silence are essential in understanding its impact on race relations at any given time in Cuban history. Most recently, as I discuss in the epilogue, this public silence on racism has started to crack in the current post-Soviet era.

Scholars writing on Cuban and Latin American race relations have also grappled with the tensions between U.S. racial paradigms and identity politics and so-called Latin American exceptionalism (for summaries of these debates, see de la Fuente 2001; Sawyer 2006). "Latin American exceptionalism" refers to a perspective that views race relations and continuing racism as inherently different in Latin America. In this view, racial inequalities do exist in Latin America, but they are not systematic. The more flexible and fluid nature of race relations marks Latin America as distinct from the nonwhite/white North American racial paradigm. Latin American exceptionalists tend to downplay the material and ideological realities of racism in Latin America. This view has been contradicted by recent studies (Sheriff 2001; Twine 1998; Wade 1993; Whitten and Torres 1998; Wright 1990) documenting the persistent and at times virulent racism in Latin America and exposing the fissures in the idea of racial democracy.

The realization that racism continues in Cuba also lays bare the limitations of Cuba's color-blind approach. The impact of the silence and the color-blind approach is best understood in the context of specific periods of Cuban history. As Mark Sawyer notes, racist ideologies are "highly adaptable to suit new circumstances and to fit neatly among a variety of state ideologies . . . and can be grafted onto what appears to be antiracist or egalitarian discourse" (2006, 13–14). The often illogical and commonsense nature of race and racism in Cuba serves to legitimate existing racial hierarchies. During the fifty-plus years of socialism the racial silence has had different generational impacts on interracial couples. My goal in this book is to deepen our understandings of racial dynamics on the island through an ethnographic account of how mestizaje works at a grassroots level and how these on-the-ground experiences are linked to broader racial ideologies and practices operating in contemporary Cuba.

To understand the racism that Tamara, Alberto, Olga, José Miguel, and many other couples encountered, I recognize the simultaneous structural and ideological nature of race and the "fluidity, mutability and historical contingencies of racism" (Mullings 2005, 674). These relationships engage with integrationist ideologies of mestizaje and socialist, color-blind equality in ways that can both undermine and

reinforce the racial hierarchy. In this book I explore the natu~~r~~
racial relationships in particular historical and contempora~~r~~
stances and examine how interracial couples face the routine
of racism. I map the ideological sea that the interracial couples navigate every day in several domains: in racialized spaces, in discourse,
and in personal and familial relations.

In a supposedly color-blind society, race speaks in socially acceptable terms through a language of space and *nivel de cultura* (cultural
level). Place and local (neighborhood) identity are central in social
relations. The meanings of blackness and whiteness in racially mixed
spaces, like neighborhoods, are multiple: growing foreign tourism adds
a global register to local and historical meanings of race and space
in Havana. The dollarized economy is re-racing space and giving new
meanings to class, blackness, whiteness, and interracial couples. The
rising number of tourists and tourism installations on the island are
creating new spaces of racial inclusion and exclusion, new visibilities
and invisibilities. For some young Cubans, interracial courtships can
be a means of escaping blackness in its social and spatial connotations.
The couples move in a physical world fraught with shifting connections
of class, race, and culture.

Despite the state's official silence, race is a pervasive presence in
everyday discourse. Popular understandings and interpretations of contemporary interracial couples draw on the commonsense racism that
Cubans openly express in conversations. Dating practices and aesthetic
hierarchies reflect racialized language, terminologies, and media representations of blackness, whiteness, and mixedness. Interracial couples
can both subvert and reinforce the racial hierarchy as they traverse
this discursive terrain. Again, the meanings of interracial couples are
never singular but are subject to both the couples' own motives and the
public's interpretations of their interracial unions.

Within the so-called private realm of the family, interracial couples
remain a volatile site in the working out of race, gender, class, and
generational dynamics. Here we see the limitations as well as the
advances the revolution has made toward remolding racial conceptualizations. The couples' narratives also demonstrate how slow and
difficult it has been to change gender relations within Cuban families

despite progressive legislation, such as the 1975 Family Code, which established the official goal that men and women should participate equally in household and child-rearing tasks. Young interracial couples are embedded in multigenerational households. In intergenerational conflicts, older family members' memories and assumptions about race can contradict the youths' lived experience of racial integration under the revolution, bringing into sharp contrast the coexisting ideologies of racism and egalitarianism. As Robin Sheriff notes of interracial couples in Brazil, "there is perhaps no other arena in which contradictory notions about the significance of race and color are brought into greater relief" (2001, 118). "Underneath the public surface of romanticized visions of interracial love," she continues, "there are stories of interracial wounding" (140). For many of my informants, the actual process of mestizaje through interracial coupling brought with it trepidation, not celebration. Generational differences regarding interracial mixing become strikingly apparent within many families.

One More Interracial Couple

There has long been a taboo on discussing or publicly acknowledging anthropologists' romantic encounters in the field. Indeed, until recently, the anthropological community implicitly assumed unmarried or unpartnered scholars were celibate in the field. This is based on an assumption "that maintaining the boundary between the scientific self of the anthropologist and the sexual self of the anthropologist is a necessary and fundamental condition for preserving the desired objectivity of the scientist from the subjectivity of the native" (S. Cole 2003, 178). Some scholars suggest that there are other reasons for this silence, including the discipline's disdain for personal narratives and cultural prudery. Ester Newton (1993) argues that avoiding such topics is a way for established scholars to silence female and gay scholars who risk their respectability and possibly their careers by discussing these seemingly personal issues too publicly (as cited in Dubisch 1995). For example, a generation ago the white anthropologist Ruth Landes had a love affair with the black folklorist and journalist Edison Carneiro while she was conducting research on *candomblé* in Bahia, Brazil. Back in the

United States a prominent male anthropologist criticized Landes's wo[rk], in part, because he considered her comportment in the field imprope[r]. Don Kulick adds that the silence about the erotic subjectivity of field-workers functions to "keep concealed the deeply racist and colonialist conditions that make possible our continuing unidirectional discourse about the sexuality of the people we study" (Kulick and Willson 1995, 4). He notes that scholars have long seen sexual behavior as the irreconcil-able difference between "us" and "them" (4).

Recent writings have begun to challenge this silence (Bell, Caplan, and Karim 1993; Kulick and Willson 1995; Pertierra 2007). Pure scien-tific objectivity is no longer the goal of most anthropological research, and personal relationships in the field are no longer a taboo subject. In fact, the reflexive movement in anthropology that started in the late 1980s all but requires ethnographers to position themselves within their research and the resulting text—to place their identities, their relationships, and their voices beside those of their informants. It is now increasingly common for anthropologists to examine how the researchers' gender, sexuality, and relationships affect the fieldwork experiences, as well as the written ethnographies. For example, Aus-tralian Filipina anthropologist Anna Cristina Pertierra (2007) tells how planning her wedding to a white Cuban man while conducting field-work on consumption in Santiago de Cuba gave her new insights into the emotional intensity and stress associated with acquiring material goods, which her informants had been recounting to her for months.

My own circumstances in the field shaped my access and experi-ences. With my Spanish and Italian ancestry and my fluency in Spanish, many Cubans did not perceive me as a "typical American," like the fair-skinned characters they saw in the weekly American movies broadcast on television. Many Cubans of all colors claimed Spanish ancestry, and this helped to build bridges between me and my informants. My white-ness in the Cuban context facilitated access to conversations about race among white Cubans in ways that might not have been possible for black scholars; and certainly my whiteness may also have shaped what my mulatto and black Cuban informants shared with me. Finally, I am not of Cuban descent, so we did not have to sort through a compli-cated and painful history of who stayed and who left, and why. I quickly developed a passion for the island, perhaps as ardent as that of an exile, but my connection to Cuba began as a purely intellectual endeavor, unencumbered (and perhaps impoverished) by issues of personal identity or family history.

My interest in Cuba emerged, in fact, from my academic background in the anthropology of education. I worked in educational research for several years and was fascinated by school ethnographies that mapped out how the social terrain of schools helped to reproduced the class and racial divisions of capitalist society (for example, Willis 1981; Eckert 1989). My interest in schooling drew me to Cuba, a socialist country touted for its achievements in education; yet nothing had been written about the social organization of Cuban schools. What social divisions—racial, class, or gender hierarchies—were reproduced or broken down in Cuban schools through students' social interactions? That was the question that brought me to Cuba in the early 1990s. However, the prospect that an outsider might uncover flaws in the universally praised education system, coupled with the controversial issue of race, apparently seemed too sensitive at that particular moment in Cuban history. After six months of negotiations with University of Havana officials and unsuccessful attempts to gain access to a school, I abandoned the school ethnography idea and instead decided to look at race relations among Cuban youth in their friendship groups and social life. It was from initial conversations with some young Cuban informants about their social lives that my eventual focus on interracial dating emerged.

Regarding my own positionality, I feel it is important to note, given what ultimately became the focus of this book, that I dated a mulato man from Cayo Hueso, whom I will call Antonio. We met during my first trip to Cuba in 1990 and lived together throughout my fieldwork. Far from being irrelevant or gratuitous to this book and my research (Wade 1993), my relationship with Antonio is analytically salient. His friends and neighbors became my friends and "informants." My experiences with Antonio informed the questions I asked other interracial couples, and our relationship facilitated my research in a myriad of ways. However, there were a few instances when my relationship also made my research more complicated, particularly in my dealings with some faculty members at the University of Havana. During the long months of negotiating my visa, one faculty member told me she could no longer help me after hearing about my relationship with Antonio because she believed I was in Cuba only for "personal reasons."

Had I found an "exotic" boyfriend? Was I engaged in a sensual and emotional encounter that Stephan Palmié (2002) called "carnal modernity" in contemporary Cuba? Was I using him to gain access to the lives of my informants and the barrio? Our relationship raised the suspicions of many people. Antonio's motives were also called into question. Many people assumed he had hopes of leaving the country by marrying a foreigner, a migration strategy employed by an increasing number of young Cubans. Some white academics were very skeptical and were certain he was a dollar-seeking delinquent from Cayo Hueso. When they met him, they realized that he was an educated professional—and, in their words, "not so black after all." Like many interracial relationships, ours raised questions of hierarchy and power, motives, and intentions. As Pertierra notes of her own courtship with an educated white Cuban, we found ourselves enmeshed "within a complex framework of gendered and racialised economics and politics" (2007, 6). Antonio and I had to contend with the many interpretations and assessments others placed on our relationship. We experienced some of the same public reactions that the couples I interviewed described. When I spoke with other couples, we exchanged stories. I empathized with their problems and admired their strength. Their stories were relevant and interesting to me in more than a professional way. I was in an interracial relationship, too, and was invested in learning about how to navigate through a social world fraught with mixed messages and shifting meanings of race in a period of economic crisis. However, while my relationship with Antonio forms the backdrop of my research, our time together is not the main subject of this book. I have made this decision for ethical reasons. Anthropology inevitably "uses" informants' lives and stories to produce texts and, ultimately, to build academic careers. As Peter Wade notes, "When a reflexive account of intimate relationships becomes a sort of personal confessional anecdote, then the ethical implications become even more problematic, since the unequal textual participation of the subjects involved is orchestrated by no more than a desire for self-revelation" (1993, 201). My intent was never to write a book about myself and my relationship, and like Pertierra, I, too, "wanted to protect my own emotions and those of the people important to me from the tumultuous debates of anthropological discussion" (2007, 11). Antonio is present on every page, but the story of our relationship remains between us.

Anthropological Fieldwork in Socialist Cuba

> Now you know it, bourgeois intellectuals and bourgeois libellants, agents of the CIA and intelligence services of imperialism, that is of the intelligence and espionage services of imperialism: you will not be allowed to come to Cuba! . . . Our doors will remain closed indefinitely, ad infinitum!
> —Fidel Castro, The First National Congress on Education and Culture, Closing Speech, 1971

Foreign anthropologists have conducted little long-term anthropological fieldwork in socialist Cuba.[6] The research attempted by Oscar Lewis and his team in 1969 and 1970 met a disastrous end. Although initially Castro and the government had approved the project, halfway through it the government withdrew what had been very generous support, confiscated thousands of pages of notes and interviews, arrested a Cuban informant, and ended the research. Ruth Lewis attributed the about-face decision to critical books published in 1970 by foreigners otherwise sympathetic to socialism (Karol 1970) and to economic setbacks in Cuba, such as the failed ten-million-ton sugar harvest of 1970. Cuba was a small country under constant threat of U.S. intervention, and could not risk the publication of another unsavory account of life under socialism (Lewis, Lewis, and Rigdon 1977). For nearly fifteen years after the Lewis team was there, it was extremely difficult to conduct anthropological research in Cuba, particularly for U.S. citizens. In 1985 the North American anthropologist Yvonne Daniel was able to conduct a year of fieldwork on dance. She commented that she "recorded few interviews and did not take copious notes. As a U.S. citizen in Cuba, [she] constantly feared that [her] work would be subject to counterrevolutionary charges or could inadvertently implicate others in problematic situations" (Daniel 1995, 23). These were not ungrounded fears given the experiences of Lewis and his team fifteen years earlier. In the late 1980s Swedish anthropologist Mona Rosendahl (1997) also conducted extensive fieldwork on local interpretations of revolutionary ideology in rural eastern Cuba. A small space for foreign researchers was beginning to open.[7]

Throughout the 1990s and 2000s, there was a slow but steady trickle of North American and European scholars conducting long-term ethnographic fieldwork in Cuba (see Roland 2004; Forrest 1999; Alfonso Wells 2004; Hill 2004; Hernandez-Reguant 2002; Crabb 2001; Ryer 2006). The mere presence of foreign anthropologists in Cuba is not to say that the Cuban government's reticence, as encountered by the Lewis team, had evaporated entirely. Some of the anthropologists felt the subtle monitoring of their activities; for others the surveillance was more obvious. Paul Ryer (2004), for example, had every letter he received from the United States carefully opened and presumably read before it was delivered to him in a sealed plastic bag with a note saying the letter had been "damaged" in transit. In a few extreme cases, the researchers were asked to leave the country (Crabb 2001; Burke 2001). Not to minimize these instances, however, the majority of the anthropologists were able to obtain visas and conduct long-term research without interference from the Cuban state. The veritable flood of doctoral dissertations based on fieldwork in Cuba on a wide range of topics attests to this fact (for an overview of recent dissertations see Ryer 2006).

Academics interested in conducting scholarship on Cuba also continue to face considerable impediments from the U.S. side as well. A remnant of the Cold War, the U.S. trade embargo against Cuba stops U.S. products and citizens from entering the island. American citizens are restricted from traveling to Cuba by the 1963 Trading with the Enemy Act, administered by the U.S. Department of Treasury's Office of Foreign Assets Control. The intent of the act is to prohibit U.S. citizens from spending money in Cuba, which would in effect be supplying monetary support to the Cuban regime. The Treasury Department controls the travel of U.S. journalists and academics by requiring them to apply for and obtain approval for a license authorizing their travel to Cuba. This can be a lengthy and difficult process. Obtaining adequate funding for research is another significant obstacle. Due to the trade embargo, research projects involving fieldwork in Cuba cannot be funded by U.S. government educational agencies that are the primary sources of funding in anthropology. Though the Cold War is long over, the situation has only gotten worse, as evidenced by the 1996 Helms-Burton Law, signed by President Bill Clinton, which further tightened the trade embargo against Cuba, and President George W. Bush's restrictions on travel and remittances from Cuban exiles living in the United States, which were finally eliminated in 2009 by President Barack Obama. The U.S. embargo not only punishes Cubans by making it more complicated and costly for them to obtain needed commodities, but also punishes the people and scholarly communities in the United States by setting nearly insurmountable obstacles on funding and scholarly exchanges with the island. How can Americans make policies or informed judgments about Cuba without scholarly knowledge? Learning and scholarship have also fallen victim to this tragic political game.

When I began my field research in Cuba in January 1992, just two years after the collapse of the socialist bloc, the Cuban economic crisis threatened the very future of the revolution. In this moment of uncertainty and economic hardship the University of Havana cautiously welcomed me. I understood the administrators' hesitations, given the icy relations between the United States and Cuba. As I mentioned earlier, I had originally proposed to study race relations among young Cubans in the context of the social organization of a school. It was only after I abandoned the idea of conducting a school-based ethnography and shifted to a focus on race relations in the context of social life among youth that I finally obtained sponsorship from the University of Havana. My student visa allowed me to live in Cuba for two years. I returned to Cuba repeatedly for shorter trips throughout the 1990s and early 2000s.

While I do not doubt that the Cuban state knew of my presence and research project, I did not feel monitored or at all restricted during my research. I went where I wanted, talked with anyone willing to talk with me, tape-recorded interviews, and took notes. On several occasions I presented papers at conferences at the University of Havana and other research institutes in Havana and received very constructive feedback from Cuban academics. Though some Cuban scholars disagreed with my interpretations, there was never any attempt to silence my views or force me to reevaluate my findings. My discussions with Cuban academics both at the university and in various research institutes have always been professional and instructive.

My affiliation with the University of Havana legitimized my research to the families and youth that I met. I focused my work in two neighboring *municipios* in Havana: the predominately working-class Centro Habana, where I lived, and the more fashionable district of Plaza de la Revolución. Few people expressed any fears or anxieties about talking with a foreigner. Only one family joked that I was a CIA spy, but I never felt this was a serious concern. More frequently, the young people and their families saw me as a resource for mailing letters to family in the United States, helping them spend their (then) still illegal hard currency, or obtaining some needed good or medicine. I was a potential conduit of goods and information who could help them *resolver* (make ends meet) in the austerity of the special period.

I spent most of my time in Centro Habana and Plaza with the people who have become the subject of this book and with the friends and neighbors I met through my relationship with Antonio. As most of my informants were in their late teens and early twenties, they were eager to talk about their love lives or those of their friends. Conversations about dating experiences provided a forum for discussing constructions of blackness and whiteness, topics more difficult to get at with broad questions about race and racism. Everyone I asked had something to say on the issue of interracial dating and either had an experience themselves or knew of interracial couples that encountered problems with their friends or families. Interracial romance was an easily accessible theme that spoke volumes about race, class, family, gender, and generational relations. As is standard in anthropological research, to protect their confidence and trust, I have given my informants pseudonyms and altered some background information to protect their identities.

To conduct my fieldwork, I learned and practiced the Cuban custom of the *visita* (the visit). Fortunately for me, it was common to stop by people's houses unannounced to sit and chat for a while, share a cup of

coffee, accompany them on errands, and then move on to the next destination. The spontaneity of this practice had its downside as well. At
times I was stuck at home and resented hosting the seemingly endless
visitas when I had planned a different agenda for the day. I know that
despite my efforts, my graciousness and hospitality never matched that
of the Cubans. It was also often difficult to predict when people would
be home and have time to talk. Throughout most of the 1990s phones
were frequently out of service and many people had no phones at all.[8]
When appointments could be made, they were casually broken as the
exigencies of daily life always took precedent. Fieldwork in Cuba could
be a frustrating process, and as one anthropologist working in the
United States aptly commented about appointments with informants,
"prior arrangements . . . were often forgotten, and I had to swallow my
chagrin at being so unimportant to them when they were so precious
to me" (Estroff 1981, 28). When we did meet, our conversations were
informal and mostly unstructured. I wrote up notes usually after our
visitas, and with their permission tape-recorded their stories of their
interracial dating experiences.

Though I deliberately present mulato, black, and white Cuban
voices, I make no claims that I represent the vast range of experiences of all interracial relationships in Cuba. Most specifically, I have
focused only on heterosexual couples. Certainly, there are also same-
sex interracial couples that not only face racial discrimination but
also must struggle to find a space in a hetero-dominant culture. Some
recent dissertations explore issues of homosexuality in Cuba, which I
could not do justice to within the scope of my project (see Allen 2003;
Fosado 2004). Among the heterosexual couples I interviewed, there
are some interracial pairs, both married and dating, who have not
faced overwhelming family protest and have felt only minimal disapproval from society at large. It must also be remembered that for many
of the couples themselves, race was not an issue or obstacle in their
coming together.

The couples' stories I present here tend to highlight the tensions
and conflicts encountered by many interracial couples because the
resistance these couples face reveals the stuff of which these social
conventions are made. As anthropologist Nancy Scheper-Hughes has

observed, "every society reveals itself perhaps most clearly in the phenomena it rejects, excludes, and confines" (1979, 13). Rules are best
observed in their breaking. The asymmetrical power relations implicit
in race, class, and gender shape the couples' experiences, even as people struggle to redefine these relations in their daily practices. Couples
who face conflicts with family members or public commentary bring
into sharp relief the competing and coexisting ideologies of egalitarianism and racism, both of which infuse the social landscape.

An examination of the lives of interracial couples is by necessity
an exploration of the general racial climate and racial understandings
that form the backdrop of their daily experiences. Framing the broader
racialized world in which the couples live is crucial. In reacting to and
interpreting interracial couples, friends, families, and strangers draw
on a repertoire of commonsense racist understandings. The revolutionary government may have been officially silent on race, but race has
never been absent from everyday life, nor have the meanings of race
been static. As Leith Mullings aptly observes, the "purposeful, func-
tional, mutable and constantly transforming nature of race" must be
reckoned with (2005, 674). Analyzing the couples' experiences and the
role of race in everyday life requires paying close attention to how race
permeates the physical spaces that interracial couples inhabit, the discursive terrain they traverse, and the households in which they reside.
As I will discuss, understandings of class and gender are never absent
when race is at issue. As interracial couples travel through the arenas of
everyday life, they create, resist, and reinforce meanings of whiteness,
blackness, and mixedness.

Coming to Terms with Race

One day, I met with a small group of university students, mostly women,
who had been involved in interracial relationships. We gathered at a
small patio area in front of the Philosophy Department under a canopy
of trees. The patio overlooked the Napoleon Museum, housed in a
sixteenth-century Florentine-style stone mansion which was built during the 1920s sugar boom, known as the *danza de los milliones*, for a private collection of Napoleon's personal effects. As was characteristic of

ɔ the side of the museum, there was another former mansion
_ɪs now a crumbling tenement house. It still clung to a vestige of
its past grandeur with a spectacular ten-foot stained-glass window of
an intricately detailed harbor scene.[9] Here, looking over (and overlooking) these juxtapositions that form the backdrop of their daily lives, I
asked these young women to tell me their own personal experiences of
juxtaposition: black with white. However, before they started to recount
their romances (which I will discuss in subsequent chapters) I asked
them how they identified themselves racially. What I thought would be
a simple question turned out to be very complex.

When I posed this question to twenty-year-old Zulema, she hesitated. "What? How do I identify people racially?" she asked. "No, what
do you consider yourself to be," I clarified. Still she paused, "Well,
blacks are those with dark skin and, as we say here, bad, hard, woolly
hair (*pasas*), and whites are—." I interrupted her again and asked,
"And you?" "What am I?" she countered. "Black (*negra*), I consider
myself black," slightly shrugging her shoulders and looking at the other
women, as if to say, "Why is she asking such an obvious question?"

Many Cubans stumbled over this question when I asked them.
Unlike North Americans, who were so accustomed to checking the
appropriate "box," Cubans had few situations in which they were
asked to self-identify racially. The policy of silence declared that racial
distinctions no longer existed in revolutionary Cuba. For this reason,
the 1970 census did not even release data by skin color (though it was
collected). On the subsequent censuses in 1981 and 2002, respondents
designated their own skin color. However, the skin color recorded on
a person's ID card (*carnét de identidad*) and in their medical records
was determined by the observer. Race or skin color, I quickly learned,
was often an assessment made by an observer, rather than an identity
asserted by an individual.

Several informants mentioned the confusion that resulted from
the skin color assignments on the ID cards. Racial identification can be
somewhat fluid in Cuba for those who fall into the middle categories,
such as mixed-race people who may be classified as mulato/mestizo or
black or, if very light-skinned, white. The racial identity of those at the
extremes of the black-white spectrum is not so negotiable. Olga, the

daughter of two mulatos, was classified as *negra* on the first carnét she was issued and mestiza on the second one. She described her father as a mulato with light skin and "good hair." His carnét identified him as *blanco*, while his biological brother was identified as *negro*. Another mulata informant noted that her light-skinned brother with "good hair" was also designated *blanco* in his carnét, and he jokingly boasted among his more obviously mixed-race siblings that he was white.

In a similar incident, as I spoke with Loli, a young white woman, about the race of her friends, she responded that her friend Elba was mulata. Overhearing the conversation, Loli's mother commented, "Oh, if she heard you say that!" Loli replied, "Well, but she *is* mulata, although she is very, very light skinned." Loli then recounted the following story of Elba's racial identification:

Elba had been registered mestiza, but when she went to have her new carnét made, apparently they looked at her and put down blanca. Oh and she was so happy. "I'm finally through with that; now I don't have to explain that anymore," she said. You see, her father is white and very fair skinned. And her mother is mulata, although you can hardly tell by looking at her. Elba turned out with blond hair and blue eyes, but she also has slightly thick lips. The only thing that would make you think that she's mulata is that her hair is so kinky. Oh, she used to hate her hair, always struggling to straighten it, but then curly hair came into style and now she leaves it curly and everyone asks her where she got her perm. Anyway, she came out looking more mulata than her mother.

Elba's desire to disassociate herself with her mixed-race ancestry was common among Cubans who could "pass" for white. This sentiment is captured in the writings of the mulato poet Nicolás Guillén. It was almost as if he were thinking of women like Elba in his poem "El Abuelo" (The Grandfather) when he wrote:

. . . que ya verás, inquieta, junto a la fresca orilla
la dulce sombra oscura del abuelo que huye,
el que rizó por siempre tu cabeza amarilla.

[One day you will see, to your chagrin, close to the cool bank
the sweet dark shadow of the fleeing grandfather,
the one who put that permanent curl in your yellow hair.]
(as quoted in and translated by Smart 1990, 167)

In Cuba, as in much of Latin America, there is great sensitivity to phenotypic variation and a vast racial vocabulary. There is, in fact, an entire doctoral dissertation dedicated to enumerating, defining, and understanding Cuban racial terms (Alfonso Wells 2004). Extensive racial lexicons and acute awareness of racial variation are also found in other Latin American countries with black populations, most notably Brazil, (Harris 1970; Sanjek 1971), Venezuela (Wright 1990), and Colombia (Wade 1993). Peter Wade asserts that in Latin America, the abundant racial terminology and its malleability attests to the institutionalization of race mixture/mestizaje (Wade 1993, 22).

In Cuba, apart from the three basic categories of negro/a, mulato/a, and blanco/a (black, mulatto, white), gradations among mulatos are marked by a series of terms that refer to skin tone, facial features, and hair texture. *Mulato/a adelantado/a* (advanced mulatto) refers to light-skinned mulato; likewise *mulato/a atrasado/a* (backward mulatto) refers to a mulato with darker skin and African features. Mestizo may also be used to identify a person of mixed race, although in the rest of Latin America this term refers to a mixture of Europeans and indigenous parentage. In Cuba, *mestizo* is often used as a more polite term for *mulato* and is the term for mixed race that is used on Cuban identification cards and census categories. The distinctions atrasado (backward) or adelantado (advanced) are generally used with implicit reference to the person's heritage, that is, one came out lighter or darker than their progenitors, and also refers to the person's position on the linear progression to whiteness that mestizaje implies. Comparisons such as this are also often made among siblings, since a wide variety of phenotypes can found in the offspring of mixed-race unions. *Mulato/a blanconazo/a* (almost white mulatto) describe those mulattos who could "pass" for white with their light skin and European features. *Jaba(d)o* is also used to refer to mulattos with light-colored eyes, skin, and hair, but with clearly African characteristics, such as hair texture and facial features. *Mulato/a achinado* refers to mulatos with Asiatic features and straight hair resulting from Chinese and black or Chinese and mulatto unions. People displaying features of Chinese or Chinese and white ancestry such as eye folds and straight black hair are denominated *Chino/a.* *Indio/a* or *moro* are used to describe mixed-race persons with features such as straight black hair and reddish brown or dark skin tone. *Trigueño/a* describes a "wheat" or olive-colored skin tone and straight or wavy dark hair (I was sometimes described by this term). *Negro/a azul* or *prieto/a* refers to very dark skinned blacks with strongly African features. Whites, the generally unmarked category in racial schemas, are sometimes designed *blanco/a cubano/a,* which refers to the fact that their apparent "whiteness" is most probably belying some history of racial mixture. Additional descriptors for hair, noses, and lips are often used in conjunction with any of the previously mentioned categories. Hair can be divided into *pelo bueno/malo* (good/straight or bad/kinky hair), *tener pelo* (to have [straight] hair), or *pasas* (literally, raisins, or bad/woolly hair). In the racial vocabulary, kinky hair is not even considered to be "hair," as is evident in the expressions *mulato de pelo* (a mulatto with straight hair) and *no tener pelo* (to not have hair, that is, to have kinky hair). Noses also fall into the good/bad categories of *nariz bueno o malo/aplastado/achatado* (good or European nose or bad/ flattened nose), and very full lips are referred to derogatorily as *bemba.* The gradations of mulatos from darker to lighter, from more African to more Caucasian, grew directly out of the project of whitening as a way of socially marking with specific nomenclature the individual's location in the trajectory from black to white. The phrase *adelantar la raza* (advance the race) shows the persistence of an evolutionary framework implicit in the vocabulary of whitening. Racial terminology is not a closed lexicon or simply a remnant from the colonial order. As Paul Ryer (2006) notes, new racial terms frequently appear in popular parlance.

The confusion over racial identification and which terms should be used and by whom reveals that racial categories are to a certain degree fluid and negotiable. The stories these women recounted demonstrate that there is some flexibility in racial identification at the edges between the middle mixed categories and the edges of white and black. However, analyzing over five hundred surveys conducted by Cuban research assistants in Havana, Mark Sawyer (2006) found that there was a very strong correlation between the researchers' assignment of race and the informants' self-assignment of race. This, he argues, indicates that racial categories are distinct despite the fluid continuum of skin color and racial terminology. According to Sawyer, "[Cubans] are able to discern who fits into what category" (2006, 138). I would agree with his assessment, except in the numerous cases, such as the examples I described above, where individuals straddle the borders of these more easily identifiable ends of the color spectrum; mulatos who are close to blancos and mulatos who are close to negros. I would also argue that the racial categories and their edges are regionally defined. "White" may include darker skin tones in Santiago de Cuba, a largely black city, than in Santa Clara, a "whiter" city, for example.

Phenotypic variation is common in mixed-race families such as Olga's and Zulema's. While Zulema's racial identity, negra, seemed apparent to any observer, it told nothing about her racial ancestry. After denominating herself "negra," she went on to describe her family's racial makeup: "Well, my mother is an advanced mulata because she has rather good hair, and my father is like jabao. My sister is much more racially advanced than me. She has good hair and lighter skin. My skin is darker than my mother's and my sister's."

Though Zulema hesitated in stating the apparently obvious *negra* as her self-identification, the term referred only to her phenotype and elucidated little of her racial heritage. Zulema was black, but she was the daughter of two mulatos. She settled on a word that best described herself phenotypically, yet in elaborating on her family's racial composition she demonstrated her sensitivity to subtle racial variations that could not be captured with a single descriptor such as negra. Our exchange revealed not a lack of racial consciousness or the social insignificance of race, as I first might have been lead to believe by her confusion when faced with my initial question. Rather, Zulema's elaborated response shows an acute awareness of the distinctions that mark differences in racially mixed people and the continued use of a vocabulary directly associated with the project of whitening.

The choice of color terms, especially on the borderlines between categories, was always dependent on the intention of the speaker, comparative assessments, and shifting contexts, as was the case in other parts of Latin America (cf. Lancaster 1992). In Cuba, racial terms were used as descriptors to refer to a third person not part of the conversation, as pejorative terms, and as affectionate terms or nicknames. In the first case, race (oftentimes along with other traits, such as age, height, weight, personality, occupation, residence, and so on) seemed to be the first word at hand to distinguish the absent party. This was often done to refer to someone who was not well known by the other party; for example, "María, the black woman (la negra) who works at . . ." Sometimes additional descriptors of hair and nose type were added for further clarification.

In situations of tension or anger, or simply if the speaker desired to establish his or her authority or social status, the same racial terms could be used pejoratively. A self-defined mulata university professor commented, "I never let anyone say to me, 'Come here, negra,' because the [speaker] hopes the black will subordinate to them." Despite this woman's strong objection to the term, it was very frequently used in exactly this manner, both by whites and black or mulato Cubans. I also heard stronger racial epithets, such as *negro/a de mierda* (black shit) and *niche* (negro) used on rare occasions during fights or street scuffles. In situations of conflict, *blanquito* (little whitey) was also used disparagingly to refer to whites, but it was a mild insult compared to the racial epithets for blacks. These terms were just as likely to be used by whites as by Cubans of color.

Finally, all of these terms (including *niche*—if used among Afrocubans) could be employed as terms of endearment or nicknames. My neighbor, an elderly white man, greeted me daily as *mi negra*. Affectionate terms such as *mi negra* and *mi china* were usually used for women, but as nicknames they were used with equal frequency for men, women, and children. For example, in an office or group of friends it was common to find individuals referred to as *el jabao* and *el chino*, both when speaking directly to them and when speaking about them. In some cases, their given names were almost never heard or used. Likewise within mulato or black families, the darkest child or relative may be called *el negro/la negra* as a nickname. Roger Lancaster (1992) suggests that color terms were affectionate and intimate precisely because they violate the rules of polite discourse. However, he also notes, "Even when motivated by affection rather than anger, such terms can never be innocent of the social relations in which they are embedded. Such terms of intimacy maintain at close range the system of contrasts that is, for other purposes and in other contexts, stigmatizing—and that might, in an argument or in a different tone, carry the force of strong invective" (Lancaster 1992, 218).

Racial terms, no matter what the intent of the speaker or how they are understood by the listener, cannot be completely disassociated from the social hierarchy from which they emerged. The racial/color categories are value laden with lightness/whiteness more desirable than darkness/blackness. Cuba is, as Sawyer (2006) notes, a "pigmentocracy," in which racial terms and color consciousness communicate positions in the ongoing racial hierarchy. As value-laden terms, racial vocabulary always carries with it the social connotations of the unequal power relations that produced them as socially meaningful markers or categories. The hegemony of whitening and racist ideology have left their mark in the lexicon of race in everyday discourse.

Two Notes on Language

First, in this book I will employ the racial terms to identify individuals as they would be most often identified in the Cuban context using either the Spanish racial terms or English translations: negro/black, blanco/white, mulato/mulatto. In Cuba the terms mestizo (mixed) and mulato are used interchangeably. Race in Cuba is not thought of in terms of ancestry or blood, but rather is mostly defined by culture, phenotype, and skin color—the term commonly used in Cuba to talk about what we in the United States would term *race.*

At times I also use the term *Afrocuban* to refer to blacks and mestizos/mulatos together. This is *not* a racial nomenclature used in Cuban speech. It is in a sense a sociological category with no people in it. The term *Afrocuban* appears most frequently in academic writings originating in Cuba to designate African-derived elements of Cuban expressive culture, such as Afrocuban music or religion. Some U.S.-based scholars also use it to refer collectively to Cubans of African descent, though this usage is *not* employed on the island. Following other U.S.-based academics, I use it here in referring to Cubans who phenotypically show signs of African descent and who would be either negro (black) or some version of mestizo/mulato in the Cuban racial lexicon. Cubans on the island might use the construction *raza de color* or *gente de color* (race of color or people of color) to refer to peoples having some African descent, though this, too, is infrequent. I use the term *Afrocuban* not to force Cuban racial terminology into a U.S. white/nonwhite paradigm, but rather to recognize that in many instances mulatos, like negros, share experiences of racism as people of African descent. Some recent research (Espina Prieto and Ruiz 2006; Sawyer 2006) has highlighted the fact that while, phenotypically, mulatos are a distinct category and Cubans perceive them to have a higher status than black Cubans, they actually do not have a higher status in any material way. Mulatos may not have any better access to resources or better economic opportunities than black Cubans (Espina Prieto and Ruiz 2006; Sawyer 2006). In light of this research, the use of the term *Afrocuban* in discussions of racial inequalities and racist ideologies is justifiable, as it encompasses blacks and mestizos/mulatos of varying shades and stresses their similarities in the racial/color hierarchy on the island. I do recognize that the use of the term *Afrocuban* is still highly contested among academics, as Paul Ryer (2006) has cogently outlined. He astutely notes that this is not simply a semantic issue, but can reflect deeply different conceptualizations of the racial system in Cuba. Knowing this, I have tried to use the term with caution and only in the contexts in which I believe mulatos and blacks share similar experiences of racism and are subject to similar denigrations due to their African heritage. Likewise, I have maintained the use of the various Cuban racial terms whenever possible and particularly in any instances when the mulato/black distinction is significant.

Second, what to call the current period of Cuban history is open to debate. The collapse of the socialist bloc in 1989 caused the Cuban economy to plummet. A 73 percent drop in imports (in 1992) and a particularly sharp cut in oil shipments paralyzed the country. The crisis intensified everyday efforts to obtain food as the long beleaguered rationing system all but collapsed under the scarcities. In 1990, the

Cuban government termed the crisis "the Special Period in Times of Peace," calling for wartime austerity in peacetime. Cuba strove to remove itself from the rubble of the socialist camp and insert itself in the dynamic global market economy through tourism and other joint ventures. My fieldwork in Cuba spans this tumultuous period of Cuban history, from the worst years (1992–1994) of the special period to the more recent economic recovery and growth (1995–present). I have decided to refer to this era as "post-Soviet Cuba." I use this term not as a eulogy to socialism but rather to distinguish Cuba's launch of a new period under Cuban socialism, what Ryer (2006) has called "para-socialism," something like and yet unlike socialism. The Soviet trade subsidies and aid that supported the island nation for decades are largely gone. What followed and follows is uncharted territory—a "transformation" into something new, not the inevitable "transition" into capitalism that the term "late-socialism" would imply. It is also not, as Sawyer (2006) terms it, "post-revolutionary Cuba," a phrase which in one sense communicates that the Cuban revolution has ended. Despite the fact that Fidel Castro has shifted power to his brother Raúl, I do not think the revolution is over. As Antoni Kapcia notes, "It has always been more helpful to see Cuba as a revolution—a dynamic process with the stresses, tensions and crises of an ongoing process of transformation" (2009, 37). I see the current transformations as very much a part of the Cuban revolution, which at its best engendered progressive ideals and visions of social justice.

All translations from Spanish are mine unless otherwise noted.

1

Interracial Couples from Colony to Revolution

Interracial couples have populated all periods of Cuban history, but their frequency, patterns, and circumstances have changed over time along with the shifts in the political, economic, and social structures of the country. From Spanish colony to independent republic to socialist revolution, understandings of race and nation influenced the nature and meaning of interracial couples.

Colonial Cuba was a plantation society and, at one time, the jewel in the crown of the Spanish colonial empire in the New World. Enslaved Africans powered the sugar plantations that fueled the colonial economy. As plantation owners increased sugar production during the first half of the 1800s, their demand for slave labor also increased. The slave population grew from 39,000 in 1770 to more than 400,000 in 1840 (F. Knight 1978). The exponential growth of the island's black population caused great concern among white Cubans. They feared that an event like the Haitian revolution (1791–1804), in which the enslaved Africans overthrew the white planter class to establish the first black republic in the New World, would be repeated on their island. This "Africanization scare" reverberated throughout the white bourgeoisie, encapsulated by the phrase "Cuba, better Spanish than African" (Duharte Jiménez 1993, 40). The Spanish government skillfully exploited the fear of a black uprising to offset some Cubans' growing discontent with colonial policies and to keep Cuba under colonial rule. In turn, discontented Cubans saw that combining Cuban independence with abolition would both satisfy the elites' desire for economic freedom and assuage their fears of a black/slave revolt. Cuba's struggle for independence began with the unsuccessful Ten Years War (1868–1878) and was finally achieved in the Cuban Independence War from 1895 to 1898.[1]

An important project paralleling these movements for abolition and Cuban independence was *blanqueamiento* (whitening). Whitening the population encompassed strategies of mestizaje (racial mixing) as well as aggressive immigration policies to attract white European settlers to the island (Rodríguez Ruiz 2004). Whitening in Cuba, as in other parts of Latin America, was rooted in nineteenth-century European theories of race and civilization that tied national progress to "racial improvement." White elites in nineteenth-century Latin American nations embraced ideas of social evolutionism which justified their own power and also strengthened intellectual connections with Europe (Graham 1990, 2). These pseudoscientific theories of race claimed to explain the superiority of one group over another and thus legitimated white rule over "inferior and backward" people. Faced with racially diverse populations, leaders and intellectuals in Latin America each shaped their own interpretations of these theories of race and progress to suit their own racial realities and considerations (Graham 1990). The ideology of whitening offered a compromise with blatant racist oppression. Progressively lightening the population from black toward white would place these nations on the road to progress. The goal was, as the term itself implied, to gradually eliminate blackness, physically and culturally, from the national panorama. Some countries, such as Argentina, were successful in attracting large numbers of white immigrants from Europe to achieve this end; in other countries interracial mixing (mestizaje) became the main vehicle for whitening. While each country approached whitening and mestizaje slightly differently, racial mixture remained the most salient feature of race relations in Latin America (W. Wright 1990).[2] The celebration of mestizaje as a national ideology in Cuba and many other Latin American countries must be viewed in this larger context of the project of whitening. Mestizaje was not an expression of racial tolerance or unqualified approval of interracial couples; it was a means to an end. In Cuba, nineteenth-century elites believed that whitening by mestizaje, only if properly managed, would allow Cuba to achieve economic development and a higher level of civilization (Patterson 1996).

Salvation versus Damnation:
The Mechanics of Whitening through Mestizaje

Whitening through racial mixing, both in its intellectual expression and in the social practices of courtship, marriage, and sexuality, betrayed its foundation in racism through the closely controlled types of interracial contacts that white Cubans allowed and encouraged or, conversely, prohibited and feared. In a similar vein, Ann Stoler's (1995) Foucauldian analysis of colonial Indonesia argued that the conjugal couple linked individual desires to social reproduction. Foucault recognized the relationship between an individual's sexuality and the security of the social body when the future of the race and the nation depended on the population's sexual practices (Dreyfus and Rabinow, in Stoler 1995, 41). In this context, the policing of sex in colonial Indonesia became the state's concern as part of its "biopolitical management of life" (Stoler 1995, 42). In Cuba the difficulties of the "biopolitical management of life" were apparent in the prohibitions on interracial marriage and the public fear of black men uniting with white women. As in other slave societies, whites feared that sexual relations between blacks and whites, if not controlled, could undermine the institution of slavery and the racial hierarchy and lead to the country's damnation. Mixing threatened white dominance by blurring the racial categories and the racial order. In these contexts, laws against fornication and marriage were mainly directed toward keeping white women and black men apart (the opposite patterns of interracial couples reinforced rather than challenged the existing system of group stratification) (Bardaglio 1999).

Given the risks inherent in mestizaje, white Cuban elites had an ambivalent attitude toward miscegenation. On the one hand, whitening the population through racial mixing was important to accelerate the progress of the nation. On the other hand, the white elites feared that mulattos were psychologically unbalanced and that the negative characteristics of the "lower races" might emerge as an even greater social problem since "whitening" also necessarily entailed "darkening" (Helg 1990).

Many nineteenth-century European theorists strongly disapproved of racial mixing and believed that the offspring of such unions were infertile and sickly.[3] Miscegenation could thus lead to barbarism and degeneration. This sentiment was epitomized in the following quote by Louis Agassiz (1807–1873), the eminent Swiss naturalist and founder of the museum of comparative zoology at Harvard University: "The production of half-breeds is a sin against purity of character. . . . [F]ar from presenting to me a natural solution of our difficulties, the idea of amalgamation is most repugnant to my feelings, I hold it to be a perversion of every natural sentiment. . . . No effort should be spared to check that which is abhorrent to our better nature, and to the progress of a higher civilization and purer morality" (Agassiz 1863, as quoted in Gould 1981, 48).

Therefore, white Cuban elites never thought of recruiting their own families to the cause of whitening through intermarriage (Kutzinski 1993). Acceptable couples included consensual or extramarital unions between elite white men and nonwhite women and, to a lesser degree, interracial relations and marriage between two individuals from the lower classes. The "right" types of couples could lead to the nation's salvation, while the "wrong" types would result in the nation's damnation. From the white perspective, sex could pollute, particularly if it occurred between white women and men of color.

Verena Martínez-Alier's classic book, *Marriage, Class, and Colour in Nineteenth-Century Cuba* (1989, originally published in 1974), explored interracial couplings as a site for understanding the dynamics of the racial, class, and gender hierarchies in colonial Cuba. Based on archival records of marriages, especially those between people of different color classifications, she examined skin color as a symbol of the division of labor in colonial Cuban society. Racial mixing, particularly in marriage, undermined the structure of the economy based on slave labor. Race relations in the colonial system, she argued, were fundamentally about class relations.

Martínez-Alier found that opposition to unions between white women and Afrocuban men was fierce in nineteenth-century Cuba.

White elites fearful of mestizaje often talked of Afrocuban men marrying white women, although the reverse type of union was more frequent. Cuban intellectual José Antonio Saco, a proponent of whitening, stated: "If mestizos were born of unions between white women and black men, this would be regrettable, indeed, because reducing our [white] population it would weaken it in every sense; but since the opposite occurs, far from considering it a menace I regard it as an advantage. . . . [T]his is the stepping stone by which the African race rises to mix with the white" (as quoted in Martínez-Alier 1989, 36).

For Saco, then, whitening of the population was to take place exclusively through women of color and white men. As Saco's statement illustrated, white women held the key to the future of the nation by determining racial purity as they were the true perpetuators of the lineage. Similarly, in anti-miscegenation campaigns in the United States, for example, many of the racial purity arguments focused on the female body as a powerful emblem for nationalist goals and desires. The discussion of women's bodies as a kind of property over which black men and white men battled for access and control (often using the vocabulary of protection) was symbolic of the political goals of controlling actual territory and empires. The Cuban female body was a metaphor to convey visions of nationalism in colonial Cuba.

White men entrusted white women with the tasks of preserving and perpetuating whiteness and family honor and the privilege and status associated with color. In slave societies, they were the point of vulnerability in the chain designed to maintain the color line (Bardaglio 1999). Men's control of female sexuality was crucial in maintaining and reproducing "racial purity." Thus the stereotypes of virtuous white Cuban women contrasted sharply with the presumed lustful, lascivious nature of Afrocuban women. Imperiled white womanhood and the image of the black male rapist threatened devolution of the species and the progress of the nation. This stereotype of white women belied white males' fear not only of black male sexuality that could threaten their "virtuous" women, but also of white women's sexuality as well. White women were "desired objects, also unruly desiring subjects . . . [and] their unmanaged sexuality was considered a threat to the social body" (Stoler 1995, 41). These divergent constructions of female sexuality were expounded upon in novels, *teatro bufo,* and popular songs which sanctioned white males' sexual advances toward Afrocuban women while supporting their protective role over white women's sexual purity (Helg 1995). Largely lost in the respective politicizations of the black and white female body was the idea of consensual sex and love between individuals of different races. Interracial sex for the most part was a male choice and either white or Afrocuban female victimization (Bair 1999, 408).

The maintenance of the elites' family system was the social glue that held the society and the racial hierarchy together in colonial Cuba. Marriage and the family were the fundamental sites of social reproduction that provided children with their social position. White parents perceived mixed unions as a menace to family integrity and honor, due to the degrading slave background of the individual of color. Since the racially inferior parent determined the group membership of the offspring, white families felt that such unions would harm the children's social status and family solidarity. Martínez-Alier (1989) suggests that the explanation for this pattern lies in the highly unequal distribution of means of production in the society. This unequal distribution was preserved by an emphasis on heredity of both property and status. Inheritance was divided equally between all offspring, both male and female, and women brought dowries of property, money, or goods to their marriages. Thus marriage choices were fundamental to the maintenance of the system. Through proper marriages, wealthy families could expand and consolidate their social and economic position, illustrating the fact that "a cardinal principle of every stratified social order is that the majority of those marrying shall marry equals" (Davis 1941, 376). In colonial Cuba this consolidation effectively served to guarantee that, among the elite, class and race would reinforce each other in an exclusionary symbiosis juxtaposed against a multiracial working class (Martínez-Alier 1989).

Given the "polluting" potential that interracial couples possessed from the white elites' perspective, the Cuban colonial government at times outlawed legally recognized marriages between whites and people of color. The public's receptiveness to these unions was very much dependent on the political and economic relations with Spain.

For example, barring such marriages during the Cuban independence struggles was a way for Spain to maintain racial boundaries of the slave society. By contrast, the Cuban independence movement used racial integration and mixing as a key strategy to combat the "Africanization scare." In turn, Spanish prohibitions on interracial marriages underscored racial fear in order to stymie revolutionary leaders' attempt at racial unity. The Cuban colonial government abolished slavery in 1886, and the government soon deemed anti-miscegenation laws outdated and finally repealed them. While abolition brought none of the social upheavals that many elite whites had feared, race remained a salient issue in the struggle for independence, as evidenced by José Martí's conceptualization of the nation based on racial inclusion.

Interracial marriages in the nineteenth century represented, at best, a tiny fraction of the total number of legally recognized unions. Although the considerable number of mulatos in nineteenth-century Cuba attests to the frequency of racial mixing, the vast majority of these people tended to be offspring of nonmarital consensual unions or rapes. The state sanctioned and encouraged concubinary relations in many colonial settlements (Mexico, the East Indies, Malaysia, Indochina, and parts of French- and British-ruled Africa) (Stoler 1995). Ethnomusicologist Robin Moore (1997) notes that in the nineteenth century, Cuban institutions such as the *casas de cuna* fostered racial mixing with the goal of whitening. Usually managed by mulata prostitutes or madams, these small dance halls served as musical entertainment venues where white men could socialize with and sleep with women of color (R. Moore 1997). These centers facilitated both interracial and interclass mixing.

Indeed, whitening provided an uneasy synthesis between desires of both blacks and whites for social and cultural advancement. Many women of color, for their part, actively sought these relationships as a means to better their social and economic circumstances. Stoler, writing on colonial Southeast Asia, notes: "Sexual desires were structured by desires and discourses that were never about sex alone. . . . [S]exual desire in colonial and post colonial contexts [has] been a crucial transfer point of power, tangled with racial exclusions in complicated ways. Such desires . . . may use sex as a vehicle to master a practical world (privileged schooling, well-paying jobs)" (1995, 190).

For Afrocuban women, those "desires" included improving their own position or at least that of their offspring by whitening or "advancing the race." As Helen Safa (2005) also noted, enslaved black women could sometimes negotiate freedom for themselves and their children through such unions. Interracial unions were an important means to manumission and contributed to the growth in the numbers of free coloreds in colonial Cuba (Safa 2005).

Martínez-Alier (1989) documented the rare cases of white women marrying men of color in the colonial period. On these occasions, the white woman had to be in such extraordinarily bad circumstances as to be ineligible for marriage within her own group (Martínez-Alier 1989). Similarly, it was often white men of low status who sought to marry women of color in colonial times. Martínez-Alier suggests that why white men of working class would make such a choice included these reasons: in gratitude for some service rendered; for romantic love, which could override social constraints; for "honor," as many men, regardless of race, had an obsessive concern with preserving female "virtue"; to give up a "sinful" unmarried life; and to provide for one's mixed-race offspring (1989, 64–68).

Class distinctions greatly affected how tolerant white families were of liaisons between white men and Afrocuban women. In unions between white men and Afrocuban women, great emphasis was placed on the woman's respectability and her family's background.[4] Wealth on the part of the Afrocuban family could at times improve the woman's status sufficiently for her be a likely candidate for a mixed marriage. Yet in terms of social status race trumped class, so even though economically the Afrocuban woman might have married beneath her, in terms of overall social status she still would have made significant gains by marrying a white man, not only for herself, but also for her children. In nineteenth-century Cuba, it was precisely working-class white men and free-born mulatas who were most likely to marry (Martínez-Alier 1989, 26).

From Whitening to a Mestizo Republic

José Martí (1853–1895), the white leader of Cuba's independence movement and an ardent antiracist who championed racial integration, offered Cuba an escape from the miscegenation dichotomy of damnation or salvation (Martínez-Echazábel 1998). Martí neither rejected nor embraced miscegenation, but rather "affirmed the mestizo condition of 'our America' as the historical by-product of conquest and colonization. . . . *His rhetoric on race . . . would permeate . . . discourses of nationalism and modernity*" (Martínez-Echazábel 1998, 32, emphasis added). Martí linked an *inclusive* nationalism with a willed blindness to racial difference, forging a mass movement for independence in the process. Drawing from the philosophical roots of egalitarianism and humanism, he saw Cuba's future in the creation of a color-blind utopian national space (Martínez-Echazábel 1998). He expressed this ideal in his often-quoted phrase, "Cuban means more than white, mulatto, or black." Martí believed that "the man of color has a right to be treated according to his qualities as a man, with no reference to his color" (Martí 1889, as quoted in Foner 1977, 308). Marti's approach was to transcend racial differences by incorporating them into "a national identity that presumed a uniqueness in color (a Cuban color)" and a sameness in national identity (Cubanness) (Martínez-Echazábel 1998, 31). Martí rejected racial labels as divisive. While this offered Afrocubans a way past discrimination in one sense, it also left little room not only for black political activism but also for black subjectivity (Ferrer 1998). His ideal of racial transcendence shrouded the racial issue in silence.

Tragically, Martí did not live to see an independent Cuba, dying in battle in 1895. Cuba became independent in 1898, but independence proved a great disappointment for many Cubans of all skin colors. Freedom from Spain was immediately followed by years of occupation by the United States, whose race policies also curtailed Martí's dreams of a raceless nation (Ferrer 1999).[5] Furthermore, on the eve of independence, the insurgent army replaced many black military leaders with white ones who the insurgents thought provided a more "civilized" face for the new republic (Ferrer 1999, 202). Martí's early death, along with the marginalization of Afrocuban military leaders, left blacks and mulatos in post-independence Cuba without their most powerful advocates. And when the newly formed republic did not respond to the concerns of the Afrocubans who had fought and died for it, Afrocubans organized into a political party, the Partido Independiente de Color, and in May of 1912 staged an armed protest in the eastern province of Oriente. The government crushed the rebellion, known as the Little War of 1912, massacring perhaps as many as six thousand Afrocubans (Helg 1995).

Throughout the first half of the twentieth century, institutional structures, discriminatory hiring practices, organizations, and legislation marginalized blacks and mulatos and denigrated African-derived culture and religions. Organizations such as La Orden de los Caballeros (the Cuban chapter of the Ku Klux Klan), founded in 1928, and La Liga Blanca de Cuba sought to bar Afrocubans from every aspect of national life (Kutzinski 1993; R. Moore 1997). Whites' fear of violence by black men against white women and the fear of using white girls and women in "witchcraft" led the state to outlaw Santería practices and prosecute practitioners of Afrocuban religions in the early twentieth century (Bronfman 2004; Helg 1995).

Whitening in its physical, cultural, and ideological dimensions remained a central theme in Cuban race relations throughout the republican period. From the start of the new republic, the state continued the project of physical whitening by means of a new immigration strategy: discouraging nonwhite immigration and encouraging Spanish and other white immigration to lighten the population. In 1902, the U.S. occupation forces imposed an immigration law prohibiting Chinese immigration and restricting the entrance of other nonwhites into Cuba. The government strengthened this measure in 1906 with new legislation that encouraged the settlement of families from Europe and the Canary Islands, along with the immigration of laborers from Scandinavia and northern Italy (Helg 1990, 1995). Immigration controls sought to diminish the nonwhite population and in the 1930s even led to the deportation of black immigrants, largely agricultural workers from other Caribbean islands.

Historian Alexandra Bronfman's book, *Measures of Equality* (2004), documents how the racist hierarchies that supported nineteenth-century ideas of whitening and evolutionary paradigms of racial progress continued into the first half of the twentieth century, now informed by the burgeoning "scientific" studies of race. This new "science" also presented conflicting views of miscegenation. On the one hand, Cuban scholar Francisco Figueros saw Afrocubans as "a race vegetating in childhood. . . .

[T]he Africans brought to Cuba musical sense, exhibitionism, and lasciviousness, and their lack of foresight" (as quoted in Helg 1990, 48). He felt that the Spanish colonial legacy similarly hindered Cuba's modernization and advancement. Cuban society could only be saved through racial mixing to whiten the population and a closer connection to the United States (Helg 1990). On the other hand, Cuban criminologists like Israel Castellanos, inspired by Lombrosian criminology, believed that miscegenation bred delinquency, and the physical mestizaje was "the most important factor in the creation of the contemporary underworld" (Bronfman 2004, 130). Bronfman argued that Castellanos's "brand of penitentiary anthropology . . . became a fixture of the Cuban state until at least 1959. His positivist view of race as a measurable phenomenon and insistence on strong ties between race and criminality updated the image of the *brujo* (sorcerer) or *ñáñigo*" (128). Likewise, for Cuban eugenicists such as Domingo Ramos, racial mixing would not improve the race, but rather lead to "inharmonious beings" (120). Strongly influenced by American eugenicist Charles Davenport, Ramos argued against mestizaje and advocated instead working to improve each race separately (Bronfman 2004). While Ramos's ideas about racial improvement through monitoring marriages and sterilizing those deemed "unfit to reproduce" were too radical to be implemented, his call for restrictions on "undesirable immigrants" helped to strengthen existing immigration policies with the goal of whitening in mind.

Whitening through racial mixing and immigration did continue despite ambivalent views of miscegenation. However, interracial marriages remained the exception, not the rule. Enid Logan's (2005) large-scale sociological study of marital practices based on Catholic Church archives found that most marriages continued to be racially endogamous in the first half of the twentieth century. Analyzing 14,500 marriage records from three Havana parishes from 1902 to 1940, she calculated that the overall rate of interracial marriage was less than 5 percent. Furthermore, her research suggested that interracial marriages became increasingly less frequent during the course of the nearly forty-year period she investigated. She concluded that the significance of race in selecting a spouse increased during the first half of the twentieth century (Logan 2005).

As in the colonial period, mestizaje persisted largely through consensual unions and other liaisons, and individuals practiced it for their own reasons within this racial landscape. In her biography, Maria de los Reyes Castillo Bueno (Reyita), a poor black woman, recounted how the racial hierarchy and racism shaped her life in a myriad of ways in the first half of the twentieth century (Castillo Bueno 2000). Reyita (1902–1997) began her life story:

> I am Reyita, a regular, ordinary person. A natural person, respectful, helpful, decent, affectionate and very independent. For my mother, it was an embarrassment, that I—of her four daughters—was the only black one. . . . She rebuked me in hurtful ways and was also saying: 'that black one.' . . . I always felt she rejected me. I was the victim of terrible discrimination on my mother's part. And if you add what was then the case in Cuba, you can understand why I never wanted a black husband. I had good reason, you know. I didn't want to have children as black as me, so that no one would look down on them, no one would harass and humiliate them. . . . [T]hat's why I wanted to 'adelantar la raza,' that's why I married a white man. (Castillo Bueno 2000, 21–22)

The darkest and thus the most marginalized child in her family, Reyita told how she consciously employed the strategy of whitening to lighten her offspring. She and her common-law white husband had eight children. Although he was not always very supportive of her or their children, she stayed with him and worked hard to ensure that their mulato children were educated and had better life chances than she herself had experienced.

Cultural Mestizaje and Cubanidad

Mestizaje was not only a physical mixing of the races but also a blending of African and Spanish cultures to create Cubanidad, a uniquely Cuban hybrid. The cultural blending was often met with as much ambivalence as its physical counterpart. Bronfman (2004) argues that some Afrocuban writers and intellectuals in the 1920s and 1930s cautiously approached the celebration of racial mixing and African cultural elements of Cuban culture. Gustavo Urrutia, a prominent black Cuban writer and columnist, condemned racial mixing since it was based in ideas of whitening and ultimately served to eliminate the black population in Cuba. In contrast, the renowned Afrocuban poet Nicolás Guillén did celebrate mestizaje as the source of Cubanidad, but still recognized and acknowledged its tragic origins. Writing of Guillén, Bronfman states, in part quoting Guillén:

> He injected into racial mixture the violence at its source. Riddled with pain and humiliation, mestizaje had not been born of harmonious coexistence but of the power struggles that permeated social relations. Thus Cuban men had repeated their fathers' habits, seeking ambivalent lovers and populating the island with a mixed race, initially outcast: "And often, following the example of their fathers, once they became men they sought amongst the black women a lover both ardent and resigned, out of whose womb would emerge, in time, the seeds of the island's future— and present—mestizaje." (2004, 150)

By the late 1920s, it became evident that neither immigration nor miscegenation would make Cuba a white country. Physical whitening had failed, and so the nation needed a new conceptualization of Cubanidad to reconcile modernity and racial diversity (de la Fuente 2001). As in much of Latin America, nationalist ideologues came to argue that the most important effect of colonialism was the genetic and cultural mixing that produced the assumed "essence" of each new nation (Klor de Alva 1995). To create this new essence in Cuba, nationalist intellectuals turned to what Alejandro de la Fuente called "the exaltation of autochthonous cultural symbols" (2001, 180). For Cuba, this meant a synthesis of white Hispanic and black African elements to create a uniquely Cuban amalgamation, a new Cuban race. The Afrocubanista literary movement epitomized this nationalist ideology through the valorization of cultural and physical mestizaje. Cubanidad now celebrated the Afrocuban contributions to Cuban culture, and black elements became central in the expressive arts— music, painting, and literature—of the 1920s and 1930s. Rather than whitening to eliminate blackness or Martí's raceless approach, the new nationalist rhetoric espoused racial and cultural mixture as the essence of Cubanidad. To be Cuban was to be mestizo or mixed race, to be of "Cuban color."

Imagining and constructing Cubanidad and negotiating the role of cultural and racial mixing in that project was neither a stable nor coherent act, but rather was an ongoing process in twentieth-century Cuba. The tensions between the African and Spanish elements of Cuban culture embedded in mestizaje continued. The *origenista* artists and writers of the 1940s privileged the *blanco-criollo* ethos and by extension the white-European aspect of Cuban identity (Martínez 2000). Art historian Juan Martínez argues that white artists stressed Cuba's Hispanic roots in order to counter the Afrocubanistas of the previous decades as well as to resist the encroaching North American popular culture. However, the Afrocubanistas did not disappear, but continued to stress blacks' contributions to the Cuban nation and also to highlight the ongoing racial inequalities on the island.

The work of the famed Cuban ethnologist Fernando Ortiz (1881–1969), the "third discoverer of Cuba," provided fuel for the fight for racial equality and the promotion of the mestizo nature of Cubanidad.[6] Born in Cuba and educated in Spain, Ortiz returned to Cuba and focused his extensive intellectual career on the study of Cuban culture. With in-depth explorations of Afrocuban music, religion, and traditions, Ortiz documented and valorized the rich African roots of Cuban culture and played a key role in promoting the idea of national culture shared by all Cubans. Through his theory of "transculturation," he likened Cuban national culture to an *ajiaco* (a traditional Cuban stew), where many elements came together to create a new fusion that was uniquely Cuban. In introducing this neologism, Ortiz writes:

> I have chosen the word *transculturation* to express the highly varied phenomena that have come about in Cuba as a result of the extremely complex transmutations of culture that have taken place here. . . . *[T]ransculturation* better expresses the different phases of the process of transition from one culture to another because this does not consist merely in acquiring another culture, which is what the English word *acculturation* really implies, but the process also necessarily involves the loss or uprooting of

a previous culture, which could be defined as a deculturation. In addition it carries the idea of the consequent creation of new cultural phenomena which could be called neoculturation. . . . [T]he result of every union of culture is similar to that of the reproductive process between individuals: the offspring always has something of both parents but is always different from each of them. (Ortiz 1995 [1947], 98–103)

His theory of transculturation continued the emphasis on a fundamentally mixed national culture and has become one of the cornerstones of thinking that continues today.

Although Ortiz's earlier works were more problematic, heavily influenced by the biological views of race and criminology of the Italian Césare Lombroso, Ortiz's views changed over time.[7] While initially advocating the progress of Cuba through the elimination not of blacks themselves but of the manifestations and atavisms of African culture, from the 1930s onward Ortiz became known for his antiracist writings (Helg 1990). Influenced by anthropologists such as Bronislaw Malinowski, Ortiz supported anthropological findings arguing that, scientifically, races did not exist, and on that basis he fought against racial discrimination in Cuba (see Ortiz, 1975 [1946]; Ortiz, 1993b). In his studies of African-derived culture and religions, he worked to valorize practices shunned by most white Cubans of his generation. Despite Ortiz's ideological shift on issues of race, Paul Ryer (2006) notes that some scholars (R. Moore 1997; Perry 2004) still question whether Ortiz's later works really engaged with the power dynamics at the heart of racial inequalities. However, his contributions in championing the fundamental notion of the hybridity of Cubanidad and his prolific scholarship continue to validate his stature and place in the pantheon of Cuban intellectuals.

Racism in the Republic

Recent historical accounts, such as those by de la Fuente (2001) and Bronfman (2004), have amply documented the material and ideological realities of racism under the first (1902–1933) and second (1933–1958) Cuban republics. Although the Cuban constitution of 1940 decreed that all races were equal and criminalized racial discrimination, racism persisted. Race remained a salient factor in determining one's access to resources and one's life chances in Cuba. Since receiving the right to vote after Cuban independence, politics and government action became central in Afrocubans' struggle for social justice (de la Fuente 2001).

A key element that exacerbated the fight for racial equality was what de la Fuente (2001) referred to as the enduring feature of Cuban race relations: the distinction between public and private spaces. Throughout the republican periods private spaces were perceived as untouchable—beyond regulation—implying that discrimination and exclusion were legal, and perhaps unavoidable, in private domains such as social clubs and resorts, private and religious schools, and homes (de la Fuente 2001). This affected blacks' access to jobs and important social networks that operated in exclusive all-white clubs and schools.

Blacks, in turn, focused their struggles in the republican periods on gaining equal access to public spaces (labor unions, government, and the workplace) and created their own private social clubs that offered recreational activities, provided mutual aid, and in some cases fostered the practice of Afrocuban religions. Though officially apolitical and nonreligious, most Afrocuban societies had political links, received government subsidies, and were used by politicians to court the black vote. De la Fuente (2001) contended that up until the revolution these societies were important venues for elite and middle-class blacks to assert their presence in Cuban society and politics. However, Afrocuban involvement in politics had negative consequences as well. De la Fuente (2001) argued that at key turning points in Cuban history, such as after the fall of the dictators Gerardo Machado (1933) and then Fulgencio Batista (1958), white leaders largely excluded Afrocubans from the process of building a new Cuba on the (false) grounds of having supported the ousted leaders. Thus, time and again, the project of nation building remained primarily in the control of whites.

At the dawn of the revolution in 1959, some Cubans saw mestizaje in its physical, cultural, and ideological forms as the hope for a future of harmonious race relations, and others viewed it with skepticism. Many black and mulatto activists found Cuba's racial heterogeneity valuable as the basis for race-based political strategies (Bronfman 2004). In this sense, mestizaje served not as a silencing veil shrouding racial inequalities but as a language that blacks and mulattos exploited in the struggle for racial justice. Mestizaje could be used to obfuscate racial conflicts, but it also could provide a space in which to struggle for racial justice (de la Fuente 2001).

The interracial couples that produced mestizos—the embodiment of the national ideal of mestizaje—inhabited a world where a racist hierarchy and ideas about improving the race through whitening persisted amid the hopes of racial transcendence envisioned by José Martí and the ideas of a hybrid Cubanidad expounded by Fernando Ortiz. Over the decades of the Cuban republics, Cubans of color had mobilized to fight for racial justice and an equal place in the nation—violently in 1912, and later through politics, labor unions, and race-based societies. On this contested ideological and political ground, the revolution attempted to sow the seeds of socialist equality, and over the next fifty years it harvested an uncertain yield.

Research on Race in Revolutionary Cuba

The new Cuban government's official position on racial inequalities was remarkably straightforward and rooted in the classic Marxist-Leninist base–superstructure division. It asserted that institutionalized racism was eliminated at the start of the revolution when its structural basis in capitalist society was dismantled. The title of Pedro Serviat's (a black Cuban scholar) book *The Black Problem in Cuba and Its Definitive Solution* neatly encapsulated the government's stance. He states: "The economic, cultural and social development of the nations of the socialist community has shown that the only theory that is scientific and can offer adequate solutions to the complex social problems of any nation is Marxism-Leninism. Because the ruling classes had a vested interest in maintaining racial discrimination as a mechanism of competition and division between the black and the white worker, and thereby profited more, it is precisely through the expropriation of these classes that the main economic factor propping up racial and sexual discrimination is eliminated" (Serviat 1986, 90).

From this perspective, the Cuban government argued that, without a structural base, residual individual discrimination in Cuba would simply disappear over time. As the elder generations passed away, racist ideas and attitudes would be buried along with them—so the thinking went. Meanwhile, the socialist revolution silenced those with lingering prejudices as the state would not tolerate or support open expressions of racism. As the Cuban anthropologist Rafael López Valdés summarized early in the revolution, "There are people, white as well as black, who keep nourishing deep in their hearts racial prejudices, no matter how much they try to conceal them. Nevertheless, these persons who feel racial prejudices abstain from expressing them because otherwise they would be . . . confronted by the government and [their actions] condemned" (1973, 23).

Silence, then, came to be a key by-product of government's structuralist approach to racial inequalities. As in colonial and republican times, the race question posed a threat to national unity. Political scientist Mark Q. Sawyer argues that "the practice of repressing black demands while paying lip service to racial democracy and national unity, which later became a key feature of the Cuban Revolution's response to race, borrowed both pragmatically and ideologically from the discourse of the early days of the Cuban nation" (2006, 41). So silence on race did not begin with the revolutionary government, but their strategy dovetailed with a long-standing historical approach to avoiding the divisive issue. After an initial flurry of announcements and investigations (which I discuss in more detail in chapter 2), the race question became a loaded gun that for decades the revolutionary government preferred not to discharge—at least not through public discourse.

In a 1992 article in the popular weekly Cuban magazine *Bohemia*, a forty-nine-year-old black woman reiterated this official position and the tenet of the color-blind approach that remaining racial inequalities should be resolved through some unspecified behind-the-scenes action: "To be sincere, I don't think you should talk about this topic [racial discrimination], rather work to eliminate the problem. But don't publish anything about it. . . . Because that could be used as a weapon by our enemies to say 'Ah look, there still is racism in Cuba.'" The journalist countered her statement, suggesting, "But one way to help resolve the problem is to recognize that it exists, and then we can think of how to solve it." The woman responded emphatically: "No. No. In the press, no.

Publicly, no, compañero" (Gutiérrez 1992, 5). Despite her protest, the article itself was part of a new opening on public discussions of race and racial discrimination on the island that began in the early 1990s (de la Fuente 2008; Fernandez 2001; Rodríguez Ruiz 2008).

For scholars concerned with race relations on the island, the race question has been politically loaded and divisive during many decades of the revolution. With the costly and deadly politics of the Cold War and the U.S. government's continuing, though now anachronistic, fight against communism as the background, the political implications of scholarship on Cuba have always been potentially explosive. In the substantial literature on race relations in revolutionary Cuba, many scholars have been caught in ideological debates in which a serious examination of race relations has often been secondary to positing one's political position vis-à-vis the revolution.[8] The resulting evaluations of whether or not the revolutionary regime "solved the racial problem" were contingent on one's acceptance or rejection of the Cuban government's position on race as outlined above and on assessments of the status of race relations prior to the revolution (Casal 1979; Nodal 1986). Alejandro de la Fuente (1995) astutely divides the debate into four camps. The first three groups agreed that the revolution inherited a racial problem but differed in that the first holds that they completely solved it (Carneado 1962; Serviat 1986), the second maintains that they did not (Clytus 1970; C. Moore 1988), and the third argues that the revolution eradicated many key aspect of racial inequality but some forms of discrimination still persisted (Casal 1979). The fourth camp posits that the revolution had a positive impact on race relations, but that its contribution was only part of a long-term trend toward racial integration in Cuba (J. Domínguez 1978; Masferrer and Mesa-Lago 1974). On the whole, both the Cuban government's structuralist approach and much of the scholarly literature on race in revolutionary Cuba often have been hobbled by ideological and political constraints.

Excellent historical accounts (Bronfman 2004; de la Fuente 2001; Ferrer 1999; Helg 1995) have done much to provide a comprehensive analysis of race relations in nineteenth- and twentieth-century Cuba, focusing on how national trends, social science, government policies, economic conditions, and different forms of social action have shaped racial inequality on the island. This research provides an important historical context in which to understand the "private spaces" and everyday expressions of race and racism in contemporary Cuba. While many scholars (Booth 1976; Casal 1979; de la Fuente 2001; Fernández Robaina 1991; Sutherland 1969) acknowledge the persistence of a "racist mentality" (also termed cultural racism, individual discrimination, and private racism), it has been difficult until the 1990s to conduct the type of indepth fieldwork necessary to examine the everyday practices of race on the island. As a result, much of the literature examining the "racial problem" in contemporary Cuba prior to 1990 tends to follow the revolution's problematic conceptual analysis of splitting racism into institutionalized or structural racism and individual psychological notions of racism. This paradigm delineates an "important" racism (that is, state policies and discriminatory actions) and an "unimportant" racism (that is, individual discourse and thoughts, images, stereotypes, and representations).

Anthropologists (Harrison 1998; Mullings 2005) concur that both ideological and structural forces contribute to persistent racism. From Michel Foucault we have learned that power is exercised in many arenas beyond state control and that hierarchies are enacted through individual actions and discourse as well as through laws and state structures. Theoretically, then, the distinction between institutional and personal racism is untenable. Philomena Essed cogently argues: "[The distinction] places the individual outside the institutional, thereby severing rules, regulations, and procedures from the people who make and enact them, as if it concerned qualitatively different racisms rather than different positions and relations through which racism operates. . . . Individual racism is a contradiction in itself because racism is by definition the expression or activation of group power" (1991, 37). This conceptualization of racism demands that we address both the ideological aspects of racism in revolutionary Cuba and the commonsense and quotidian expressions of racism in order to achieve a fuller understanding of racial dynamics on the island. Structures of racism do not exist external to agents but rather are made through peoples' actions and discourse.

The historically situated and variable nature of racial dynamics on the island, detailed in accounts of nineteenth- and early twentieth-century

Cuba (Bronfman 2004; de la Fuente 2001), are beginning to be explored in revolutionary Cuba as well. In the final section of his groundbreaking book *A Nation for All: Race, Inequality, and Politics in Twentieth-Century Cuba*, de la Fuente (2001) documents the policies, progress, and obstacles the revolutionary government faced in battling racial inequality on the island. De la Fuente (2001) asserts that in one sense the revolution did the most to eliminate racism compared to any previous Cuban government, yet it also did the most to silence discussions about its persistence. The revolution's impact on racial inequalities, de la Fuente concludes, has been complex and contradictory. With measures for integration and a color-blind social equality in place, the revolutionary government took racial equality as an achieved fact rather than a continuing challenge. As a result, racial inequality became a taboo subject in public debate except in the realm of culture and international politics. De la Fuente convincingly argues that the lack of public debate about racism facilitated the survival and reproduction of the racist stereotypes that the revolution claimed to oppose. Achieving racial equality in revolutionary Cuba, de la Fuente argues, was largely dependent on government performance—which began to falter in the 1990s with the onset of the special period. He suggests that in the special period racial inequalities and tensions have increased substantially, and persisting racist ideologies have excluded blacks from the more lucrative positions in the new mixed economy.

In his recent book on racial politics in Cuba, the political scientist Mark Sawyer (2006) also looks to fluctuations in government performance to predict and explain the shifting racial climate on the island. Sawyer develops the idea of "race cycles" to capture the structural, ideological, and dynamic dimensions of racism. During the course of the revolution, he argues, Cuba has cycled through periods in which racial inequalities have been ameliorated and periods in which racism has been re-entrenched. In focusing on the role of the state, he concludes that periods of state crises can result in progress for blacks and more equality, while subsequent state consolidations have produced stagnation and increased inequality. His theory incorporates ideology, structure, events, and agency into a nonlinear perspective. In Cuba racism and the racial hierarchy have proven perfectly compatible with the revolution's color-blind rhetoric. Sawyer argues that these seeming contradictions find expression in what he terms "inclusionary discrimination," where patterns of racial inclusion and exclusion exist simultaneously. The revolution, he argues, made some advances toward racial equality, but these were limited by the persisting "inclusionary discrimination" and the adaptability of racist ideologies. His book is notable for contributing this dynamic model of race relations at the state level and for its sophisticated conceptualizations of race and racism.

Scholars on the island have also recently acknowledged the continuing racial inequalities in Cuba and noted that even so-called benign prejudice does indeed have material implications. This is evinced in the lucrative tourism market, where highly desirable positions are given to applicants with *buena presencia* (good looks), a thinly veiled attempt to specify someone white or at least light-skinned (Espina Prieto and Rodríguez Ruiz 2006). Scholars both in Cuba and abroad (Fernández Robaina 1991; McGarrity 1992; Pérez Sarduy and Stubbs 1993; Espina Prieto and Rodríguez Ruiz 2006; Morales Domínguez 2008; Rodríguez Ruiz 2004) agree that racism remains alive in the thinking and practices of many Cubans, both overtly and in "inferential" forms (Hall 1981). It is by no means merely an ideological system. Pedro Pérez Sarduy and Jean Stubbs observe that in Cuba "blacks continue to be marginalized in personal, social, and cultural relations . . . [and] blacks continue to predominate in older, poor neighborhoods. . . . There [are] more blacks [than whites] in the country's jails" (1993, 11). This clearly suggests that Afrocubans still shoulder the burden of racism in socially and materially consequential ways.

Research on Interracial Couples in Revolutionary Cuba

> In a very fundamental way, we all distinguish those who are of
> our kind from those who are not of our kind by asking ourselves
> the question, "Do we intermarry with them?"
> —Edmund Leach

In contemporary Cuba, assessing the actual number of interracial couples is a Sisyphean task for numerous reasons. First, shifting definitions of race and the problems of racial identification make it very difficult in some cases to identify exactly which couples are, in fact, interracial. Second, the revolution's color-blind approach to race, again combined with the complexity of racial identification, has made statistical and census data on this issue unavailable or of questionable reliability. Third, many couples are not in legal marriages but in consensual unions that the state cannot count and record with the same accuracy as formally registered marriages. Examining census data, de la Fuente (1995) speculates that the high growth rate in the number of mulattos between 1953 and 1981 reflected an increase in the frequency of interracial unions. Other references in the literature (Booth 1976; Clytus 1970; Nodal 1986; Safa 2009; Taylor 1988) to the frequency or increase of interracial couples across the island have been mostly impressionistic for the above reasons.

The frequency of interracial couples also varies across Cuba due to the regional differences in racial composition on the island (Booth 1976; Rodríguez Ruiz et al. 1994). The eastern provinces (Guantánamo, Santiago de Cuba) have traditionally had a higher percentage of darker Cubans, and here interracial mixture is more accentuated and mixed couples are more common. The central provinces, such as Camagüey, Ceigo de Avila, Las Tunas, Holguín, and Las Villas, are known to be whiter and more racially endogamous by comparison. The western provinces (Pinar del Río, La Habana, and Matanzas) have a higher percentage of both whites and blacks than the national average, but fewer mestizos. Havana is more racially mixed, especially because, as the capital and the island's most populous city, it has been the destination for many migrating from the provinces.

Among the different modes of interracial unions, legal marriages continue to be the exception, as they were in the republic and colonial periods, though laws no longer prohibit them.[9] Indeed, many scholars cite the resistance to interracial unions as an indicator of persisting racial inequalities and racial prejudices (Beatriz 1990; Calderon et al. 1993; de la Fuente 1995; Gutiérrez 1992; Hoffman and Hoffman 1993; Pérez Sarduy and Stubbs 1993). When it comes to courtships and marriage, even slight differences in skin color matter, testifying to the continuing significance of race and to the fact that nowhere is race more ent than in romance. In over eighty interviews conducted on racial attitudes in Santiago de Cuba by Cuban sociologist Rafael Duharte Jiménez, the most commonly articulated theme by black, mulatto, and white informants was an aversion to interracial unions (Duharte Jiménez and García 1998). In my research, I learned that some blacks and mulattos and many whites entered these relationships with hesitancy and fear, conscious of the racial norms they were transgressing. Given these prevailing social attitudes, it was not surprising that Cuban researchers (Reca Moreira et al. 1990; Rodríguez Ruiz 2008) concluded that the vast majority of unions in Cuba are still racially endogamous, especially for whites.[10] The ongoing strong racial endogamy among whites is also substantiated by the 2002 census data. The Cuban population by skin color shows that the percentage of whites remained relatively stable between the last census taken in 1981 and the one in 2002 (66 percent and 65 percent, respectively).

Starting in the early 1990s the Havana-based Instituto Cubano de Antropología (formerly known as the Centro de Antropología) has conducted several pioneering studies on contemporary race relations in Havana. The findings have been described in a series of articles and unpublished reports (Alvarado Ramos 1996, 1998; Perez Alvarez 1996; Rodríguez Ruiz 1997, 2001, 2004, 2008; Rodríguez Ruiz et al. 1994; Serrano Peralta 1998). The studies were the first large-scale, systematic investigations on contemporary race relations in Havana and focused on structural issues such as educational achievement, employment, and socioeconomic class as well as family relations, prejudice, and continuing discrimination. While limited to a few barrios, the studies presented the most comprehensive on-the-ground look at race relations conducted by Cuban researchers to date. The studies provide insights into the frequency and nature of interracial unions in Havana.

One study was based on a total sample of close to eight hundred households (2,776 people) living in two predominantly working-class, racially mixed barrios in Havana: Carraguao in municipio Cerro and el Barrio Chino in Centro Habana.[11] Researchers collected both statistical and qualitative data on race in relation to class, housing, occupation, education, marriage, and family. The study indicated that of the sample 32 percent of the families were interracial, while the nationwide rate was only 14 percent, according to 1981 census data (Rodríguez Ruiz 2004). Among interracial unions, researchers included black/white unions, black/mulatto unions, mulatto/white unions, and people of Chinese descent with whites/mulattos/blacks. The researchers speculated that this high incidence of interracial couples could be due to the fact that the areas were predominantly mestizo/mulatto and black (55–58 percent), the barrios were largely working class, and researchers employed a broad definition of interracial couples.

The study also found generational differences in the frequency and pattern of interracial couples. Mixed families comprised 34 percent of families with the head of household under thirty years of age, while only 20 percent of the families were interracial when the head of household was over the age of sixty-five. Interestingly, unions between darker men and lighter women predominated in couples under thirty-five, while those between darker women and lighter men were more prevalent in the couples over sixty. This represented a marked generational shift in the kinds of couples formed. The authors attributed this difference to changing values and family attitudes in post-revolutionary Cuba, the improved economic position of blacks and mulattos, and possibly a greater degree of independence among young women. Unfortunately, the researchers did not discuss in further detail this fascinating generational difference or how the factors they listed might have shaped the patterns of interracial couples.

Socioeconomic class also influenced the frequency of interracial couples. Researchers found that these unions were more common among the working class than among the professional/managerial class. Interracial couples in the sample tended to be intraclass unions (Rodríguez Ruiz et al. 1994, 102). By contrast, 70 percent of all racially endogamous couples in the sample were interclass unions. Finally, including black/mestizo couples as interracial, the study noted that these types of interracial unions were more common than those between whites and mestizos or those between whites and blacks. The researchers attributed this to the resistance of whites to "darken," despite the opposite and still pervasive desire of blacks and mulattos to "whiten" (Rodríguez Ruiz et al. 1994, 145). Pablo Rodríguez Ruiz (2004) argued that racist stereotypes still stigmatize blacks, making it more difficult for them to form relationships with whites; and when they do, they are most likely to encounter difficulties (as I will discuss in detail in subsequent chapters). In the study, when people did form these black/white interracial unions, it was whites in the poorest material condition and blacks in middle- or better-class positions who tended to be involved. This pattern followed the classic economy of marriage model, in which partners exchange status characteristics. In this paradigm, higher-achieving black men "marry up" with lower-class white women. In the working-class barrios studied, whites in better material/ class positions were less likely to mix racially, and the same held true for blacks in the poorest conditions (Rodríguez Ruiz et al. 1994, 145). Interracial couples were also more likely to be found living in *solares* (tenements) rather than apartments or houses, again an indication of the mixing being more prevalent in the poorer areas.

Based on the research, Rodríguez Ruiz (2004) identified a series of factors that favored the possibility for an interracial union. Interracial couples were more likely to be found in extended or what he called "complex" families. Larger households headed by younger couples or headed by women were more likely to be interracial, particularly if they were from the working class and if they lived in solares. Interracial unions were more frequent in second or third marriages/unions, and mestizos/mulatos were the most likely to involved in interracial unions. Close to 47 percent of the interracial unions in the study were between mestizos and whites, 25 percent were between mestizos and blacks, and slightly less than 2 percent were between blacks and whites. The remaining unions were combinations involving Chinese descendents together with blacks, whites, or mestizos. Overall, researchers concluded that mestizos/mulatos, rather than blacks, were the force behind continuing mestizaje in the barrios they studied, and the racial mixing continues to come from the more humble (poorer) segments of the population.

In a more recent study conducted in the early 2000s, researchers from the Instituto Cubano de Antropología focused on immigrants from the eastern part of the island (*orientales*) living illegally in a marginal shantytown on the edge of Havana (Rodríguez Ruiz 2008). The migrants are drawn to Havana in the hopes of obtaining better employment and more access to material goods than are available in the eastern provinces

of Cuba (Oriente). However, without legal residency in Havana they
forced to work in the informal sector, and many are unemployed (S
2009). The majority of the population of this shantytown is black and
mulatto. Residents are very low income and live in extremely poor
material conditions. Researchers were surprised to see that the whites
who lived there were totally integrated into the community. The majority of the whites were in interracial relationships with either blacks or
mulattos, which was an atypical pattern for whites, who tend to be the
most racially endogamous group in Cuba. The researchers concluded
that in this extremely marginal community racial differences were not
as significant as in other parts of the city. The shantytown residents
were isolated and stigmatized and generally formed relationships with
each other. Community members collectively struggled for daily survival
regardless of racial distinctions; poverty and stigma in this illegal settlement has leveled racial and class differences (Safa 2009).

The Cuban research on interracial couples provides a backdrop on
which to situate the stories and meanings of the romances that I present in this book. The Instituto Cubano de Antropología studies outline
the frequencies and types of interracial couples found in various barrios in Havana. Building on this, my research explores what these interracial couplings mean for the individuals themselves and their families,
as well as why couplings between black and white Cubans are so infrequent and often meet with so much resistance. It is in these cases of
conflict we can best see the ideological aspects of racism at work. As
Stuart Hall (1981) notes, pernicious and tenacious negative images, concepts, and premises about race are not so much found in official state
declarations or institutionalized structures, but rather are embodied in
commonsense logic that informs everyday social practice and provides
the frameworks through which people represent and interpret visible
physical differences. It is here that the focus on interracial couples provides a lens to examine the ideological dimensions of racism enacted
in commonsense logic, the material implications of racism as they are
manifested in barrios and the new dollarized spaces, as well as a view
of generational differences and differing perspectives on the grassroots
practices and meanings of mestizaje—the pervasive icon of Cubanidad,
but one so fraught with ambivalence.

2

Socialist Equality and the Color-Blind Revolution

The elimination of racism would be one of the plausible social reforms that with firmness and tact could be achieved by the present revolutionary government.

> –Fernando Ortiz, "Cuba puede y debe dar el ejemplo en cuanto al desvanecimiento de los funestos racismos"

I didn't say to anyone here that we were going to open the clubs exclusively so that blacks would go there to dance. I didn't say that. People can dance with whomever they wish, go out with whomever they wish, and get together with whomever they wish. Who is going to force anyone to dance with someone they don't want to? . . . I met one man who said to me, "Listen, do you think that it's correct that a black man *piropee* a white woman?" And then I said to him, "And do you think that it is correct that a white man *piropee* a mulata?" In my opinion it is better that no one *piropee* anyone, that women are respected when they are in the streets. Because basically if all of the *piropeadorea* were poetic the women would be listening to something beautiful, but the *piropos* that are heard in the street . . . are indecent in most cases. . . . Everyone has the obligation to respect women and not insult them in the street."

> –Fidel Castro, "El Espiritu Renovador va a Superar al Tradicionalista"

Just two months after seizing power, Fidel Castro voiced the need for greater racial integration. In his historic speech of March 23, 1959, Castro presented the "four great battles for the well-being of the people" (Castro 1959a, 24). First was the battle against unemployment; second,

54

to reduce the cost of living; third, to raise the salaries of the lowest-paid workers; and fourth, to end racial discrimination in the workplace. He pledged that his government planned to address racial discrimination in two major domains: in the workplace and in recreation and cultural centers (Castro 1959a). The public response to this announcement of a commitment to racial integration was intense (Booth 1976; Fernández Robaina 1991; C. Moore 1988). Here finally was a government that had placed racial equality at the forefront of its agenda, the first to make ending racism a central goal (de la Fuente 2001).[1] Afrocubans rejoiced, but many white Cubans were horrified.

Interestingly, white Cuban men were not afraid that Afrocubans would take their jobs or share their offices; rather they worried that black and mulatto men would enter their exclusive beaches and their private clubs. Even some whites who supported the revolution thought Castro had gone too far. Historian Alejandro de la Fuente argued that Castro's new policies violated "one of the central tenets of Cuba's complex system of race relations: the separation of public and private spaces" (2001, 264–265). Citing the Afrocuban journalist Sixto Gastón Agüero, de la Fuente noted, "The notion that blacks and whites would attend public dances together had created the strongest opposition" (264). Interestingly, de la Fuente suggests that middle-class mulattos—who had risen in the socioracial hierarchy though education and income—felt such integration would threaten their precarious social position. I would go a step further and assert that the public protest that arose around the issue of blacks and whites sharing the dance floor encapsulated the underlying fear of interracial sexual unions, particularly white women with black men. A century earlier in colonial Cuba, the "Africanization scare" led white men to voice the same fear of black and mulatto men possessing white women. The imagined threat of a voracious black male sexuality crystallized white fears of racial integration in colonial Cuba as it did at the start of the revolutionary period. Along with their clubs and their beaches, white elite men sought to "protect" their families.

What kind of nation was this new revolution trying to create? Castro's speeches had struck a central nerve of Cuban race relations—interracial unions. Race mixture through interracial couples was so inextricable from Cuban history and central to national identity, yet racial endogamy remained the "bastion of white inviolability" (Casal 1979, 20)—the ultimate social norm that should not be violated. Castro's plan to integrate private as well as public spaces precipitated public outcry. Haitian poet René Depestre pointed out that after Castro's speeches on integration, "respectable white ladies" fled the country to escape the threat of sexually predatory black men (1965, 124). In an attempt to assuage many white Cubans' fears, Castro delivered another speech (quoted in the epigraph to this chapter). The revolution, he clarified, was not forcing blacks and whites to "dance" together. In this follow-up statement, Castro suggested that the integration of private and personal spaces would happen gradually. The revolutionary government opposed fighting discrimination through legislation; instead it hoped to achieve racial integration (particularly of the private spaces) though color-blind education and persuasion (de la Fuente 2001).

Castro's statement, however, did not dissipate white elites' fear of Afrocuban men pursuing white women. Rather, that fear grew as the revolution's new policies brought blacks, mulattos, and whites together as equals in many social situations. The gradual color-blind approach to integration was an implicit part of the mass volunteer movements, such as the agricultural brigades and the 1961 literacy campaign. Young men and women (often only in their early teens) were sent off together to work in remote rural areas of the island as part of these mobilizations. In a short story first published in 1976, Cuban writer Mirta Yáñez tells of the trepidations of a middle-class, white mother whose fifteen-year-old daughter was going off with a volunteer brigade to pick coffee in the mountains: "And who knows if the coffee-picking mightn't turn your head so much that you even fall in love with a Negro, she says in a powerless rage. You know what it means to be a nice white girl. . . . For a white girl must receive maximum care. . . . She cannot go alone out onto the street" (1989, 41).

The mother's overriding desire to protect her daughter's honor/ virginity echoes nineteenth-century concerns for family honor and status that took the form of control over female sexuality. The mother continues: "And if afterwards her period, her menstruation, is one, two months late, what will the family think of this child who has risked losing her honor going to do volunteer work? For though it is not actually said, honor is not something you can touch, or see, it is only something you lose" (Yáñez 1989, 40). The mother is still concerned with family honor, which for her is tied to her daughter's virginity and, ultimately, a proper—white—partner for marriage. The mother fears not just any sexual union, but an interracial one, and the possibility of a mixed-race or mulatto child that such a coupling would produce. Implicit is a fear that the young woman's sexuality might be unleashed by the sexually predatory nature attributed to Afrocuban men.[2]

The story also suggests a generational rupture between people raised within the new social, political, and economic context of revolutionary Cuba and the older generations. The mother grew up in a world that the revolution hoped to make a memory. The daughter, meanwhile, committed to the revolution, is coming of age in a new world governed, in part, by the ideals of an egalitarian and color-blind society. Historical specificity is essential in understanding each cultural configuration and pattern. This is especially true in societies that have experienced dramatic revolutions and tremendous political and economic upheavals. Cohorts in these societies have different historical experiences. Some generations witnessed and helped to created epic social changes. Others who came later inherited the structures and institutions already established by the previous generations. Each generation became heir to the previous generations' successes as well as their failures.

The Cuban revolution, now in its fifth decade, seems monolithic as a metaphor for transformative social change. Fidel Castro stated in a 1963 speech: "The Revolution is a developing, dynamic process. But there is only one Revolution. If it is not a revolution, there is no revolutionary process. And if it stops, it is not a revolution. . . . If it is a revolution from the first step, it will remain a revolution to the last one" (Castro, 1963, 4). The revolution is not a moment in time, but an ongoing process of change. This works as a metaphor, but the revolution is deeply fissured as an ongoing social practice. From the standpoint of different generational cohorts, "the revolution" has had different meanings and effects over the course of its reign. Whether we divide the revolution analytically into generational cohorts or periodize it by changes in the organization, ideology, and outcomes of the economy (Hamilton 2002), or by cycles of crisis, debate, and certainty (Kapcia 2009), it is difficult or perhaps simply imprudent to make blanket claims about the revolution, particularly in regards to racial issues. The impact of the revolution's egalitarian policies, its color-blind approach, and its silence on race might better be understood conjuncturally, that is, in the context of particular historical, political, and economic moments. Generational differences in acceptance or rejection of interracial unions illuminate the successes and limitations of the revolution's color-blind approach. A conjunctural analysis demands we ask, Exactly who was "dancing" with whom in those early years of the revolution? And what did it mean to be an interracial couple in the midst of revolutionary euphoria?

Amalia and Eduardo

Amalia's sparkling eyes shone above her pink cheeks as she told me of her relationship with her husband, Eduardo, a dark-skinned black Cuban. Amalia, the only child from a well-to-do family in Santa Clara (central Cuba), attended Catholic schools in the 1950s before moving to the capital to enroll in the University of Havana in the 1960s. She is now a lawyer, and the couple lives in a middle-class section of Havana's municipio Plaza de la Revolucíon. Amalia first met Eduardo at a university dormitory where he worked as the building's superintendent. In addition to maintaining the building, he often did small jobs such as fixing students' irons or installing shelves in their rooms. Their friendship developed over the years while Amalia was a student living in the dormitory. After she had graduated, she continued to rent a room in a nearby building. While Eduardo was very kind to her, she never considered him as a romantic partner until she had known him for several years. At that time she had just ended another relationship. She recounts:

> I [sought a relationship with] Eduardo not because I was depressed, but because I realized I was no longer in love [with the other man]. [The other man] wasn't what I was looking for. [So I thought about] all of Eduardo's good qualities and traits. Maybe before I didn't think about Eduardo in that [romantic] way

because I knew that [a relationship with] him would be a source of problems because he's black. . . . I knew I would have to face a lot, so I thought [carefully] about it before I responded [to his interest]. . . . So we started to have another kind of friendship. I took my time because I didn't want to hurt him and I still wasn't sure. I didn't want him to get any illusions and then have to tell him no. . . . So little by little our relationship began to change.

Amalia didn't tell her parents about her relationship with Eduardo until they had been together almost a year and had decided to marry. She returned to Santa Clara alone to tell her parents, as she didn't want to place Eduardo in an uncomfortable position. She knew her parents would not respond positively to the news. She told her father first, as she was more confident that he would respect her decision. Her father responded that he did not like the fact that they were marrying, as he felt, citing the popular aphorism, *cada oveja con su pareja* (each sheep with its matching mate), but it was Amalia who was to marry and she should choose her partner. Her paternal aunts and uncles were also somewhat accepting of her relationship to Eduardo. Amalia attributed this to the fact that hers was not the first interracial couple in her father's family. Her paternal grandmother was a mulata and her grandfather a white Cuban.

With her father's support, she told her mother, who was, as she had feared, very upset by the news. Amalia said:

She [her mother] had worried so much about me. She had put me in the best private school so I could become a professional. Now I should look for someone like myself. What would she tell her friends and family? What kind of public image would this make? My mother was more upset about what others would think than she was about the fact that I was marrying a black, working-class man. The ideal [for her] would have been if I married a white professional with a car. Instead, I was marrying a poor person without a house, without a car, and without the possibilities of getting one, since he was a worker. She felt [Eduardo] was beneath me and below what my aspirations should be. I tried to appeal to her religiosity by citing the Bible and that Joseph, Mary's husband, was also a worker, carpenter, but this did not persuade her. She refused to come to the wedding and refused to tell my grandfather about it, even though he was very revolutionary and at the time it was seen as very revolutionary to treat blacks and whites as equals.

I returned to Havana and told Eduardo that my father would come to the wedding but not my mother. So we made arrangements for my father and then a week later we get a telegram saying that my mother would also come. . . . Well, they attended the wedding, but they didn't really participate in it. You can see them in the photos, very serious. It was a day full of tension. . . . We [Amalia and Eduardo] had a project to convince my parents to accept Eduardo. We would win them over and show them that a person's color is not important. I was careful never to talk about his weaknesses or to complain about him. I always defended him. It was really to protect both of us. . . . After [years], my mother finally grew to accept Eduardo. She said she finally realized that he was whiter than many whites she knows. . . . But the rest of my relatives in Santa Clara never accepted our relationship.

She later showed me the wedding pictures, and, indeed, her parents appeared as dark clouds over an otherwise joyous event.

Amalia and Eduardo's marriage is one of many interracial relationships in Cuba. What is remarkable about their marriage is that it is not only an interracial union but an interclass one as well. Moreover, Amalia is a white professional, the most unlikely type of person to become involved in an interracial marriage according to a recent Cuban study (Rodríguez Ruiz 2004). Though they met by circumstance in the same building, the revolutionary ideology of racial equality provided a discursive space and even justification for their relationship. They met and married at a time when there was a belief that a color-blind Cuba could really become a reality.

Like many coming of age in the 1960s, they were caught up in the revolutionary fervor and enthusiasm. Amalia, born in 1944, and Eduardo, in 1936, belong to the generations that built and mobilized the revolution's projects, according to María Isabel Domínguez, María Elena Ferrer, and María Victoria Valdés's (1989) extensive study of the generational structure of contemporary Cuban society. The study was conducted from 1988 to 1990 with a sample of 3,719 people between the ages of about fifteen and sixty-five, living in six different provinces across Cuba (Havana City, Havana Province, Cienfuegos, Camagüey, Santiago de Cuba, and Guantánamo). They divided the population into the following cohorts by their year of birth: 1922–1943, 1944–1949, 1950–1961, 1962–1975, 1976–1988. Researchers determined this generational structure of contemporary Cuban society not by decade but by the historical, political, and social contexts that shaped each cohort's experiences. The study highlights the profound impact of transformative historical events on individual biographies.

According to this generational structure, at the start of the 1960s the tasks needed to build a new society were numerous and concrete and required mass mobilizations of people. The literacy campaign, efforts to increase industrial production, sugar cane and coffee harvests, and public works construction gave people like Amalia and Eduardo direct roles in building the new Cuba.

Likewise, their generation's level of political participation was notably high. Indeed, revolutionary identity and nationalist discourse required engaged citizenship and active political participation of their generations. To be Cuban was to be a revolutionary, a Fidelista, a follower of Fidel. These generations gained leadership roles in political organizations, the military, government, and in the country's new and expanding industries. Furthermore, the economic and political restructuring of the early revolution, coupled with the mass emigration of many middle- and upper-class professionals to Miami and other points of exile, created a unique window of opportunity for Eduardo and Amalia's generations (Martín Chávez 1990). The expansion of public works, the nationalization of industries, and the agrarian reform helped the government implement its commitment to full or nearly full employment for the workforce. A new class of intellectuals and professionals replaced those who had left (Martín Chávez 1990). As the generations that built the revolution, they still are largely responsible for controlling it. Members of these generations have remained in crucial positions of power in all areas of Cuban society for more than forty years.

Mobilization →
Integration
new
intellectuals

Perhaps the most revolutionary of all the changes was the government's decision to officially open all positions in all sectors of the economy to black and mulatto Cubans.[3] Mass volunteer movements also fostered racial integration. According to Pedro Serviat, a black statesman and revolutionary, the mass mobilizations and organizations (FMC, or Cuban Women's Federation; neighborhood CDRs, or Committees in Defense of the Revolution; labor unions; PCC, or Communist Party of Cuba; UJC, or Young Communists Union, and so forth) brought people together to achieve some greater social good or project and to translate the ideals of the revolution into material realities (1993, 89). This is exactly the situation depicted in the short story cited above about the young girl going to harvest coffee. The hands-on involvement available to Eduardo's and Amalia's generations contributed to the romantic atmosphere of those early years of the revolution. Many Cubans, black, mulatto, and white, felt that they could resolve even the country's most intractable problems, like racism, with good intentions and hard work (Arandia Covarrubias 1994). Working toward the goal of socialist egalitarianism gave meaning and direction to their lives.

In these first decades of the revolution, equality was not a hollow philosophy or simply political rhetoric, but was manifested in tangible material changes. The early revolutionary reforms secured housing and basic material needs for many members of these generations, and as a result they tend to have better living conditions than many of today's youth. The revolution immediately reduced rents by 50 percent and eventually gave tenants permanent tenure in their apartments.[4] The revolutionary government distributed old mansions abandoned by the fleeing members of the upper class to the new revolutionaries. A significant byproduct of this redistribution of property was that some previously all-white neighborhoods became racially integrated. The housing and neighborhood integration fostered the kind of egalitarian interactions that the revolution sought to promote. It also increased the possibility of interracial couples and social networks due to residential proximity and neighborly interdependence.

Eduardo, in particular, coming from a large poor family in eastern Cuba, was transformed by the politics of the revolution. Amalia describes him as a very politically involved person, and his political participation was very important to her: "One can think that there would be a big distance between [a worker] and a university-educated person, but [Eduardo] is a very political person. He has read a lot, has many interests, is intelligent, and has taught himself many different trades—carpenter, mason, locksmith." Eduardo participated in some of the mass mobilizations that were the political baptism of his generation, such as the literacy campaign of 1961. Despite his political commitment, Eduardo did not benefit materially from the revolution as others of his generation did, nor did he gain access to new or better-remunerated employment. As he was without his own apartment before the revolution, he did not benefit when tenants were given permanent tenure in their homes. He and Amalia both suffered from the housing shortage in Havana, and despite their political activism and Amalia's professional position neither were able find adequate housing. The couple eventually had to make do by joining together two small rooms that now comprise their tiny one-bedroom apartment.

Amalia was also very politically involved, and her break from her conservative middle-class upbringing was as much a political action as her involvement in student and political organizations at the university. Her marriage also had political significance, both in the sense that it was the political commitment of the couple that bridged their class differences and, as she states, "that in the context of the time, it was seen as very revolutionary to treat blacks and whites as equals." When they married in 1973, she commented, there were few interracial couples in her social circle, and she and Eduardo were doubly discriminated against because Eduardo was both black and working class. Ideologically, the revolution created social space for couples like Eduardo and Amalia, but the ideology of equality battled with the persisting racist ideas for hegemonic terrain.

Amalia was very conscious of the social norms she was crossing in marrying Eduardo. Their differences were especially apparent when they traveled together to visit Amalia's family in Santa Clara, a region historically more racially segregated before the revolution. Eduardo said that their arrival in Santa Clara just after they were married created a sensation everywhere they went: in the airport, in the hotel, everywhere, people stared in shock. In addition, at all of Amalia's family functions, Eduardo was the only black person present. Many relatives gave him a polite but chilly reception.

In explaining her own acceptance of Eduardo, Amalia cites her religious education as contributing to her egalitarian outlook and remembers as a child visiting poor, racially mixed neighborhoods with the nuns from her school, where she saw many interracial couples among the lower classes. Although Amalia asserts that she was raised without racial prejudices, she also realizes she was raised to live in a white world. Only after she became involved with Eduardo did she become conscious of her whiteness, and then she realized that Cuba was more racist than it seemed. Racism had persisted despite the changes of the revolution, although sometimes it manifested itself in subtle and less direct ways. Amalia herself has suffered from her association with Eduardo. People sometimes did not take her seriously as a professional because she married a worker with little formal education. She also encountered difficulty when Eduardo moved into her apartment in the building, fighting with the building administration to legalize his residency there, a struggle she eventually won. Her friends and colleagues have come to accept Eduardo but continue to see him as an exception among blacks. People tell her that he's black, but really white.

When I spoke with Eduardo, a taciturn man, about their relationship, he downplayed the conflict with Amalia's family and instead stressed how her family had come to accept him. He had expected they would react negatively at first, as mixed couples, especially in that region of the country, were not very common, and their class differences exacerbated the situation. For him, the most important element of his history with Amalia was not her parents' racism but rather how he had won them over and convinced them of the kind of person he was. He also noted the generational changes that have occurred during the revolution. The integration the younger generation has grown up with has shaped how interracial couples meet. Today's youth, according to Eduardo, see interracial couples as something more normal, more common.

When I asked Eduardo if he had dated other white women, he replied: "I've had mulata, white, and black girlfriends. I didn't dedicate myself to looking for white women. That wasn't my profession, but after my first white girlfriend I never had another black girlfriend. I met many white and black women, but this is how destiny has decided it should be." He explained his choice of partners not in terms of preference but simply as something beyond his control. Yet his choices or his "fate" reflected the enduring valuation of whiteness in the color hierarchy on the island.

Eduardo's family accepted his marriage with the same intensity with which Amalia's family initially rejected it. While his parents had died years before they married, Eduardo was extremely close to his siblings, especially his three sisters living in Havana. His siblings readily welcomed Amalia into the family. This is not always the case. The white family is often not alone in its rejection of an interracial couple. Elana, a dark-skinned mulata biologist of Eduardo's generation, married a white doctor. While her husband's family welcomed her warmly, in her own family there was always a certain disdain for their marriage. She described it as a subtle, reserved attitude, which occasionally was expressed in comments such as, "You married him because he's white." As a result Elana distanced herself from her own family and associated more frequently with her husband's kin and a circle of white friends. She also had a black friend with whom she had been very close prior to her marriage. After the marriage, he would not even speak to her. She said it was as if she had betrayed her race. Other Afrocuban friends told her that her marriage was a great conquest, the ultimate prize . . . a white husband (and lighter-skinned offspring). Elana found this instrumental view of her marriage equally offensive. In black Cuban families interracial couples often provoke the contradictory feelings of betrayal or triumph. Both responses are rooted in the racist project of whitening. Old meanings die hard and are easily layered onto new realities.

Amalia and Eduardo met by sharing the same physical space, but as social unequals, inhabitants of two social worlds that, prior to the revolution, would not have likely come together at an intimate level despite their physical proximity. However, they could be life partners because the politics of the revolution and the articulated ideology of equality gave them a common ground on which to meet. So the white middle-class university student and later lawyer shared a political commitment and activism with the black working-class building superintendent. The revolution and their accompanying political activism gave Amalia and Eduardo a common social and ideological space in which to incubate their romance.

Sofia and Fernando

Sofia, a mulata who works as an engineer, was born in 1950, and her white husband, Fernando, an art historian, was born in 1952. This generation was too young to remember many of the formative events of the 1960s. Sofia's and Fernando's generation (1950–1961), as defined by María Isabel Domínguez (1989), benefited from the educational reforms and institutions established by the revolution. Cuban identity and nationalism were still very much based on revolutionary involvement. At the same time, there was a lessening of the mass social activities and mobilizations that marked the earlier generations. Later generations had significantly less participation in social/political activities. The revolutionary euphoria had passed, and in some ways the future had arrived, or at least was said to have arrived. Now involvement meant the administrative oversight of the established political institutions and social programs. This tedious process of institutionalization and bureaucratization occupied much of the 1970s. In general, the political agenda since then focused on promoting ideological consensus among the people and sustaining established mass organizations rather than on the directly productive and institution-building activities that marked the earlier decades (Domínguez, Ferrer, and Valdés 1990, 30).

As part of what Domínguez (1989) terms the "transitional generation," Fernando and Sofia took advantage of many of the educational reforms and opportunities instituted by the revolution and, in fact, met while they were both studying in the former Soviet Union. Sofia comes from a middle-class family in Havana and Fernando from a working-class family in the Havana countryside. Both of their families supported their relationship. For Sofia, the daughter of a black mother and a white father, racial mixing was already part of her family history. Sofia insisted that the family history of mestizaje did not influence her relationship with Fernando. She commented:

We were not thinking about that. We looked for the person's values inside, not outside. It didn't matter if they were gray, yellow, green—we looked for other things. If he's black, black. If he's white, white. You have to find understanding and harmony. . . . There are people that don't like to mix [racially], and there are others that do it for aesthetic reasons, personal taste—I like dark skin or a man with blond hair. There are others [who don't mix] because of prejudice—a black, Ah! A white, Ah! Yes, both parts [can be prejudice], not just whites toward blacks, but blacks toward whites. It's possible that there are black men who would like to kill me for marrying a white man. No one has ever said that to me, but there are people like that. . . . I remember an incident that happened to a mulata friend who was studying medicine. A mulata woman who suffered a stroke came in to the hospital, and the mulata doctor treated her. Her son, who was white, was so grateful to the doctor for her attention to his mother. He said to her, "I would have loved my mother to see that a mulata, like herself, tried to save her life! I had a mulata girlfriend once and my mother never liked her. . . . She really made me suffer because she didn't want me to marry a mulata." . . . [Although the mother was mulata herself,] she wanted her son to *adelantar* (advance the race).

For Sofia interracial relationships were not about whitening or mestizaje, but rather were set in a color-blind framework. Race did not disappear, but it was irrelevant in choosing her life partner. This was not necessarily the frame of her mother's marriage or of the story she recounts of the white man and his mulata mother, where advancing the race was the goal of intermarriage. For Sofia the revolution's color-blind ideology resonated with her own beliefs and supported her view that skin color is irrelevant in choosing a partner.

Fernando also was not the first person in his family to be in an interracial relationship. His paternal uncle married a mulata and had a long and happy marriage that Fernando felt paved the way for his own relationship. Apart from his family history, Fernando believed that his education with a racially mixed group of people also profoundly shaped his social interactions: "I was in boarding school for thirteen years with people of all colors and types. And we shared everything from a glass of water with sugar to a case of beer. On the weekends we all went out together. . . . I think that here in Cuba this really helped our generation. This mix [of people] would all go to the beach together or all go to do *trabaja productiva* (productive work tasks such as agricultural labor while in the boarding high school)."

Fernando literally lived the revolution's color-blind agenda. The state had targeted education—particularly boarding schools, where the youth would be away from family influence and supervision—to make race disappear as a variable for the future generations. Here the revolution's educational institutions and policies brought together diverse groups of young people as social equals in the same physical space. For Sofia and Fernando, such conscious political motivation was not so integral to their meeting, but the pervasive color-blind ideology did shape their union. As Fernando put it, "We were raised in an environment where racism didn't exist, at least officially—as it's stated in our constitution. Although there were [racist] people, it was seen as something bad."

If shared political commitment had bonded Eduardo and Amalia even closer to each other in the early revolution, in later years, new opportunities for all classes and races provided literal spaces—schools, neighborhoods—for people like Sofia and Fernando to meet and feel comfortable with each other. Moreover, the revolution's ideological insistence on "racelessness" and egalitarianism across racial and class lines provided a sociocultural and ideological space for interracial couples. But both Sofia and Fernando knew of other couples whose experiences were not so positive. Fernando commented:

> I know of a couple, friends of mine. She's blond and he's black. . . . [W]hen her parents found out about their relationship they kicked her out of the house. They didn't accept it. Luckily, his family took them in and considered her like another daughter. Now they've been married twenty years and have two beautiful, healthy children. I think that with time her parents had to accept him. They resigned themselves to [the fact that she

married a black man], but they never really connected with him although he was a great person. He was the person that made their daughter happy. . . .

There are people that don't externalize their racism. They say, "My best friends are black." They say that, but then the day that their daughter decides to marry a black man, then their racism comes out. They may say it's not because he's black, and they start to invent a million excuses. But in the end you realize what it is.

As Fernando observes, interracial relationships violate the long-standing social norms by overstepping the boundaries of acceptable interracial contacts and cordiality from the perspective of many white families. Interracial friendships are fine, but not interracial courtships in the eyes of some Cubans, often regardless of skin color.

The color-blind approach provided one framework for how the races should interact. But it also competed with many other racist ideologies and frames of reference for understanding interracial relations. The ideologies of whitening and the racial hierarchy lurked behind the official silence, and many couples continued to face racism in a myriad of venues.

Silence and the Color-Blind Approach

While the 1985 Cuban movie *Se Permuta* (House-Swap) provides a comic look at the housing shortage in Havana, the subplot of the movie is concerned with another enduring drama in Cuban society: interracial romance. The young middle-class white heroine is first courted by a white man who has a good job, a car, and, most importantly (from her mother's perspective), a nice house. However, one day the daughter is home alone and a handsome mulatto plumber comes to repair the kitchen sink in the apartment she shares with her mother. The plumber does not have any of the material advantages of the white suitor. He is poor and shares a room in a *solar* (tenement house) with his black father. But the attraction between the two is apparent instantly. The young woman, to her mother's dismay, falls madly in love with the plumber and decides to marry him, thus ruining her mother's schemes ıagling a new house and a socially desirable husband for her ıter. The mother resigns herself to her daughter's decision. The young couple moves off together to La Isla de la Juventud, where they work on a micro-brigade to construct a new house for themselves. The movie ends with them standing in the frame of their unfinished new home, a metaphor not only for their future life together but moreover for the new revolutionary color-blind society—still a work in progress— that they are constructing with their interracial relationship.

The process of nation-building is a process of race-making (Williams 1989). In nineteenth-century Cuba, interracial unions were part of the explicit nation-building project of whitening the population. In contrast, the interracial couplings of the early revolutionary years were not intended to whiten or darken the population. They were a celebration of neither the Spanish nor African contributions to society. They were not an exaltation of the mestizo nature of the Cuban population or culture. Yet like their nineteenth-century counterparts, the interracial couples in socialist Cuba were part of a nation-building/race-making project, but a peculiarly paradoxical one. Under the revolution, the goal was to create a raceless society—a socialist, revolutionary society that would transcend race. A century earlier Cuban independence leader José Martí said that to be Cuban was to be more than black, more than white, more than mulatto. Likewise for Castro, to be revolutionary (which was to be Cuban after 1959) was to be more than black, more than white, more than mulatto. Revolutionary identity, now conflated with national identity, was to remove race as a significant variable from the social panorama. The interracial couples under the revolution did not produce *mestizos*, but rather socialist revolutionaries. Color would not *disappear* through intermarriage and racial integration; rather, it would become *irrelevant*. Interracial couples, like the young couple in the movie *Se Permuta,* were part of building a society in which "difference made no difference," and their very presence demonstrated how little difference race might make (Hernandez-Reguant 2005, 287).

Though the statements and programs initiated at the start of the revolution were a tremendous step toward racial equality, these efforts were always carefully couched in a color-blind language or the idiom of class, not as any type of affirmative action or race-specific policy (de la Fuente 2001). After 1962, the initial campaign against discrimination waned, and the government took the ideal of racial equality as an accomplished fact rather than a continuing process (de la Fuente 2001). The revolutionary government would resolve the racial issue through gradual, nonconfrontational policies, "through the color-blind education of new generations of Cubans" (de la Fuente 2001, 266) rather than antidiscrimination legislation or racial quotas. Once the revolution's programs for social redistribution had leveled the class contradictions, the cultural elements of race would serve to enhance continuing national synthesis (Hernandez-Reguant 2005). From the mid-1960s onward, race surfaced in public debates only regarding cultural themes, such as Afrocuban dance, and international politics, such as racism elsewhere. Paul Ryer (2006) notes that the Cuban state media gave full attention to the racism in capitalist societies abroad, especially racial conflicts in the United States, while remaining silent on racism domestically. The paradoxical result was what Ryer called a "now you see it, now you don't" treatment of race (2006, 85). The color-blind approach went hand-in-hand with a requisite silence on racial issues at home.

However, the silence on racial issues did not begin with the Castro government. Since the war of independence against Spain, Cubans have perceived discussions of race as an obstacle to national unity and have thus continually attempted to silence the issue through the rhetoric and imagery of nationalism (de la Fuente 1998a). The revolution's silence was in part a perpetuation of these traditional cultural tendencies to mute open reference to racism. While this type of "cultural censorship" is common throughout Latin America (Sheriff 2000), within revolutionary Cuba the silence dovetailed with an additional repertoire of socialist ideological and political agendas that helped to reinforce the silence. An arsenal of old and new motifs buttressed the silence; coupling these with centralized state power that controlled all outlets of the media created an official silence on Cuban race relations that was deafening. Certainly, the new regime viewed the subject as politically charged and potentially divisive at a time when maintaining unity was a paramount concern for the fledgling state. Echoing the words of José Martí, Castro called on all Cubans, regardless of race, to unite and ground themselves in their national identity—an identity inextricably yet ambivalently grounded in race. As anthropologist Ariana Hernandez-Reguant argues, "Revolutionary discourse forged an absolute identification between nation and revolution. . . . [P]otential signifiers of difference like race, gender, sexuality, and generation which could weaken national unity would be neutralized through ideological education. . . . [T]he 'monolithic ideological unity of the people' was a pressing goal" (2005, 288).

Castro's 1961 declaration that the revolution was socialist added another layer to the silence on race. Writings by Cuban intellectuals (López Valdés 1973; Serviat 1986) communicated this perspective in their proclamations that the revolution had successfully eliminated racism. Adopting a Marxist perspective in theory and practice produced an official blindness to difference other than class (Hernández-Reguant 2005). Under this paradigm, the revolutionary government treated racism as a by-product of class divisions. In the classic base-superstructure formulation of Marxism-Leninism, race and other forms of social inequality were epiphenomenal to the basic contradictions in the relations of production. These social inequalities would simply disappear once their roots in the capitalist economy were eliminated by socialism. The Marxist-Leninist doctrine, coupled with the state's emphasis on national (not racial) identity, kept racial issues from emerging onto the terrain of ideological struggle in revolutionary Cuba.[5] True revolutionaries could not be racist.

Cuba's national racial paradigm of inclusion also complimented socialism's need for social homogeneity. Anthropologist Katherine Verdery (1996) notes that communist parties in Eastern Europe pursued social policies designed to create social homogeneity by decreasing income inequalities as well as gender and racial/ethnic discrimination. By homogenizing society, the party could justify its claim to represent and serve the interests of the entire population, a collective subject from which it had erased any meaningful differences. "[This] homogenization served neither an ethnic nor a citizen nation, but a socialist nation that was a kind of extended family" (Verdery 1996, 93). Ethnomusicologist Robin Moore cites Cuban scholar Reynaldo Fernández Pavón, who commented directly on the government's need to promote a united, homogenous citizenry: "A social entity for and with the socialist cause, a single undivided mass . . . when the leadership was faced with expressions of ethnic identity among various groups manifest in folklore, they viewed them as something that needed to be eliminated or erased because they demonstrated difference and the leadership didn't know how to manage such difference" (as quoted in R. Moore 2006, 174).

In revolutionary Cuba, the ideology of mestizaje, the foundational myth of the nation, helped to sustain this vision of a unified national "we" (Hernandez-Reguant 2005). The revolutionary government affirmed Cuban mestizaje as a deeply constructive and enduring process and did not subject it to critical examination despite the notion's racist underpinnings and its ambivalent role in nation building in the previous centuries. For example, the mulatto poet Nicolás Guillén (and white Cuban intellectuals Fernando Ortiz and Elías Entralgo) celebrated mestizaje as a process of "both natural miscegenation ('improvised and precipitated love') and cultural synthesis which resulted in a mulatto nation void of racism" (Hernandez-Reguant 2005, 290). As Cuban intellectual Roberto Fernández Retamar noted, "Our culture is that of the mestizo people and the oppressed classes" (as quoted in Hernandez-Reguant 2005, 289). Fernández Retamar and Cuban official discourse offered a homogeneous mestizo cultural identity (Cubanidad) for all Cubans.

However, this homogenized Cuban "mestizo" culture failed to completely transcend or fully synthesize the races as it drew predominantly on white-Hispanic culture (Caño Secade 1996; Carbonell 1961) along with an uneasy incorporation of selected Afrocuban traditions. The revolutionary government continued to support Western bourgeois "high culture" by creating a network of schools, galleries, and theaters to promote "high art" (Hernandez-Reguant 2005). Afrocuban folklore could theoretically be even more revolutionary than "high culture," as it emerged from the oppressed groups in society—the poor, the workers, the blacks. However, folklore required much closer scrutiny and research to differentiate the authentic types of folklore that could be encouraged from the superstitions and spontaneous disruptive expressions (like some religious ceremonies) that conflicted with revolutionary ideals and should be eliminated (Hernandez-Reguant 2005).

Incorporating Afrocuban folklore in Cuban mestizo culture required close policing and critical selection procedures by folklorists who became "the guardians of the nation's purity" (Hernandez-Reguant 2005, 293). Robin Moore noted that "cultural advisors wished to 'elevate' folk expression, professionalize it, and make it more intelligible for urban audiences" (2006, 186). Yet even these limited attempts to integrate and institutionalize some Afrocuban elements (such as rumba) into national culture also met with resistance from white Cubans who did not accept lower-class, Afrocuban cultural forms as valued contributions to the national culture but continued to see these cultural expressions as belonging to blacks (Daniel 1994). Referring to the government's early support for the Afrocuban music and dance troupe the Conjunto Folklorico Nacional, scholar Catherine Hagedorn noted that "underneath the newly varnished layer of Revolutionary enthusiasm . . . were several layers of mistrust and wariness, as well as a hair-trigger readiness to lose faith in the endeavor" (as quoted in R. Moore 2006, 186). Color-blindness and the silence left other Cubans with no way to name or protest this dismissal.

Meanwhile, black and mulatto Cubans themselves did not share a common view about the process of national and racial integration or racial mixing (de la Fuente 2001). For example, Juan René Betancourt, the black Cuban lawyer, believed in the need for a racially defined autonomous movement to promote the interests of Afrocubans. Betancourt elaborated some of his ideas in his 1959 book *Negro: Ciudadano del Futuro*, which met with official resistance and forced him into exile soon after its publication (de la Fuente 1998a). The type of agenda Betancourt was proposing was impossible to pursue under the revolution. Attempts by other black Cuban intellectuals, such as Walterio Carbonell, to raise the racial question directly early in the revolution were also quickly extinguished. Without a free press, and with the closure of the Afrocuban societies in the early 1960s,[6] black intellectuals lost their primary voice to the public; and the Cuban idiom of race relations based on an idealized shared mestizo national culture and racial fraternity undermined mobilization along racial lines.

The color-blind approach, however, resonated with other black and mulatto intellectuals. Some agreed with the government's view that saw race-based initiatives and organizations as threats to redefining revolutionary civil society (de la Fuente 2001). From this perspective a race-based approach would only perpetuate segregation, resentment, and isolation among Cubans of different colors. In this light, the Afrocuban societies, for example, were obstructions to national integration. Black and mulatto Cubans have historically attempted to build racial solidarity without promoting segregation (Schwartz 1998). Many have long rejected race-based appeals, including Marcus Garvey's return-to-Africa platform, which he tried to promote in Cuba in the 1920s (Fernández Robaina 1998).

Many Afrocubans feared that Black Nationalism would lead to U.S.-style racial segregation (Schwartz 1998). Indeed, from the Cuban perspective, the U.S. system, by contrast, seemed the very essence of racism—the embodiment of an unrelenting oppression of and aggressive antagonism between clearly distinct groups. Violent clashes and racially motivated abuses, such as the Miami riots in 1980, the Rodney King beating in 1992, and the subsequent riots in Los Angeles, were broadly covered in the Cuban press (Ryer 2006). These incidents supported the Cuban government's characterization of the United States as a racist country and implicitly forced Cubans to compare their own more racially integrated lifestyle with the United States. While the official silence prohibited addressing race relations in Cuba directly, press coverage of racial violence in other parts of the world told the Cubans who they were by telling them who they were not.

Despite the fact that Black Nationalism never took root in Cuba, Castro was an ardent supporter of these movements in the United States. According to Carlos Moore (1988), a black Cuban scholar in exile since 1963, Castro's interest in supporting black power movements was a strategic attempt to foster U.S. domestic unrest in the hopes that it would weaken U.S. power internationally. However, on the domestic front, Moore asserted that the Cuban government feared that black power could awaken black consciousness in Cuba that might lead to demands for a more equitable distribution of political and economic resources. During the 1960s and 1970s, Cuba hosted or offered political exile to a number of prominent African American black power leaders, including Kwame Toure (Stokely Carmichael), Assata Shakur

(Joanne Chesimard), Eldridge Cleaver, Robert F. Williams, William Lee Brent, Huey Newton, Fela Olatunji (Charles Hill), and Angela Davis. Moore suggested that Cuban leaders used race strategically to further their domestic and foreign policy agendas.[7] Among African American militants and intellectuals there was no consensus on Cuba's racial achievement. Some saw Cuba as a racial paradise (J. Cole 1986), while others quickly became disillusioned with the revolution and race relations in socialist Cuba (Clytus 1970).[8]

The ambivalence of African American intellectuals and activists toward Cuba's color-blind approach was patently evident during the one-week symposium on Malcolm X that I attended in Havana on my first trip to Cuba in May 1990. The symposium commemorated the sixty-fifth anniversary of Malcolm X's birth and the thirtieth anniversary of his historic meeting with Fidel Castro in Harlem's Hotel Theresa in 1960. Rosemari Mealy, an African American activist and journalist, organized the conference, and the twenty-four U.S. participants included African American academics and activists such as Kwame Toure (Stokely Carmichael). Interestingly, while Mealy noted that the symposium was in recognition of Malcolm X's contribution to the worldwide struggle for justice and equality and of Cuba's acknowledgment of his achievements, the conference did not once address the issue of race relations in contemporary Cuba. The Cuban academics participating in the symposium spoke on issues such as third world socialism, Cuba-Africa relations, African roots of Cuban culture, and Afrocuban religion—sticking strictly to the prescribed domains for discussions of race in revolutionary Cuba: culture and international relations (de la Fuente 2001). Meanwhile, the U.S. delegates discussed Malcolm X's worldwide impact and legacy, Cuba's solidarity with Africa, and Malcolm X's influence on contemporary movements in the U.S. black community. At the close of the symposium our delegation met with Fidel Castro, where he commented, "We have always been in solidarity with the struggle of Black people, of minorities, and of the poor in the United States . . . and they have been in solidarity with us" (as quoted in Mealy 1993, 60). The U.S. delegation in its closing declaration also acknowledged Cuba's efforts to aid in "the cause of Black liberation, both on the African continent and in the African diaspora" (as quoted in Mealy 1993, 81). Despite these

joint recognitions of solidarity, neither the Cuban nor the U.S. delegation mentioned the racial situation in contemporary Cuba. The subject
was too controversial to approach and was still shrouded in silence. Furthermore, the Black Nationalist agenda of Malcolm X seemed to speak
to race relations elsewhere, not in Cuba. Outside of the conference,
several black journalists in the U.S. delegation did conduct informal
interviews with black Cubans that they met on the streets about Cuban
race relations. They were told of continuing discrimination and racism.
However, conference presentations or discussions did not address this
aspect of the contemporary Cuban reality. In fact, a black Puerto Rican
journalist traveling with the delegation was chastised by Mealy for trying to raise this topic among some of the delegates (Santiago 1990).

The silent color-blind approach and the vivid dream of equality
did have a positive impact on some generations of Cubans. In Cuba,
despite familial resentment, it never became a political "necessity"
for blacks to court and marry only other blacks. In the United States,
by contrast, some Black Nationalist movements were explicitly against
racial "miscegenation." In a most unlikely pairing, Marcus Garvey, for
example, teamed up with white supremacist groups in 1920s Virginia
to fight interracial unions and sexual liaisons (Bair 1999). The common
ground between the Garveyites and the white supremacists was a belief
in protecting racial purity and a separatist vision that for Garvey meant
a black homeland in Africa. For both groups, racial purity arguments
focused on the female body, which became a powerful symbol for their
nationalist goals and desires (Bair 1999).

The rigidifying of racial fault lines affected many U.S. interracial
couples during the 1960s as well. In her memoir, Hettie Jones, the white
ex-wife of black writer and activist Imamu Amiri Baraka (Le Roi Jones),
noted that by the mid-1960s people were beginning to see Baraka as a
hypocrite—"He talked black, but married white" (Jones 1990, 218). Others were more direct in their criticism of their relationship, saying that
"he was laying with the Devil" (218). Baraka left Jones in 1965, and she
observed that during that period there was pressure on all black people
to end their interracial relationships (Jones 1990).

The historical context for U.S. interracial couples stands in sharp
relief to that of Cuban couples of the same period, as we see in the

narratives of the couples in this chapter. Despite the fact that at the start of the revolution the fear of black men "dancing with" (possessing) white women resurfaced and embodied white trepidations about the revolutionary project and the future of the nation, the concurrent presence of the revolution's equalitarian ideology and the historical creed of mestizaje offered a counter vision that could nurture, not thwart, interracial courtships.

The silence on racial issues in Cuba was a double-edged sword. It was both an obstacle to racial equality and an opportunity for racial integration. From the start of the revolution, both openly racist acts and attempts to debate the limitations of government's stance on racism became counterrevolutionary (de la Fuente 2001). Coupled with the revolution's egalitarian agenda, the silence provided a space for the ideology of socialist equality to take root. At the start of the revolution, egalitarianism was realized (albeit partially and imperfectly) through policies that fostered racial integration in education, housing, and health care and prohibited blatant racial discrimination in the workplace and in social centers. The structural changes instituted by the revolution actually contributed to a decline in racial inequality in a number of crucial social indicators such as life expectancy, infant mortality, and education levels (de la Fuente 1995), thus in very material ways making race seem less pertinent as a social concern. Thus, though it is evident that there were cracks in the color-blind utopia the revolutionary government attempted to construct, and the raceless society never completely became a reality, the attempts to reach that utopia produced distinctive race relations and mixing. Completely discounting the color-blind approach hinders our understanding of the nature and meaning of interracial couples in contemporary Cuba. The color-blind approach to equality should be understood conjuncturally, that is, within the context of different generational cohorts.

The narratives of the interracial couples formed during the early period of the revolution attest to the political consciousness and real changes fostered by this new social agenda. There was a dream of equality that people believed they could achieve. The material transformations and ideological fervor at the start of the revolution strongly shaped the generation of young adults that came of age in the 1960s.

Amalia's, Eduardo's, Fernando's, and Sofia's stories attest to the power of this ideology. As Alejandro de la Fuente notes, "The facts that racial brotherhood had become the ideal and that people felt required to act accordingly where themselves significant achievements in a country in which racial barriers, and even segregation, had been rampant only a decade before" (2001, 278). As Fernando said, "We were raised in an environment where racism did not exist, *at least officially*" (emphasis added). This dream should not be taken lightly, even though it did coexist with racist ideologies that worked to reinforce the very racial hierarchy the revolution hoped to dismantle.

However, when interracial couples in Cuba encountered actual racism and discrimination, it was all the more difficult to label and combat. Amalia's paradoxical position embodies racism in a "raceless" nation: while she took strength from the revolution's egalitarianism and shared this with her black, working-class husband, she also expressed surprise that their relationship had revealed to her that racial prejudice, even after the revolution, still permeated Cuban society. Accepting the integrationist philosophies presented its own set of problems and obstacles to racial equality. Even in the paradigm of inclusion "fences were inexorably erected—fences that blocked a more realistic assessment of the racial question" (Fernández Robaina 1998, 126).

The interracial couples that embodied the socialist dream of building an egalitarian revolutionary Cuba were caught in this ideological crossfire. Cubans continued to live in *both* a racialized social world and, in many instances, a raceless socialist society. The revolution's dreams of racelessness were sown on a terrain historically stratified by race, class, and gender inequalities. Race may have become a classic nontopic for the government, but as the interracial couples realized, race was far from being a non-topic in daily life. It simmered through conversations and quotidian interactions and reverberated through housing patterns and public spaces. Complete silence, even in a totalitarian socialist state, could never be fully achieved.

3

Mapping Interracial Couples

Race and Space in Havana

Cultural difference is spread over geographical space by virtue of the fact that social relations become concrete in spatialized form.

–Peter Wade, *Race and Ethnicity in Latin America*

Even casual observations in Havana will affirm the racially integrated nature of the city, and especially in areas like Centro Habana. Dark-skinned Cubans can be found living next door to light-skinned Cubans in most areas. Whites, mulattos, and blacks stand in the same lines for food and the same queues for buses. Their children are in the same schools and play together in the same parks. The numbers, in fact, attest to the multiracial nature of the city as a whole, though there are darker and lighter municipios.

The three-and-a-half-square-kilometer municipio of Centro Habana is one of the most densely populated sections of the city with well over forty-eight thousand inhabitants per square kilometer, and it includes areas zoned for a mix of residential, industrial, and commercial use. It is nestled between the historic core of the city, Habana Vieja (Old Havana),[1] and the municipio of Plaza de la Revolución, which by contrast has just under fourteen thousand residents per square kilometer and includes several of Havana's more middle-class residential neighborhoods, like Vedado (Comité Estatal de Estadísticas 1981, vii). The housing conditions in Havana's municipios reflect the age, poverty, and density of the districts. According to 2001 statistics, in all of Havana 64 percent of the housing units were in good condition, 20 percent in fair condition, and 16 percent in poor condition

TABLE 3.1.

Cuban Population by Skin Color

Year	Total	White (%)	Black (%)	Mestizo (%)	Asian (%)
1981	9,723,605	66	12	22	<1
2002	11,177,743	65	10	25	<1

SOURCE: Cuban Comité Estatal de Estadísticas, "Censo de población y viviendas 1981, La poplación de Cuba según el color de la piel" and "Censo de población y viviendas 2002, La poplación de Cuba según el color de la piel."

NOTE: At best, we can use these census statistics as very rough estimates of the racial composition of the population. Respondents chose their skin color classification from among these categories: white, black, mestizo, Asian. With the tremendous racial mixture in Cuba, skin color or racial identification is subjective. As I discussed in the introduction, racial classification in Cuba is complex and often contextual.

TABLE 3.2

Havana Population by Skin Color, 1981

	Total	White (%)	Black (%)	Mestizo (%)	Asian (%)
Havana total	1,929,400	63	17	20	<1
Centro Havana	169,300	53	19	27	<1
Plaza	164,500	69	13	18	<1

SOURCE: Cuban Comité Estatal de Estadísticas, "Censo de población y viviendas 1981, Provincia de Cuidad de la Habana," vol. 3.

NOTE: Only a limited amount of data has been released from the 2002 census, and this particular breakdown by of the population of Havana's *municipios* by skin color was not publicly available.

(Coyula and Hamberg 2003). Furthermore, there were sixty thousand units that were deteriorated beyond repair and needed to be replaced (Coyula and Hamberg 2003). Much of this substandard and dilapidated housing is located in Centro Habana and Habana Vieja. By the mid-1990s, 35 percent of the Centro Habana population lived in *solares* (tenements), while that was true of only 11 percent of the people in

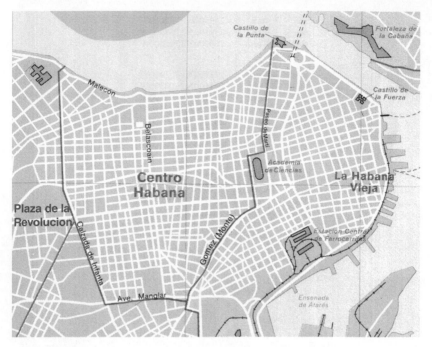

Map of Havana. From the U.S. Central Intelligence Agency, Washington, D.C., 1992.
Maxx Berkowitz edited and formatted the map.

Plaza (Coyula and Hamberg 2003). Studies conducted in the mid-1990s
by Cuban researchers concluded that blacks tend to live in the worst
housing conditions, evincing a persisting structural inequality (Espina
Prieto and Rodríguez Ruiz 2006).

When I first moved to Havana, academics and other professionals
I met would immediately ask me where I was living. When I responded
that I was living in the Cayo Hueso neighborhood of Centro Habana,
they rolled their eyes, expressed concern about my safety, and then
concluded that no one could tell me stories—because I was living *la ver-
dad,* the real Havana, not some cleaned-up version presented to groups
of foreign visitors. Years later this perception of Cayo Hueso still held
true. In a 2004 article on the neighborhood park, Parque Trillo, posted
on the Web site for the National Center of the Committees in Defense
of the Revolution, the author, who grew up near the park, cited similar
experiences: "Despite the contradictory legends and stories, I never
saw any act of violence that would distinguish it from other areas in

Havana. Nevertheless its infamy reigns. When you say you live a block from the Trillo Park, people look at you in such a way that it is not difficult to imagine what they are thinking" (Guimeras 2004).

Like this author reading people's reactions, I quickly figured out that I was living in the Cuban equivalent of the South Bronx. Like blighted areas of U.S. cities, Cayo Hueso carried the stigma of a bad neighborhood. The dilapidated housing stock, the numerous solares, the largely poor and working-class population, the perceived presence of *guapos,* and even the thriving Afrocuban culture, all confirmed the marginality of the space for many white and middle-class Habaneros. The racial integration enhanced by the revolution was evident in the neighborhood, but at the same time the accompanying egalitarianism was undermined by a persistent conflation of race, poverty, crime, and space that ultimately culminated in the barrio's reputation.

Discourses about the barrio's reputation reveal divisions even within "racially integrated" areas. Closely reading the topography of Havana, or more specifically of the barrio Cayo Hueso, we can find the racial hierarchy echoed in the spatial arrangement of housing. The residents of Cayo Hueso, in general, shared this dominant negative view of the barrio but had a much more nuanced understanding of the source of this negative reputation. The fine-grained distinctions and micro-hierarchies that were not apparent to outsiders were crucial to residents who sought to distinguish themselves from the barrio's reputation and escape "territorial stigmatization" (Wacquant 1993).

Its rich history as a working-class neighborhood of tobacco rollers and notable architecture not withstanding, Cayo Hueso did not have much social cachet or, in Bourdieu's terms, cultural capital. In fact, for Cubans, living in places like Cayo Hueso could be a social liability. Local identity was extremely important and was among the first bits of information Cubans exchanged upon meeting each other. The long-enduring nature of barrio reputations often had deleterious implications for past and present residents of slum areas (Butterworth 1980). This was especially true if your skin color reaffirmed the barrio's "black" character. Such a struggle formed the central theme of Sara Gómez's classic Cuban film, *De Cierta Manera,* in which the mulatto protagonist attempted to distance himself from his past in a slum area that the revolution demolished and replaced with new housing. The themes of marginality and space were also found in the 1979 play *Andoba*, written by Abrahán Rodríguez, in which an ex-convict returned to Cayo Hueso only to become embroiled in conflicts in his solar. In 2005 the play was performed for the first time in the Parque Trillo, the staged drama mirroring the realities of the surrounding barrio. As Mette Berg (2005) noted, residents of such barrios often try to distance themselves from the reputations of their spatial origins. Her university-educated mulatto informant, Pablito, from Habana Vieja provides one example. Talking about his university life in Vedado, Berg quoted Pablito as saying, "I never mentioned I was from Old Havana. I would get off the bus and arrive [at university] walking so nobody would realize I was from Old Havana" (Berg 2005). As Pablito's comments attest, one's barrio communicated much about a person's background and respectability and in some cases must be hidden or denied to build another identity for oneself.

While the university provided an escape and new identity for Pablito, interracial courtships could serve a similar function for some people. Javier, the young mulatto man I interviewed, was involved in a number of relationships with white women. He was from Habana Vieja (Old Havana) and described his barrio and its residents in the following terms:

> The blacks, they themselves, have defined their characteristics and don't permit people of their own color to overcome these characteristics, understand? So, for example, they don't want to accept that a black goes to the university. . . . It's a problem of communication. In this barrio I cannot have a conversation with anyone. All of their arguments are in extreme—either the revolution is great or it's awful; either you are good or you're bad. There can be no discussion, no real thinking about the points. . . . I'm more and more convinced that what they [blacks] want is to stay in that barrio. They have concentrated themselves there and they don't want to leave.

For Javier the barrio was not just a physical place, but a racialized culture—a set of characteristics ascribed to people and concretized in a defined space. Javier envisioned himself as a calm, peaceful person with a certain level of education and culture. The encounters he had in the barrio—filled with aggression and vulgarity—fed his dislike of the neighborhood and the people in it. He tried to interact with his neighbors, but he said that the other residents themselves put up barriers. His neighbors called him bourgeois or homosexual because he did not fit the local schema of male behavior. The young black and mulatto men in his barrio viewed intellectual activity as unmanly. Locals teasingly called him "Lenin" because he spent all of his time reading instead of hanging out in the street. In this environment Javier was, in his own words, "an anomaly." He did not fit the *guapo* notion of black/mulatto masculinity dominant in his barrio. Javier saw that the only solution was to distance himself from his neighbors; and generalizing from this experience in his barrio, he concluded, "That's why I don't get along with people darker than me—lower than my color." And for Javier that included dating only white women. For him blackness was both a physical space and a set of social and cultural characteristics that he longed to flee. The barrio, the social and economic position of its residents became an intrinsic part of their blackness, a tough-guy image of masculinity and values from which Javier fought to dissociate himself. His interracial courtships were part of his distancing strategy, as whitening had been a century earlier. In this context, his interracial relationships did not so much reflect racelessness but rather in his view moved him up a rung on the cultural-racial hierarchy.

Javier's comments on his barrio illustrate the often occulted relations between sensuous physical space and various social and cultural processes. Racialization draws upon spatial relations in complicated ways. Since the early 1990s scholars have increasingly turned their attention to how identity and difference are rooted in space, place, and locality (Low and Lawrence-Zúñiga 2003; Pred 2000). Cuban neighborhoods are not only geographic entities that we can trace out on a map, but racial formations as well—sites that generate symbolic associations between skin color, place, and a host of traits ascribed to blackness and whiteness. Within the racialization of space in Cayo Hueso, blackness takes on competing and conflicting meanings as national, local, historical, and emerging perceptions of blackness and space come into play. Interracial couples traverse these webs of meaning as black partners, especially those from stigmatized places like Cayo Hueso and Habana Vieja, struggle against centuries-old conceptions of blackness rooted in barrio reputations. As Allan Pred proposes, there is a "dialectical fusing of space and identity" (2000, III). Identity and difference are rooted in space, place, and locality. The meanings and identifications associated with particular places shape people's reactions to interracial couples and the experiences of the couples themselves. In Cayo Hueso, race emanated through the geography of spatial inclusion and exclusion, in the discourse of barrio stigma and reputation, and in the recent valorization of the barrio as a "cradle of Afrocuban culture" in the eyes of foreign tourists. As Pred (2000) notes the meanings of race inscribed on a locality are not singular: just as hegemonic power is always contested and shifting, so too are the spatial and racial meanings.

Integration and Stability

The revolution's housing reforms in the early 1960s reduced rents and gave tenants secure tenure in their apartments. The housing policy also had the consequence of making it very difficult for people to move or change homes. The housing system is such that you cannot legally sell your home, only trade it with someone else. The limited options for moving and an inadequate supply of new housing has resulted in cramped living conditions for many growing families.[2] In Centro Habana, several generations often live in endlessly subdivided apartments in turn-of-the-century buildings that are on the verge of collapse. Despite the cramped quarters and the teetering buildings, many people have few options but to stay put, making the populations in many barrios very stable.[3] Neighborhood stability is one of the less recognized aspects of Havana's housing shortage. For better or worse, this stability gave people a true sense of place. In fact, it is local identity/ barrio identity that people often use to define themselves (or distance themselves from, as Javier and Pablito illustrated); even Cubans in exile will not only proclaim themselves as Habaneros but refer to the specific section of Havana where they lived.

The apartment I shared with Antonio is a good example of both the stability and racial components of the barrio. Antonio's great-grandmother had rented the one-bedroom apartment mid-1950s shortly after it was built in what was then a mostly white, working-class neighborhood. As a black woman, she was at first barred from renting by the building's owner (who left for Miami at the start of the revolution). Only after a relative who was a lawyer intervened was she allowed to rent the apartment that would stay in the family's possession for more than half a century. Antonio and his grandmother moved into the apartment in the late 1960s after his great-grandmother died and the surviving relatives decided that they should have the apartment since they shared one room with Antonio's unmarried uncle in a nearby solar. When Antonio's grandmother passed away in 1990, Antonio became the legal resident of the apartment, and one of the few young Cubans in Havana to live alone. When he left the country for Spain in 1996, his half-brother, who had been sharing a room in a solar with his paternal aunt, moved into the apartment and continues to live there today.

Residential stability fueled the face-to-face character of daily interactions. In the barrios, people were known, predictable, and familiar. Like Antonio, many had been living in Cayo Hueso all their lives, and often so had their parents and grandparents. Daily life centered around a few blocks in which most everyday interactions occurred among people who had known each other and who had lived together for generations. Here the barrio was defined and demarcated by its population.

Perhaps the truest visual markers of my barrio were not the buildings, but rather my elderly neighbors who could be found standing like sentinels in their customary posts day after day. At one end of the block, Kiko, a white man in his late seventies, dressed in his undershirt and a pair of khakis, stood in his doorway every morning surveying the street scene and greeting me as I opened our second-story balcony doors when I awoke. He lived in the row house in which his seventy-five-year-old wife, Rosita, had been born. Later in the day, Kiko's front stoop was occupied by Panchito, a mulatto in his sixties who lived around the corner and who was sort of the block's personal message center. He would tell us who stopped by while we were out, and likewise informed the visitors when we were not home. As with many apartment buildings, we had no doorbell, so visitors would have to stand in the

street calling out our names so we would come downstairs to unlock the
entrance door. So all the neighbors knew of and watched our comings
and goings and those of our visitors with as much interest as if they
were their own.

The impromptu nature of visiting in Cuba meant that one had little
privacy. One day I needed to retreat from the world for a few hours
and closed the balcony doors to indicate that I was not home. Soon
Antonio's best friend, Lazaro, appeared and was calling my name in the
street. I decided not to answer the door, as I had no energy for a visita.
Daisi, my inquisitive nine-year-old neighbor, who could hear me moving around in my apartment, called down to Lazaro, "She's home, but
she doesn't want to see you now." Lazaro later recounted to me that he
left feeling simultaneously amused and annoyed.

Seated at the far end of the block was the largely silent and truly
ancient Walterio, whose dark skin was a sharp contrast to his shock of
white hair. Rosita loved to tell me in a conspiratorial whisper that he
was a *garotero* (a loan shark) before the revolution. Now Walterio's most
important daily transaction was to shift his small wooden bench from
one side of the street to the other as the afternoon sun ate the morning
shade. The slight variations in Cuba's climate would be reflected in his
hat, which would alternate between a dilapidated straw boater in the
summer and a dusty gray felt fedora in the winter. Arrayed around his
bench would be odds and ends for sale: sometimes cigarettes, sometimes current—but mostly old—newspapers, a few books, and occasionally some vegetables. I once asked him if he had the day's newspaper,
and he replied, "No, but these are very clean." I thus discovered the
market for week-old newsprint—as toilet paper.

Tere, another octogenarian regular, lived in her labyrinthine
ground-floor apartment with several generations of her family. She
would enjoy the shade on her side of the street by opening the shut-
tered doors on her fifteen-foot windows and placing a small cushion,
made especially for this purpose, on the flat top of the cement railing.
She would then pass the hours resting her liver-spotted white forearms
on the pillow, peering out at the bustling street scene, and chatting
with passers-by. She frequently grabbed my arm as I passed to share
with me tales of her latest bouts of constipation or to tell me how

well the laxative I brought for her from the United States had worked. The repetition of this theme was more regular than she was and never seemed to bore her. I soon became accustomed to the intimate level of health and bodily information people shared. I had my own experience with stomach ailments shortly after I arrived in Havana. When I finally emerged from the house several days later, I was greeted with inquiries about the state of my health and the details of my illness.

Rosita, who I affectionately referred to as the national public broadcasting center, would disdainfully call Tere an unabashed gossip for spending her day hanging out the window. Rosita at least had the decency to gossip inside her house—beckoning to passers-by as they walked passed her always open door or more frequently chatting with them as they came to use her phone, one of the few functioning phones on the block in the early 1990s. This phone privilege gave Rosita direct access to details of many of the neighbors' lives, as the phone was strategically placed in the living room within earshot of all present. She also received all the mail for eight apartments in my building, since either she or Kiko were always home and our building had no mailboxes. This was an arrangement she personally had made with the postman. She would then contact the neighbors to tell them they had letters—and where and whom they were from. She would even sometimes spend a few days flipping through the foreign magazines that would come for my neighbor who was a journalist before delivering them to their fifty-year-old owner, whom she had know since he was born and whom she still called by his childhood name, Tico. These living landmarks of the barrio were complemented by the physical ones, which both united the barrio and marked its divisions.

Blackness at the Center and in the Margins

The neighborhood unfolded around the Parque Trillo, which occupies one square city block in the heart of Cayo Hueso. The park itself was crisscrossed with walkways connecting to the large paved circular center. It boasted several very large *ceiba* (cottonsilk) trees, whose religious importance in Santería makes the base of their trunks preferred repositories for charms of various sorts pejoratively known as *brujería* (witchcraft). I quickly learned to distinguish the small brown paper bags, the blackened bananas tied with red string, the bits of cloth, bundles of herbs, feathers, and coconut shells of Santería from the randomly strewn garbage that littered the rest of the park and the surrounding streets. Antonio, like many Cubans, did not practice any religion in an orthodox sense but believed in everything,[4] so he advised me to spit as I passed the packets, so the charms would not stick to me.

The cycle of a day in the Parque Trillo had a generational rhythm. In the early mornings it served as the site for the *circulo de los abuelos* (grandparents' club), the elderly barrio residents who come every morning to stretch and exercise. During the day, it functioned as the playground and gym for the elementary school two blocks away. At night, with most of the lights in the park smashed, the few cracked and broken-down concrete benches became the living room for many of the residents of the surrounding solares.[5]

Presiding over all this—visitors old and young, activities sacred and profane—was a statue of the black independence fighter Quintín Bandera, who achieved the rank of general for valiantly leading the western invasion during the war of independence against Spain. The statue of Bandera was first unveiled in 1948 by Cuban president Ramón Grau San Martín.[6] Bandera was a fascinating figure to grace the center of a park in a barrio such as Cayo Hueso. While most people knew of his military prowess, few in the general public remembered that he was court-martialed and stripped of his rank and position in 1897, shortly before Cuba gained its independence. Bandera's accusers, most of whom were white, argued that he had avoided military combat and had very publicly ensconced himself with his concubine in the army camp near the central city of Trinidad. Bandera did not deny these accusations, but in his defense argued that the presence of lovers in camp was common practice among military leaders and he was being singled out because of the racism of local officers. However, historian Ada Ferrer suggests that the charge of racism cannot fully account for the case against him (1999, 174). She argues that Bandera's behavior defiled the moral purity and honor of the rebel cause. A national hero was to derive his political and spiritual authority by resisting the temptation of women—renouncing corporal pleasures that might distract him from his mission. Bandera's questionable moral actions were exacerbated by his deliberate lack of discretion and the reputed character of the predominantly black men under his command, who themselves were thought to be lacking moral rectitude according to insurgent leaders (177). Bandera considered himself to be a "rustic," uneducated man and drew little cultural distinction between himself and his soldiers. On the contrary, Máximo Gómez, a white hero of the independence war, felt that leaders should serve as moral examples for the soldiers; they were to subdue, not reflect, the inclinations of the poor, uneducated enlisted men (177). Bandera's dismissal was rooted not only in lack of military discipline, but moreover in issues of morality, civility, and refinement—all racially coded traits. He did not serve as an appropriate role model for the citizens of the emerging republic. Yet, less than fifty years later his statue was placed by President Grau San Martín in a location of honor at the center of this small urban park situated in "*la parte más ciudad de la ciudad*" (in the most "city" part of the city)—as Centro Habana is described by Cuban troubadour Silvio Rodríguez.

Exactly because of his history, he is perhaps an all-too-appropriate icon for Cayo Hueso. Bandera's past, his glory and subsequent banishment, can be read as a metaphor for the barrio itself. His self-proclaimed "rustic," uneducated nature still accurately reflects the popular impressions of Cayo Hueso, where residents are thought to be tough and unrefined. How apropos that Bandera, a black national hero—first valorized, then maligned—should be ensconced as the central image in the barrio's main public space. His history echoes the ambivalence toward the barrio and the park as decidedly black and reputedly dangerous spaces. In fact, despite its mixed population, the barrio's reputation comes largely from the alleged and actual behavior of its poorest and darkest inhabitants, who live, for the most part, in separate social and physical worlds—the solares—"black" spaces within the racially integrated Cayo Hueso.

Solares: Black Spaces

The level of racial integration and stability is impressive by any standard, but the reality of living in a barrio like Cayo Hueso is, of course, more complex. Even in a highly integrated neighborhood like Cayo Hueso there are distinctions, perhaps not noticeable to the passer-by, but part of the tacit knowledge of every resident. Race, history, housing, and poverty interconnect to create a finely grained map of the barrio for the long-time residents—a map that carefully delineates the independent social worlds of insiders but for outsiders conveys only the barrio's reputation in the crudest and most pejorative strokes.

Cayo Hueso is a barrio punctuated with solares and is indeed defined by all of the negative racial and social implications associated with them. In Cayo Hueso alone there are approximately 204 solares; 40 to 50 percent of all housing units in the barrio are solares (Coyula and Hamberg 2003). In the urban landscape these vest-pocket slums are tucked in between apartment buildings or sprawl on empty lots, and they function to spatially locate and socially isolate the predominantly black, poor solar residents. Even when found in more middle-class neighborhoods, sandwiched between single-family homes in areas such as Vedado, solares still signify poverty, blackness, and low culture—the unrefined masses represented in the statue of Quintín Bandera.

Solares (*cuarterías, casas de vecindad, ciudadelas*) are single or multistory buildings with single-room apartments opening onto a central courtyard. Traditionally, solares have only a communal toilet and water tap located in the courtyard. In some, tenants have managed to install running water and toilets in their individual units. Each single-room apartment is often home to entire families. Sometimes lofts (*barbacoas*) are built to accommodate the numerous people who must share these tiny spaces. Ventilation is poor, making solares sweltering in the tropical heat and dank during the rains.

Solares have housed the poorest and darkest residents for more than a century (Booth 1976; J. Domínguez 1978). Irene Alice Wright, an American journalist living in Cuba, writes in 1910 of "Havana tenements teeming with mulattoes and blacks" (2002, 105). David Ames, an American scholar conducting research in Havana in 1948, defined solares as "Negro tenement houses, stem[ming] from the days when Negros built little shacks on empty lots. . . . In each solar observed, Negro tenants were in the majority, although many whites and mulattoes were encountered" (1950, 159). Solares have continually been linked to marginality, crime, and promiscuity—traits frequently used to characterize blackness (de la Fuente 2001). Alejandro de la Fuente (2001) documents the identification of solares as problematic spaces in the first half of the 1900s when negative media reports of these tenements and their inhabitants served to validate social hierarchies and further marginalize the city's darkest and poorest residents.

Decades later the reputation of the solares persists. For example, in the summer of 1993 when severe oil shortages led to massive blackouts throughout the city there was an increase in street violence and vandalism in certain neighborhoods such as Cayo Hueso. As a result, the barrio was designated a "dangerous zone," and the nighttime blackouts in the area were drastically reduced. Irma, my neighbor, convinced the alleviation of the blackouts was due to the recent stint of rock throwing, applauded the rock throwers and commented to me, "If it means fewer blackouts, I hope they keep throwing rocks even if they have to break every window in Havana." However, there were no statistics available to document whether the vandalism and disturbances in Cayo Hueso really were disproportionately high during those particularly austere years of the special period. I would argue that government reaction to the vandalism in part came from and reinforced the barrio's negative reputation. An earlier Cuban study (conducted in 1987) found that supposed high-crime areas like Cayo Hueso in most cases did not have a higher than average crime rate (de la Fuente 2001). But even facts could not alter the negative image of the barrio, which was based in part on perception and an enduring racial/spatial ideology and in part on the reality of disturbances in this run-down, densely populated urban district.[7]

Street fights did erupt periodically in some Cayo Hueso solares in the early 1990s. Usually these occurred on Saturday nights between the two American movies that were broadcast on Cuban television. The frequency of the fights seemed directly proportional to the distribution of the rum or alcohol ration. When the fights spilled out of the solar next door to my apartment building, the call *"bronca"* would rise from the street. The sounds of screaming and dogs barking announced the fight, and apartment residents quickly assembled in their doorways, balconies, or windows to watch. Solar residents poured out into the street and surrounded the fighters. In Cayo Hueso, a street scuffle was a public cle, something you ran *toward*. The street filled with dozens of ₂ who followed the opponents (usually male) as they ran up the street or around the corner. The disturbances ranged from heated and threatening verbal exchanges to bottle and rock throwing to sticks and clubs and, on rare occasion, machetes and knives, which seemed to be brandished more for intimidation purposes than for inflicting injury.

As my white neighbor said to me, leaning over his balcony toward mine during one of these events, "Opening the balcony doors is like watching TV; there is always some commotion taking place." The barrio scuffles highlighted the clear social division between the residents who lived in apartments and those who lived in problematic solares, between those who watched from their balconies and doorways and those who ran out into the street—the respectable versus the marginal. My apartment-dwelling neighbors of all skin colors watched with a mix of fascination and disgust. Shaking their heads, with raised eyebrows and pursed lips, "There they go again," was a comment passed among the "respectable" apartment residents who nonetheless stayed glued to the scene until it passed out of view or dispersed. "They" were the predominantly darker-skinned residents of the solares. Despite the generally high level of interdependence on neighbors and the frequent face-to-face interactions, especially at the bodega and other shops distributing rationed food, many Cayo Hueso residents rarely knew or interacted with the people who lived in the solar next door.

The day after a street scuffle my neighbors would speculate about the causes of the fight: circulating bits of gossip and innuendo but having little direct contact with the solar residents, the discussions remained inconclusive. In one sense, the truth was irrelevant, as the apartment residents constructed their own version of reality—a vision that perpetuated the social isolation and negative reputation of the solares. Olga, the young black university student in an interracial relationship, summarized this common perception: "The racial problem in Cuba was always among concentrations of people who live in very poor conditions, in socially difficult environments. . . . [For example,] the solares in Havana are typical of black people. I cannot defend or admire people who stab and fight others, and when I look and see everyone there is black, then [I think] all the blacks are bad." Low culture and blackness resided in the solares. The occasional fights in Cayo Hueso only served to confirm residents' conceptions of blacks and mulattos and these "black" spaces and for many white Cubans reinforced a more generalized negative stereotype of Afrocubans, particularly those from places like Cayo Hueso.

For many Cayo Hueso residents, regardless of color, many solares represented dangerous spaces that they did not enter. By corollary, the simple fact of residency could socially blacken those living in solares regardless of their actual skin color. Living in a solar could virtually cast individuals, especially black men, in a negative light—as people who are problematic, prone to delinquency and violence—as *guapos.*

Guapos

> In a *solar*, the good person becomes bad. . . . [T]he men have to become guapos.
>
> —Lázara Menéndez and Raquel Mendieta,
> "Cayo Hueso: Una experiencia cultural"

As this quote suggests, the solar environment is purported to turn people bad and make men guapos. While solares spatially locate and contain blackness (both its folkloric/cultural and negative aspects), guapos are the iconic characters that populate these black spaces. They are nearly mythological figures that embody both marginality and hypermasculinity, with roots tracing back to the eighteenth century.[8] The term *guapo* itself glosses race, poverty, culture, and history into a socially acceptable discourse. Like Quintín Bandera, these modern day "rustic men" are simultaneously valorized and maligned, and they become a way to talk about race without mentioning the word.

Cayo Hueso has a reputation as a barrio of guapos, a place filled with solares and people of low culture, like other darker and poorer neighborhoods, including Habana Vieja and Marianao. Indeed, while the presence of solares is undeniable, actually defining and finding the supposed guapos is much more difficult. References to guapos surface in research on social problems conducted by various state agencies in the 1980s. One study by the FMC (Federation of Cuban Women), for example, examines the high incidence of antisocial behavior and what the author called *desviaciones socio-morales* (socio-moral deviations) among youth in a poor neighborhood in Camagüey (an eastern province): "In our analysis of the ten-block area that was surveyed we found: nine [blocks] with disorder, nine with frequent public disturbances, nine with guapos, nine with residents [who practiced] religious beliefs—usually santería, five with alcoholics and residents with antisocial behavior, and one with homosexual residents" (Montane Valdés 1986, 86).

In the Cuban social science of the 1980s, researchers defined guapos as social deviants, along with a cast of others who manifested behaviors or beliefs considered problematic from the state's perspective, including religious practitioners, rock music fans, and homosexuals. Many of the white youth I spoke with were quick to generate lists of "antisocial" behavior attributed to guapos. Guapos were described as always fighting among themselves, speaking badly, using vulgar words, fighting in the street, yelling, dealing on the black market and in illegal business, looking for the easy life, not working or studying, trying to scare people, and having a very low cultural level (*muy bajo nivel cultural*). The guapos were most often described by my informants as *conflictivo* (problematic, conflictive/trouble-makers). One white young man summed up the guapos, saying, "El dia que no se fajan, se sienten mal" (The day they don't fight, they feel bad).

When I asked my young white friends how these present-day guapos could be distinguished, they generated a long list of styles. Their descriptions concentrated exclusively on male guapos and included the following: guapos wear wide-legged pants, well-ironed short pants, short wide-bottomed pants; they carry a comb in their pocket, a knife in their pocket, a pistol in their pocket; they have strange haircuts, short haircuts; they have silver or gold front teeth; they wear boots with heels, shiny shoes with white socks, well-ironed clean shirts, open shirts, Santería beads; they have their neck and chest full of talcum powder, long fingernails, handkerchiefs in their hands; they walk with a bouncy step, with a skip step, with a wide step. Guapos were also distinguished by their musical taste: the Tropical, Los Van Van (a famous salsa band), and casino (salsa) music.[9] As one young white man noted, "[They like] dance music, a more national thing, music from here [Cuba]." Despite the detailed dress styles meticulously and consistently described by my friends, during my years in Havana, I saw no one that fit this commonly cited physical description of a guapo. Jafari Allen (2003) also found that his informants would consistently describe and demonstrate guapo mannerisms but could not identify a definite individual who would be considered a guapo. When I posed this paradox to my friends, I was told that these styles are rarely found now in Havana. Some of the youth speculated that they still may be seen in the countryside—which was where many of young people had spent some time at schools or agricultural camps. However, in my experience, guapos referred much less to this visually differentiated dress style and near mythic characterization than to speech patterns, actions, gathering places, barrios, leisure activities, and, of course, race and class. According to Allen, they were the local Cuban reputational figure par excellence (2003, 122). For my white friends, the guapos' most distinguishing trait was that they were almost always Afrocuban. Allen refined this claim, arguing that the racialization of guapos was primarily from a white perspective. Black Cubans, he argued, do not necessarily associate guapos or *guaperia* and low culture solely with blackness (2003).

While on the one hand guapos were often considered delinquents, on the other hand their hypermasculinity and bravery harmonized with Cuba's rebel image and its gendered project of constructing the "new socialist man." The new image of the proper revolutionary citizen, particularly in the early years of the revolution, encouraged homophobia and the "most brutish expressions of machismo" (Lumsden 1996, 59). This masculinity, of course, also resonated with dominant patriarchal ideology that the revolution inherited. Martín Morúa (1857–1910), a black senator and author, noted in his 1901 novel, *La Familia Unzúazu*, that a great number of youth both black and white were proud to be associated with these valiant types. It was thought that women would look on this with favor. According to Morúa, each youth would boast of being *"un hombre ñon,"* that is, a man who inspired dread, a fearless man (1975). This link between guapo behavior and an exalted image of masculinity (and homophobia) was still present in post-Soviet Cuba, as expressed by black Cuban social scientist Gisela Arandia Covarrubias in the following quote: "For Cubans, in general, . . . being guapo is nothing bad. On the contrary, being guapo is something very good. Because in our social context, the opposite of the guapo is the homosexual. Since we are Hispanic, in our consciousness homosexuality is something historically taboo or negative. In general, the Cuban man is guapo. Here the one who is not guapo is a fool. The Cuban man is guapo. They teach him to be guapo since he is a boy. When someone tries to snatch his snack in school, he goes home and his family tells him to fight for his food."[10]

The exaltation of the guapo for his hypermasculinity resonated with the traditional patriarchal culture and also with the state's militarism. Whether pursuing universal literacy or large sugar cane harvests, state policy initiatives were couched in military metaphors as "campaigns" or "battles," and frequently Cuba portrayed itself as a state under siege, due in part to the ever-present threat of U.S. intervention. The state's unwavering defensive position depended on an image of aggressive masculinity like the one the guapos presented. The guapo himself may have been socially peripheral, but his image was symbolically central. Though long maligned in the urban landscape, images of the guapos reflected, as Peter Stallybrass and Allon White (1986) argued, the "striking ambivalence to the representations of the lower strata in which they are both reviled and desired" (1986, 1).

Guapos in contemporary Cuba held a paradoxical position: stigmatized as delinquents and valorized as icons of masculinity. The term *guapo* was a way for residents and state agencies to couch unmentionable social divides in a socially acceptable, albeit racially coded vocabulary. Guapos and solares communicated the dangerousness associated with blackness and black spaces; however, these were not the only meanings of blackness circulating in the barrio.

Valorizing Blackness and Solares

The negative depictions of Cayo Hueso, solares, and blackness have not gone uncontested, and struggles over the meanings of blackness have taken place on both the domestic and international stage. The growth of mass tourism in Cuba had very local manifestations and effects for black Cubans and neighborhoods like Cayo Hueso. Tourism brought with it conflicting meanings of race—both blackness and whiteness.

Cayo Hueso, as many urban areas, was what Setha Low calls a "contested space"—where conflicts over meanings invested in sites echoed broader social struggles over deeply held collective myths, in this case myths about blackness (Low and Lawrence-Zúñiga 2003). Thus the barrio's blackness spatialized in the solares and in the park—the source of the barrio's vilification—became the source of an alternative representation of Cayo Hueso as a cradle of Afrocuban culture, a source of barrio identity and solidarity, and potentially an attraction for foreign tourists. While not denying the blackness associated with Cayo Hueso, cultural efforts sought instead to celebrate it.

Cultural production has become the fulcrum around which various forms and significances of blackness are enacted. References to solares as nodes of Afrocuban culture surface repeatedly in popular music. Song lyrics, written as early as the 1920s and as recently as 2001, make reference to the music and dance radiating from solares. The songs tend to highlight a folkloric image of the solar as a place where Afrocuban culture flourishes, as the following excerpt from "Ay! Mamá Inés" illustrates:

Belén, Belén, Belén	Belén, Belén, Belén
Adónde estás tú meti'a	Where have you been
Que por to' Jesús María	For God's sake
Y te buscá y no te encontrá.	And I looked and I couldn't find you.
Yo estaba casa madrina,	I was in my godmother's house
Que ayer me mandó a buscar	She sent for me yesterday
Del solar de la esquina,	From the *solar* on the corner,
Ella vive en El Manglar.	She lives in El Manglar.
Ay! Mamá Inés, Ay! Mamá Inés	Ay! Mamá Inés, Ay! Mamá Inés
Todos los negros tomamos café.	All the blacks drink coffee.
Nos vamos pa' la solar	Let's go to the solar
Donde va tanto negrito,	Where all the blacks go,
A bailar el congrejito,	To dance the *congrejito*,
Taitica, vamo' al Manglar.	Hey, let's go to El Manglar.

"Ay! Mamá Inés," written by Eliseo Grenet in the late 1920s, not only refers to solares as black spaces, but is written/sung in *bozal* speech, a truncated, lower-class Spanish associated with slaves or former slaves. From the lyrics we can envision not only a black social space pulsing with music and Santería ceremonies but a place of poor, lower-class, uneducated blacks who speak nonstandard Spanish. A more recent example, "Suave, Suave," from Nueva Trova artist Gerardo Alfonso, appears on his 2001 album *El Ilustrado Caballero De Paris*.[11] Nearly a century later the solar is still a site of rumba and a cradle of Afrocuban culture—though, in this case, it is a foreigner who seeks out the "authentic and exotic" black cultural life that solar residents offer, in "Suave, Suave":

Una sueca vino al país	A Swedish woman came to the country
A aprender la rumba como se toca aquí	To learn how they play rumba here
Su marido fue a Malecón	Her boyfriend went to the Malecón
A comprar tabacos y botellas de ron	To buy cigars and bottles of rum
En la Habana todo se intenta	In Havana everything is attempted
Lo que no se puede se inventa	What you can't do, is invented
Todo el mundo quiere salir	Everyone wants to escape
De su derrotero	Their destiny
Ella caminó toda la cuidad	She walked all over the city
Ella se metió en cualquiere lugar	Entered all kinds of places
Ella preguntó en cada solar	Asked in every *solar*
Y en un patio descubió	And in a courtyard found
Un negrón tocando tambor	A big black man playing the drum
Con los brazos fuertes como de un gladiador	With arms as strong as a gladiator
En los hombros el brillo del sol	The sun gleaming on his shoulders
Casi encandilaba	Almost dazzling

The songs depict the touristy quaintness of solares as "authentic" black places filled with drumming and carefree dancing. In the late 1980s, the Cayo Hueso Cultural Center attempted to capitalize on this image. Under the auspices of Central Havana Municipal Cultural Office (Dirección Municipal de la Havana), the cultural center organized events in barrio solares as a means of community development and in a sense tried to "re-image an African descendent identity" (Mullings 2004) in Cayo Hueso. This effort consisted of organizing rumbas in solar courtyards. In an interview with Margarita Saez Saez, a representative of the local Casa del Cultura, she told me she wanted to "rescue and revitalize *rumba de cajón* (rumba played on wooded boxes) inside the solares." Her goal was not solely to spread and keep rumba alive, but rather by working inside the solares she hoped to use culture as a point of entry to get residents, especially youth, involved in this community project and reconnected with society and neighborhood organizations. Saez deliberately selected solares that had problems among the neighbors and frequent fights—places that were physically neglected, dirty, and rundown. Staging the events in the solares was designed to encourage solar residents to take more responsibility and pride in their solar and hopefully work together to maintain it and keep it clean. The project was an attempt to emphasize the solar as a site of culture rather than of marginality. Using rumba highlighted and spatially located blackness in the solar but tried to valorize blackness and Afrocuban culture—certainly an attempt at what Leith Mullings called a "racialization from below" (2004). This project was plagued by a lack of resources, as its start coincided with the worst years of the early 1990s, and by the late 1990s its efforts seemed to have been usurped by the emergence of what has become the barrio's main tourist destination, the Callejón de Hamel.

In the 1990s a local Cayo Hueso artist, Salvador González, painted a mural on the wall of friend's house on the small alleyway, Callejón de Hamel. Salvador, a light-skinned mulatto (sometimes considered white) and practitioner of Santería, draws heavily on Afrocuban religious symbols and elements in his art. During the 1990s, his murals slowly expanded to cover more than one hundred meters of wall in the alleyway and most of the back walls of the six-story apartment building facing the alley where Salvador lives. By 2000 Callejón de Hamel had become a multidimensional outdoor art space complete with live music and weekly rumbas. It also included a shop where Salvador sold his art-work in hard currency, a bar that sold cold drinks and snacks in hard currency, and even a stand selling rum to Cubans in pesos. Salvador gained international reputation as a muralist and has been commis-sioned for murals in countries around the world.

Despite the fact that Callejón de Hamel may have started as a space celebrating Afrocuban culture in an effort to help revitalize Cayo Hueso for the residents, the alleyway now serves a much broader audience: namely, foreign tourists. A recent Google Internet search on "Callejón de Hamel" resulted in over five thousand hits. The Callejón draws much of its authenticity from its "spatial fix" in the largely black, working-class barrio of Cayo Hueso (Colantonio and Potter 2006). A Cuban Web site, Radio Coco, describes the alleyway as a cultural center of Afrocuban traditions "so rooted in the municipio of Centro Habana . . . it is a center of social and culture activity where art, dance and music coexist with religious syncretism and the patriotic feeling of this *ajiaco* (stew) to which Don Fernando Ortiz compared the cultural identity of our country" (G. González 2008). Canadian- and U.S.-based Web sites echo this sentiment, citing how the alleyway highlights the importance of African influences on Cuban culture, "a public temple" and "an obligatory stop" on the tourist agenda (Pérez Sarduy 2001). The local community cultural agency in Cayo Hueso also includes the Callejón on its Web site, stating that the alleyway's activities for all ages are geared toward "enriching our cultural wealth and allow all those who visit to know [our culture]."

The religious symbols depicted in the Callejón are derived from the widely practiced Afrocuban religions which were brought over by enslaved Africans from various ethnic groups, including the Bantu, the Yoruba, and the Arará. The myths and practices of these religions have, as Ortiz observed, "transculturated" into a variety of syncretic spiritual practices. The Yoruba people (known as Lucumí in Cuba) from the southwestern area of current-day Nigeria had the greatest influence on the blended religious systems that emerged in Cuba.[12] The Yoruba belief system changed as it encountered and melded

with other African religions and with Roman Catholicism. This syncretism resulted in the religious system known as Santería or Regla
de Ocha, which centers around the worship of the *orishas* (deities) of
the Yoruba pantheon and their Catholic saint counterparts (Barnet
2001). As Cuban scholar Miguel Barnet notes, "The rituals, music,
symbolism and also the rich mythology and hagiography attest to
the complexity of the system" (2001, 26). The devout must keep the
diverse pantheon of deities fed and happy through ritual ceremonies and offerings. Every deity or corresponding Catholic saint has
specific music, foods, colors, objects, symbols, and places associated
with them. Believers adorn home altars with symbols and offerings
for their orisha/saint. They also may wear beaded necklaces (*collares*)
in their orisha's colors or leave offerings for their orisha in sacred or
favored locations. The symbols and evidence of Santería worship were
pervasive in Cayo Hueso.

In an interview with Pedro Pérez Sarduy, Salvador himself (originally from a province in central Cuba) describes the barrio of Cayo
Hueso in the following terms:

> [It] is a barrio of the people, with a great cultural force which has
> given rise to some magnificent artists. . . . [H]ere the traditional
> *comparsas* (carnival street bands) of our barrio are very impor-
> tant. So too all the rumbas formerly played in Trillo Park. This
> is also a place steeped in popular religion. You can walk down
> the street and hear a "toque." Abakuá plants (for initiations) are
> found all over. The barrio has its own "potencia" of the secret
> Abakuá religion. . . . This barrio has a strong contingent of Black
> people. . . . The great importance that Callejón de Hamel holds
> for us, [is] it preserves those values which for many are archaic,
> primitive, but which nevertheless have their origin in one of the
> oldest cultures on earth—the Yoruba culture which in Cuba is
> lived . . . with living elements of a strong cultural identity which
> prevails in our food, in our education in our manner of speech,
> . . . in the way we express ourselves. . . . [O]f course foreigners
> who don't know our culture . . . they look for the exotic side of
> this [Afrocuban] theme. (Pérez Sarduy 1998)

Later in the interview Salvador laments that some artists and artisans cater the to tourists' curiosity by selling them Santería trinkets and talking to them about the deities without any real grounding or knowledge of the religion (Pérez Sarduy 1998). Others have voiced a similar concern that cultural promotion for tourism is often entrusted to whites, many of whom are ignorant about Afrocuban cultural traditions (Fernandes 2006, 163; Martínez Furé 1993).[13]

These references to the Callejón de Hamel and the surrounding barrio of Cayo Hueso use the blackness of the barrio to reinforce the authenticity of the performances and representations of Afrocuban culture that take place in the Callejón. In other similarly marginal and rundown barrios, community development projects have also tapped into Afrocuban religious folklore as a venue for showcasing local traditions and earning hard currency. As part of an effort to revitalize older inner-city neighborhoods with dilapidated housing stocks, failing infrastructures and services, and numerous social ills, the Comprehensive Development of the Capital Group (Grupo para el Desarrollo Integral de la Capital, or GDIC) started a series of Comprehensive Workshops for Neighborhood Change (Talleres de Transformacion Integral del Barrio, TTIB, or Talleres) in 1988. The Talleres used professional architects, planners, and social workers to work with local residents to help residents refurbish their own dwellings and communities. This grassroots effort has been largely overshadowed by the higher-profile, vast commercial project to restore Habana Vieja, though the work of the Talleres have caught the attention of a number of scholars and international development projects (Hearn 2004; Kapcia 2005; Wolfe 2000). The Talleres sought to engage popular participation of the residents as subjects rather than objects in the remaking of both the physical and social environments of their barrios (Coyula, Oliveras, and Coyula 2002). The revitalization was to stimulate the most positive cultural values of a barrio, maintain and keep its cultural traditions alive, and at the same time encourage new ways of acting and thinking that were socially positive (Coyula, Oliveras, and Coyula 2002). Talleres tried to promote a sense of solidarity and belonging within a barrio so that residents developed a heightened sense of personal responsibility for the physical and social condition of the barrio. The Talleres were located throughout the city, including some in Centro Habana and Habana Vieja.

Adrian Hearn (2004) describes several collaborative community development projects in the early 2000s in the similarly poor and black barrios of Habana Vieja and Cerro (Atarés). In each of the three cases he presents, the activities began as community-generated civic actions from established Afrocuban religious groups, but each transformed (to a greater or lesser extent) into a folklorization of religious rituals or dance performances for tourists as part of what one community leader called "folklore-development tourism." In each case, Hearn argues, it was difficult to balance the commercial opportunities with the barrio's original interests and goals of empowerment. Though two of the three did manage to get back to organizing more community-focused activities along with those for the tourists, Hearn remained cautiously optimistic about the potential for community improvement that these types of projects could generate.

With the increasing tourism in Cuba and the foreign fascination with Afrocuban culture in particular, some scholars (Hodge 2006; Martínez Furé 2000) have critiqued the resulting "cultural commodification." Kevin Meethan, however, suggests "that in the context of globalization and consumer culture . . . seeing commodification as negative does not give credit to the producers or consumers for their agency in re-writing the meanings of signs" (as quoted in Roland 2004, 214). I would suggest that Callejón de Hamel offers the potential for generating multiple significances of blackness and of space (namely, the barrio) in the context of global tourism. It certainly sells Afrocuban culture, but it also attempts to validate Afrocuban culture in the barrio and brings local and international attention and potentially increased resources to a space and a population that was formerly seen as socially marginal within Havana. Whether or not the Callejón project will become a source for civic action and community development remains to be seen.

At the very least, the similar cases Hearn presents and the presence of tourism in Cayo Hueso layer yet another meaning of blackness—a global one—onto Cayo Hueso and similar barrios. Most locals now view the alleyway as exactly what it seems to have become—a tourist attraction. Many young Cubans, especially young black men, can be found hanging out there—some hoping to meet foreigners, others coming to enjoy the live music and the availability of rum. The Callejón roots its authenticity in the persistent image of Cayo Hueso as a black space; however, it simultaneously displaces blackness onto the exotic black diaspora sought by foreign tourists. While Cayo Hueso may have been transformed from a stigmatized place to a destination in the eyes of some, it is now a place where the constructions of blackness are played out both locally and on the global stage. Standing silently at the heart of Cayo Hueso, Quintín Bandera still epitomizes the uncertain place of blacks and blackness in the nation.

The attention to race and space in this chapter is essential as interracial couples inhabit physical places—spaces laden with racial significance. They live in a city shaped by both historic meanings of blackness and current and shifting valuations of color. Interracial couples navigate the competing webs of meaning around race, blackness, and space. Racial inequalities are occulted in physical spaces and coded terms like *guapos* and *solares,* but inequalities and meanings of blackness and whiteness were also openly expressed in conversations, as Javier's comments at the start of this chapter attest. The integrationist policies of the revolution could not completely expunge inequities from the physical landscape, nor could the policy of silence remove race from daily interactions.

4

The Everyday Presence of Race

Jaime, a young, white, working-class man, lived with his extended family in a cramped apartment in a rundown section of Centro Habana. He dated Madaleis, a mulata, and I visited his house often. In the following chapters, we will hear more about this couple's story. On one visit, I entered the cluttered living room and found the room filled with family members and neighbors. Jaime's sister was rocking a neighbor's child to sleep in her arms. Another neighbor, a white man, Armando, who was often present in the apartment, looked at the black toddler sleeping in her white arms and commented, "She sure is black. Black, black [Prieta, prieta]." Jaime's uncle added, "The mother was black, and the father was blacker." Everyone laughed. Then Armando said to Jaime's father, implying that the child belonged to him, "Oh, I thought you'd been dipping in the petroleum." Again, the room resonated with laughter. Jaime's sister smiled awkwardly. Continuing the joking, Jaime's uncle turned to me and said, "Can't you see her [the black toddler] swinging around in her cage." I winced at the blatantly racist banter. Amid the renewed laughter, Jaime's sister gently castigated her uncle, "Oh, you're so bad," and then carried the sleeping child off into the bedroom.

The fact that Jaime's sister was babysitting the neighbor's child showed the close interdependence among friends and neighbors of all skin colors. The cordiality and the circulation of favors, goods, child care, and information among neighbors stretched across race lines. There was genuine fraternity among neighbors of all skin colors.

form of Closeness

Same w/ husbands

KEY

However, instead of erasing color distinctions, these neighborly cross-racial encounters often provided opportunities to reinforce and re-exert racist thinking. The sharing and mutual aid did not necessarily imply a degree of color blindness. In some cases, like in Jaime's family, the close interracial neighborliness created situations ripe for racist jousting and joking. The white family's racism did not result in social distancing or avoidance of their black neighbors or in fiery verbal or physical confrontations, but instead, the racial hierarchy was main-tained through humor. Since such jokes were easy to brush off as inconsequential, in the context of sincerely friendly relations, racist ideologies could go unchallenged. This paradoxical and contradictory situation was emblematic of the complexity of race relations in Cuba. As Mark Sawyer states, this type of "inclusionary discrimination" is not a question of inclusion or exclusion based on race, but rather "deter-mines the *terms* of inclusion" (2006, 19).

In the banter Armando chided Jaime's father for "dipping in the petroleum," that is, sleeping with black women and thus begetting a mulatto child. In this instance the racist joke focused on interracial sexual encounters. These potentially reproductive unions (like Jaime's relationship with Madaleis) often threatened the white family. In this scene, it was not coincidental that a white male was teased about hav-ing a black lover. The reverse pairing (white women with black men) seldom was the topic of a joke. Such opposite pairings produced appre-hension in many white families, as I will discuss in the following chap-ters. It is Jaime's father who was accused of "dipping in the petroleum," not Jaime's sister, who was holding the child. The aphorism evoked images of white males seeking Afrocuban women as pleasure objects in relationships or encounters whose primary objective was sexual enjoyment—a historically grounded and more socially permissible type of interracial pairing from the perspective of many white families. So humor served to frame the boundaries of cross-racial neighborliness by reminding those present of the types of interracial relations that were acceptable from the white family's perspective.

With the official "silence" on race, when I arrived in Cuba I expected to find exactly that, silence. I thought race might be something no one mentioned, something that I would only be able to tease out after months

of fieldwork—a subterranean discourse whispered among confid
I was wrong. If direct mention of race was largely absent from
ment declarations and public (published) dialogue or was pres
racially coded vocabulary, it saturated daily life with an astonishing raw-
ness (like in the scene I described above). I was surprised to hear racial
and sexual stereotypes, jokes, and sayings easily slip uncontested into
conversations, regardless of the racial makeup of the audience or the
speakers. The terrain of everyday interactions in Cuba *was not* filled with
explosive or violent interracial encounters, but it *was* rife with knowing
gestures and looks, under-the-breath comments, and out-in-the-open
jokes through which people made their racial views known. There was
no notion of "political correctness" to filter even the most blatantly
racist remarks. I was struck by what seemed to be schizophrenic—the
everyday cross-racial cordiality and interdependence and the numerous
interracial relationships that coexisted with a pervasive denigration of
blackness and valorization of whiteness and lightness.

Recently some scholars (de la Fuente 2001, 2008; Espina Prieto and
Rodríguez Ruiz 2006; Sawyer 2006) have noted an increase in racial discrimination and prejudice on the island, but I would argue that these tensions have been present in revolutionary Cuba all along. The economic
crisis of the special period did not create racism; it only created opportunities for racist thinking to take on new forms and expressions. As Katherine Verdery noted, "Historical enmities must be reproduced into the
present. . . . [T]heir continuity cannot be simply presupposed. . . . No set
of issues simply hangs around for forty years awaiting resurrection, much
has happened in the meantime" (1996, 95). Noting the diffuse nature of
power, Michel Foucault commented on the tenacity of social inequalities
in the former Soviet Union: "I do not mean in any way to minimize the
importance and effectiveness of State power. I simply feel that excessive
insistence on its playing an exclusive role leads to the risk of overlooking
all the mechanisms and effects of power which don't pass directly via the
State apparatus, yet often sustain the State more effectively than its own
institutions, enlarging and maximizing its effectiveness. In Soviet society
one has the example of a State apparatus which has changed hands, yet
leaves social hierarchies, family life, sexuality and the body more or less
as they were in capitalist society" (1980, 73).

In Cuba, as Foucault stated for the Soviet Union, people continually remade the racial hierarchy and racist ideologies despite revolutionary changes that gave Cubans an alternative non-racist discourse, an inclusive ideology of national identity, and real structural changes that fostered racial equality and integration. Despite this context, Cubans voiced and reinforced racial hierarchies in negative stereotypes, representations of blackness, and views about interracial couples. Alejandro de la Fuente (2008) noted that the Cuban government had been less than successful in dismantling Cuba's racist culture.[1] Racist ideologies persisted precisely because they were able to mutate, transform, and adapt to new social and political circumstances. In Cuba, the question was not so much *when* or *if* racism had returned or resurfaced in the special period, but rather *how* racist ideologies continued to permeate daily life in taken-for-granted ways. As Peter Wade (1997) posited, the point is to understand how racial flexibility and racism coexist in Latin American countries. The power to maintain and reproduce racial inequality was diffuse and manifested itself in everyday social and personal interactions. De la Fuente observed that "a multitude of aphorisms, popular sayings, and jokes continued to denigrate blacks as naturally inferior and predisposed to crime and violence" (2008, 713). Far from being a "nontopic" in revolutionary Cuba, race remained tightly interwoven into the weft of commonsense thinking, everyday discourses, and quotidian life. These racist ideologies were reproduced in part *despite* and in part *because of* the revolution's color-blind stance on the racial question.

Racial Jokes and Aphorisms

Both race mixture and the racial hierarchy are ensconced in Cuban literature, popular icons, and everyday discourse and aphorisms. These two competing images of race relations find voice in widely heard sayings. While "Desde San Antonio hasta Maisí, el que no tiene de Congo, tiene de Caribalí" (From San Antonio [western Cuba] to Maisí [eastern Cuba], one who doesn't have blood of the Congo has the blood of the Calibar) celebrates racial mixture, *"juntos pero no revueltos"* (together but not mixed) and *"cada oveja con su pareja"* (each sheep with its own kind) counter that national ideal and instead endorse racial separateness.

Renowned Afrocuban poet Nicolás Guillén reworks these aphorisms in his celebration of Cuban mestizaje: "The national mestizaje . . . comes from our fundamental double root. For that reason in Cuba, the white is mestizo, the black is mestizo, and the mestizo is mestizo. . . . [T]ogether and mixed, they create Cubanness, something new, neither Spanish nor African, or better said, African and Spanish, in a profoundly national synthesis" (1959, 3). In this quote Guillén inverts the popular aphorism "*juntos pero no revueltos*" (together *but not* mixed) and instead insists Cubans are "together *and* mixed," stressing the fundamentally mestizo nature of Cubanidad. However, along with this powerful ideology of mestizaje were equally common aphorisms devaluing blackness.

As I spent most of my time visiting friends in their homes, it was there that I witnessed and overheard these aphorisms and racist exchanges—like the scene I described at Jaime's apartment. These types of interchanges were common in many of the white families I visited. It was particularly the middle-age parents who would participate, and if the younger members were present, as in Jaime's case, they would simply laugh along or downplay the exchange. I was always struck by the naturalness with which they flowed into daily conversations in white households, but also in black and mulatto households I visited frequently.

On one occasion I attended a party at a black friend's home. As the party at Maité's solar was winding down, an argument erupted between a sober black man and his white wife, who was drunk. The angry husband chased his wife out the door and down four flights of the dark, steep stairs of the tenement house. Many of the guests followed in close pursuit. Observing the incident, Maité, the black hostess, commented to me that a white man never would have become so enraged at the antics of his obviously drunk wife. The black husband exploded because "*está en la pinta*" (it's in his color/blood), she said, citing a popular phrase and rubbing her index finger on her forearm, a gesture used to indicate blackness. Other guests overhearing the comment nodded in agreement and shrugged their shoulders, attesting to the inevitability of the man's actions. With that, the subject was closed.

Once the hostess stated "*está en la pinta*," nothing more needed to be said about the event. The commonly shared assumptions embodied in the saying did not need to be articulated. The discussion was truncated. What exactly is in *la pinta* was understood. In fact, this lack of specificity allows such popular phrases great flexibility and applicability. Those unnamed negative characteristics and traits associated with blacks can be reconfigured, adapted, and called upon to fit any situation, attesting to the "practicalness and naturalness" of these commonsense expressions (Geertz 1975).

Aphorisms foreclose discussions by drawing on a shared wisdom that is assumed to be true. The naturalization of these ideas in popular conceptions and assumptions often make them difficult to contest and, as a result, curtail further comment, as Antonio Gramsci states: "In a whole range of judgments common sense identifies the exact cause, simple and accessible" (1971, 348). Maité's comment had a distinct air of naturalness—things are as they are—and it was met with an attitude of "Of course, it figures." Common sense about race represents things as being precisely what they seem to be. "Religion rests its case on revelation, science on method, ideology on moral passion; but common sense rests its on the assertion that it is not a case at all, just life in a nutshell. The world is its authority," Clifford Geertz writes (1975, 7).

Stuart Hall argues that it is this "taken for granted terrain . . . of conceptions and categories on which the practical consciousness of the masses of the people is actually formed" (1986, 12). The notion of common sense captures the negotiable and often contradictory nature of race relations in Cuba. Robert Miles observes that racism may take the form of a relatively coherent theory, exhibiting a formal and logical structure such as exclusionary laws or practices, but it may also appear as an amalgam of stereotypes, attributions, and explanations which are constructed and employed to negotiate social interactions in everyday life (1989, 79). Ann Laura Stoler refers to the intrinsic and paradoxical power of racist discourse, a "scavenger" discourse, saying that racism "provides truth claims about how the social world once was, why social inequalities do or should persist, and the social distinctions on which the future should rest" (1995, 91). Racial discourses, she argues, derive force from a "polyvalent mobility, from the density of discourses they harness, from the multiple economic interests they serve, from the subjugated knowledges they contain, from the sedimented forms of knowledge that they bring into play" (204). While others (Miles 1989; Stoler 1995) have noted the commonsensical nature of racism, it is Hall (1986) who explicitly draws on Antonio Gramsci's notion of common sense and applies it to "complexify" the study of race and ethnicity.[2]

According to Gramsci, "common sense" refers to the uncritical and taken-for-granted worldview (1971). It proceeds from an incoherent set of generally held assumptions and beliefs, a chaotic aggregate of disparate conceptions. Entrenched racial ideologies of black inferiority are prevalent in commonsense thinking. These everyday ideologies are grounded in the idea of an essential and static human nature, not mediated or clouded by the historical struggles that truly generated contemporary race relations (Hall 1986). Common sense provides understandings and explanations that legitimate the status quo.

Some of the negative assumptions ascribed to blackness in Cuba were painstakingly detailed on a neatly typed sheet of racist jokes that circulated in Lazaro's engineering class and highlighted the commonsense racial lens through which actions by blacks and whites are interpreted. Lazaro, a dark-skinned black man in his early thirties, was from a very poor family. He had studied with Maité in high school and was Antonio's best friend. Like Antonio, he was educated at a university in the former Soviet Union. Now he worked as an electrical engineer. In 1993 Lazaro was attending a professional development course in engineering in Havana. Among the dozen or so students (all professional engineers close to Lazaro's age), Lazaro was the only black. One day the following page of jokes was passed among the students. (I have added the English translations.)

CLASIFICACION DEL NEGRO [CLASSIFICATION OF THE BLACK]

- El negro es una especie animal parecido al hombre que se diferencia del *mono* porque camina erguido y tiene *carne de identidad.* [The Black is a species of animal similar to man and different from the ape because he walks erect and has an ID card.]
- Su cuerpo se divide en *patas y rabo.* [His body is divided into feet and tail (penis).]

CARACTERISITCAS GENERALES [GENERAL CHARACTERISTICS]

- nariz achatada [flattened nose]
- olor inconfundible [distinct odor]

- siente miedo al agua y al trabajo [is afraid of water and work]
- tiene pasion por las blancas, las grabadoras y las gafas (navajas) [has a passion for white women, tape recorders, sunglasses, and knives]
- Solo es inofensivo, pero en manadas es peligroso. [Alone is not a threat, but in gangs is dangerous.]
- Se diferencia del blanco en que este cuando muere se vela y al negro hay que velarlo desde que nace. [He is distinguished from the white in that when the white dies he is mourned, and the black is mourned from the day he's born.]
- Estudios sobre las razas han determinado que es una especie africana y que por desgracia se adapta a climas tropicales, calidos, templados. [Studies about race have determined that he is an African species and unfortunately adapts to warm, tropical, temperate climates.]

SEMEJANZAS Y DIFERENCIAS SIN DISCRIMINACION RACIAL
[SIMILARITIES AND DIFFERENCES WITHOUT RACIAL DISCRIMINATION]

- Blanco con uniforme [White in a uniform] . . . Militar [Soldier]
- Negro con uniforme [Black in a uniform] . . . Maletero [Bellhop]
- Blanco con pistola [White with a pistol] . . . Precavido [Cautious]
- Negro con pistola [Black with a pistol] . . . Asaltante [Assailant]
- Blanco subiendo loma [White climbing a hill] . . . Alpinista [Mountain climber]
- Negro subiendo loma [Black climbing a hill] . . . Buscando comida [Seeking food]
- Blanco con maletín [White with briefcase] . . . Funcionario [Bureaucrat]
- Negro con maletín [Black with briefcase] . . . Ladron [Thief]
- Blanco con chofer [White with chauffeur] . . . Millonario [Millionaire]
- Negro con chofer [Black with chauffeur] . . . Detenido [Under arrest]
- Blanco comiendo mucho [White eating a lot] . . . Se alimenta bien [Well-fed]
- Negro comiendo mucho [Black eating a lot] . . . Muerto de hambre [Starving]
- Blanco jugando billar [White playing billiards] . . . Elegante [Elegant]
- Negro jugando billar [Black playing billiards] . . . Vicioso [Vice]

- Blanco con uñas largas [White with long nails] . . . Pepillo [Fashionable]
- Negro con uñas largas [Black with long nails] . . . Maricón [Gay]
- Blanco leyendo periodico [White reading newspaper] . . . Intelectual [Intellectual]
- Negro leyendo periodico [Black reading newspaper] . . . Buscando Trabajo [Job hunting]
- Blanco con sandalias [White in sandals] . . . Turista [Tourist]
- Negro con sandalias [Black in sandals] . . . Bugarrón [Gay]
- Blanco rascandose [White scratching] . . . Alérgia [Allergies]
- Negro rascandose [Black scratching] . . . Sarnoso [Mange]
- Blanco corriendo [White running] . . . Deportista [Athlete]
- Negro corriendo [Black running] . . . Carterista [Pickpocket]

¿Que más se puede esperar de un negro? [What more can you expect from a black?]

No effort was made to shield Lazaro from seeing the list. The jokes, circulated with the "best intentions," were met with hearty laughter from all present, as Lazaro recounted the incident to me later. Lazaro's reaction to this was, he said, "to laugh along, of course. If I show that I'm offended, they'll think I'm *pesado* (a spoilsport). But, of course, I feel bad hearing these things." Lazaro gave me the list but informed me that I could only keep it for a day or so, as his classmate wanted it back. The list had such widespread circulation that several years later it appeared in an article by a Cuban social scientist on racial discrimination on the island (see Caño Secade 1996).

Folklorists argue that jokes, as a particular type of folklore, can also serve as socially sanctioned outlets for expressing taboo ideas or subjects. Ethnic and racial humor conveys a message about power relations, and, in fact, these types of jokes actively help to keep that power decentered. While the content of jokes may reflect the broader social hierarchy, the telling of jokes speaks to the more immediate, often ambivalent social relationships among the actors involved. Hall echoes this focus on power, urging that racial jokes and sayings require special analysis: "Racist jokes told across racial lines in conditions where relations of racial inferiority and superiority prevail, reinforce the difference and reproduce the unequal relations because, in those situations, the point of the joke depends on the existence of racism. Thus they reproduce the categories and relations of racism, even while normalizing them through laughter" (1981, 43). It is not the individual's intentions (good or bad) that are the central issue in the joke telling, but rather the larger social milieu in which the joke takes place that grounds its significance: "Intentionality is not a necessary component of racism. It is not the nature of specific acts or beliefs that determines whether these are mechanisms of racism, but the context in which these beliefs and acts operate. . . . Racism often operates through seemingly nonracial practices" (Essed 1991, 45).

In the case of Lazaro, in a classroom of all-white professional engineers, he reads the list of what are ironically titled "Similarities and Differences without Racial Discrimination." The list is a sort of social map to decode apparently similar behavior or traits among blacks and whites. The jokes represent stereotypical images of black males as criminals, lower-class, lazy, dirty, and sexually insatiable. Most importantly, blacks are seen to possess these traits "naturally," with several references to blacks as a distinct "species" predestined to embody these characteristics and fulfill these roles.

Ironically, the form of these particular jokes highlights Lazaro's position as the only black engineer present in the class. It is almost as if to this list we might add "a white in an engineering class . . . an engineer; a black in an engineering class . . ." Well, that's difficult to say. As a result, the unspoken couplet can only be completed by laughter. Obviously, Lazaro's presence is something that is noticed, something out of the ordinary, something in need of explanation. As is often commented in these types of black-white encounters, "Well, so-and-so isn't really black"—a statement that essentializes black identity in pejorative stereotypes. Perhaps sharing the jokes with Lazaro affirmed that his classmates did not see him as "socially" black. Or perhaps it was to remind him that although he was an engineer, he was still black and could never distance himself from all of the negative connotations associated with blackness. The laughter masked the anxiety of the situation, but its overriding effect, even though Lazaro laughed along, was to marginalize him and to remind him of the differential in power and the unequal valorizations of blackness and whiteness.

Situations such as Lazaro's, involving encounters with professional or educated Afrocubans, often evoked another set of aphorisms that attempted to account for the excepted (and thus accepted) individual. Some educated Afrocubans had distanced themselves far enough from the negative stereotypes of blackness as to gain "honorary white" status. The black person who was culturally and socially considered white may be referred to as *blanco por dentro* (white on the inside) or *un mulato de cachet* (a stylish, high-class mulatto). Many white academics frequently used these phrases to refer to Antonio after meeting him and being surprised by his "high cultural level" (*alto nivel cultural*—more on cultural level in chapter 5). The discourse of the "exceptional" black also expressed racist ideology.

Aphorisms and jokes reinforced negative assumptions ascribed to blackness, and these were complimented by disparaging visual representations of blacks in the media. For years Cuban scholars and actors have bemoaned the stereotypical typecasting of blacks in the media and the lack of opportunities for Afrocubans in the fields of radio, television, and film (Cervera 2000; Fernández Robaina 1991; A. Knight 2000; Ramos Cruz 2000; Rosete Silva 1994). New civic organizations, such as the Confradía de la Negritud, have taken up this issue as well. De la Fuente (2008) notes that the Confradía has "petitioned for an effective and proportional presence of blacks and mulattoes on television, ballet and in movies" (711). Its work has brought new attention to a problem that has persisted for decades.

Media Representations of Afrocubans

The reality of race in any society is, to coin a phrase, "media-mediated."
    —Stuart Hall, "Race, Culture, and Communications"

Being black is the bane of any black Cuban actor.
    —Elvira Cervera, "Todo en Sepia: An All-Black Theater Project"

One day as Antonio and I watched an American thriller on television, he turned to me and said, "There can't be so much racism in the U.S. Look, in this movie, the lawyer is black, the police chief is black, and the criminals are white." I had just lost another round in our ongoing comparisons of racism in the United States and Cuba. He was right, at least in part; in the United States the media was much more conscious of their portrayals of blacks and sensitive to viewer reactions and critiques. In Cuba all venues of media (radio, television, and print media, newspaper and magazines) were financed, operated, and controlled by the state. The media and programming were not shaped by commercial interests as much as by the state's policies, agendas, and revolutionary propaganda. As in the United States, intellectuals and media professionals know that the media functions as a principal means of ideological production: "What [the media] produce is, precisely representations of the social world, images, descriptions, explanations and frames for understanding how the world is and why it works as it is said and shown to work" (Hall 1981, 35). In the last several decades in the United States, the media has attempted to project less stereotypically negative images of people of color, and at the very least there has been a consciousness about the impact of media images. Elvira Cervera (2000), one of Cuba's foremost black actresses, concurred that the media plays a very important role in shaping people's vision and perceptions, and in the case of black Cubans the media was constantly lacerating their self-esteem, both as actors and spectators.

During an interview, I asked Irene Ester Ruiz, a black woman who worked as a program manager at ICRT (Instituto Cubano de Radio y Televisión), to comment on racial images projected in the media. She responded with the following anecdote: "TV images don't correspond with the achievements of the revolution. Blacks are not represented on TV. This doesn't reflect the level of education achieved by blacks, their acting talent, etc. Recently on *Contacto* (a Cuban TV program), the Cuban comic Alexis Valdés made a joke saying that when TV was first developed it was in black and white. Then technology kept advancing and produced TV in color, but now here in Cuba we have TV in white only because we don't see blacks anywhere." The joke revealed a truth poignantly recounted by Cervera. She described the difficulties and frustration she experienced as a black actress during her career in radio, television, and film, and she lamented the limited opportunities blacks still confront in these fields. Cervera stated:

At the start of the 1970s the management of ICRT met with the workers to hear their complaints. I said blacks continue to be excluded [as actors]. My attitude was considered unrevolutionary and my statement inappropriate. I felt harassed. They wanted me to change my idea. I didn't think this would happen under the revolution. . . . The revolution gave liberties to the blacks in many areas, but in the dramatic arts, nothing changed. . . . Basically, in the director's mental designs there are no blacks, and they separate us [blacks] by reflex. The problem is not resolved by decree or by law. No one tells you that it [the problem] doesn't exist, but everything functions as if it doesn't exist; that is to say, it doesn't matter that it exists. . . . To hide that problem is simply dishonest. (as quoted in Rosete Silva 1994, 28)

Scholar Tomás Fernández Robaina (1991) noted that when ICRT did attempt to respond to this absence and broadcast an adventure series with a mostly black cast, the public reaction was negative. They complained that the show was nothing more than crowds of blacks on the screen.[3] These observations by Ruiz, Fernández Robaina, and Cervera contradicted earlier perceptions which posited that by the mid-1970s blacks were frequently seen and accepted in a variety of roles on Cuban television (Booth 1976). In fact, Alden Knight (2000), a renowned black Cuban actor, commented on this change. In the first decades of the revolution, the actor's union was part of ICRT and had a say in programming and casting. During this time the ethnic and racial representativeness of the shows were taken into account. Now, however, the actor's union and ICRT are independent bodies, and ICRT takes full responsibility for programming and casting. Knight observed that now there is a rupture between the actor and television. Actors can no longer make demands on television directly. This has muted their voices, and the result has been the all-white television that has become the norm.

Cervera bemoaned not only the absence of blacks in the media but also their stereotypical typecasting as slaves, historical black figures, or poor, uneducated people. She wondered when black actors would be recognized as actors and not as blacks, and, citing the success of black screen stars in the United States, she concluded that the Americans "as

bad as they are, are less separatist in the dramatic arts than the revolutionary Cubans—which is a shame" (as quoted in Rosete Silva 1994).
One example of the roles in which blacks were typically found was on
Sabadazo, the variety show broadcast on Saturday nights in the early
1990s. The program presented a series of comic skits with a recurring
cast of characters. Within this cast, the black character was portrayed as
a vulgar, uneducated, tenement-dwelling tough guy who spoke in nonstandard Spanish. Guillermina Ramos Cruz observed that blacks were
often satirized on television with "deformed speech" (2000, 152).

In an attempt to counter this trend, Cervera launched an all-black
theater project titled Todo en Sepia (All in Sepia) in the late 1990s. Her
project was to break the barriers that kept black actors from taking
roles in theater and to "document, analyze, denounce and reject the
evident limitations on the dark-skinned actor professionally on the
Cuban stage" (Cervera 2000, 97). Cervera met with harsh criticism for
the project's all-black cast and was encouraged by film, TV, and theater
officials to integrate the cast. Her retort to them was, "If TV programming and films . . . have all fair-skinned casts, what right have they to
tell me not to do it with all dark-skinned ones?" (Cervera 2000, 100).
Her chief complaint was that the problem of black representation and
discrimination within the media was not recognized by media institutions and officials: "I think there's a residual sub-esteem of canons of
beauty, of mental approach, which ends up being prejudicial to those
who do not have the necessary conviction to place the black actor on
a par with other actors. . . . This explains the generalized attitude of
ignoring the existence of the problem, attempting to silence the voices
or denunciation, twisting the concepts as 'inopportune,' 'complex,' and
'inverse racism'" (Cervera 2000, 107).

By relegating blacks to such roles as poor, ill-mannered people or
delinquents, the media contributed to what Hall (1981) terms "inferential racism," which naturalized these images of blacks. This representation of the familiar stereotypes becomes layered along with other
negative views of blackness in forming commonsense racist ideologies.
Inferential racism, Hall (1981) argued, was more insidious and widespread than overt expressions of racism, as it remained largely invisible
even for those whose worldview was shaped by it.

Racial terminology, sayings, jokes, and visual images all contributed to molding and sustaining racist culture and the racial hierarchy in Cuba. These representations had real consequences in social interactions and personal relationships, particularly for people involved in interracial romances. Commonsense notions of race affected the choices of dating partners and shaped public reactions to interracial couples. In the style of the racist jokes Lazaro encountered, we might speculate what couplets racist interpretations of interracial couples could produce.

Meanings of Interracial Couples:
Mythic Sexuality and *Interés*

Given the commonsense assumptions about blackness, whiteness, race, and class, interracial couples raised questions in the minds of many Cubans. Their unions were much more than simple romantic relationships. Their existence often begged for further explanation or the divulgence of some mitigating circumstances that brought these two individuals of different shades together.

Historically, in Cuban literature and arts interracial couples were not depicted as the cultural ideal or the champions of mestizaje, but rather as romantic tragedies laced with stereotypes and shrouded in ulterior motives. A nineteenth-century literary genre centered on the theme of mixed race couplings, usually interracial love triangles with a sensual mulata caught between two rival suitors, one black or mulato and one white. In the typical scenario, the honest black man sincerely loved the mulata, while the ambivalent white suitor desired only an ongoing sexual relationship with her. The white man would never dare marry her, in part for fear of his family's reprisals. In this script the mulata preferred her white lover and rejected the more honorable advances of the black man. Trapped in this context of conflicting desire and restraining social convention, the affair inevitably ended tragically. This was the basic plot of the classic Cuban novel *Cecilía Valdés* by Cirilo Villaverde (first published in its entirety in 1879).[4] Cecilía Valdés, the mulata protagonist, fell in love with a well-to-do white man, Leonardo Gamboa, neither one of them knowing they were half-siblings. Cecilía herself was the offspring of an affair between her mulata mother and Leonardo's father. Cecilía's father clandestinely maintained his illegitimate daughter and her grandmother, while Cecilia's mother was driven insane, as her relationship with Cecilía's father could never be legitimated. The next generation repeated the tragedy, as Cecilía dreamed Leonardo Gamboa would marry her. Meanwhile, she spurned the advances of the honest mulato man who truly loved her. The novel ended with her mulato lover killing Leonardo on the day he was to wed his white bride, who he did not love but was forced to marry under pressure from his family. Leonardo's death plunged Cecilía into madness, and she joined her mother in the asylum.

Ethnomusicologist Robin Moore (1997) noted that similar love triangle imagery was so common in light opera (*zarzuelas*), comic theater (*teatro vernáculo, teatro bufo*), and other artistic expressions that it deserved recognition as one of the most pervasive tropes of Cuban culture from the nineteenth through the mid-twentieth century.[5] The recurring character types of the *negrito* (comic black man, played by a white man in blackface), the *gallego* (Spanish businessman or shopkeeper),[6] and the mulata (or light-skinned mixed-race woman) were central tropes for seventy or eighty years (R. Moore 1997). The genre helped to reinforce and naturalize the belittling traits associated with Afrocubans, such as greed, lechery, stupidity, incompetence, wanton sexuality, and deceit (R. Moore 1997). The performances presented the "dominant society's perspective on Afrocuban culture" (R. Moore 1997, 46). Moore observed that the negrito was typically depicted as a hustler who made sexual advances to all mulatas and light-skinned women. In one example, *La canción del mendigo* (The Song of the Beggar), an orphaned black boy was taken in and raised by a white family but was thrown out when he fell in love with a white woman (R. Moore 1997). For the negrito character, who was often depicted with a predatory sexuality, interracial romance was forbidden with white women and elusive with mulatas. For mulatas, the pressures of whitening (lightening their children) led them to value and pursue relationships with white men, even if they were likely only to be transient affairs. These cultural scripts assume that mulatas sought relations with white men either for the genetic or material advantage these men would give

them and their children. White men meanwhile sought mulata love\
for their iconic sexuality and sensuality that continued to be lauded in\
contemporary Cuban poetry, theater, and song.

A typical song in this genre, "Que Mulata," by renowned musician
Chano Pozo, was laden with sexual connotations:

Que sabroso tu bailes mulata	How deliciously you dance mulata
Y traes una rumba que me mata, ay, ay	You do a rumba that kills me, ay, ay
Que me mata, que me mata.	It kills me, it kills me.
Cuando te agarras la bata mulata	When you grab the drum mulata
Y sacas la pata, mulata	And start to move, mulata
El tambo se desbarata	The drum falls apart
Mulata, mulata, mulata, y mulata	Mulata, mulata, mulata, and mulata

In expressive arts since the nineteenth century, whitening, material
advantage, and sexual potency all appeared as justifications for interracial couples.

Even in contemporary Cuba, racist ideology informed reactions to
interracial relationships and often led people to interpret them as relationships *por interés*, that is, relationships with some ulterior motive—be
it sex, status, whitening, or money.[7] Slang classifications and vocabulary reinforced ideas about these relationships as being purely status or
pleasure motivated. Olga described her light-skinned mulatto brother
as *"un piolo hasta lo último,"* meaning he exclusively dated white women,
even though Olga said he repeatedly encountered problems with his
girlfriends' parents. Her two paternal uncles, who were black, were also
fixated on the idea of whitening according to Olga. She recounted: "In
Cuba it's that the mulato wants to lighten so they look for white women.
I'll give you an example. . . . My two uncles always thought about this
[lightening]—with a girlfriend it [race] didn't matter, but when they
want to marry it's with white women. My [one] uncle messed up and
married a mulata darker than me, but the other one did marry a white
woman. But I remember [them saying,] '*Negra, negra buena para pasar el*

tiempo' (Black woman, black women good for good time)." Conversely, *petrolero, negrero,* and *mulatero* were slang terms that referred to whites (especially white men) who preferred black lovers. These terms carried with them the connotation of an assumed hypersensuality of black and mulata women, making them more desirable as sexual partners. From the stock cultural models of teatro bufo and the racially loaded slang terms still circulating in contemporary Cuba, the process of mestizaje did not conjure up iconic images of national ideals and idyllic romance, but rather sensual relations motivated by some kind of sexual or material interés.

Young Cubans confronted these images in their interracial romances. Yanet, a young white woman, commented on how these issues arose in reactions to her relationship with Victor, her black boyfriend. In Yanet's case material interest was often suspected, given Victor's class position. Yanet stated: "Other relatives and some of our friends began to treat me as if I were with Victor only for ulterior motives (por interés), because he has a car and lives in a nice house. People still think that way. It's the only way for them to understand how a girl like me could be in this relationship." Yanet also felt the judgmental looks of strangers on the bus or in the street: "There is always that stare that follows you. There's that person who tells me, 'You'll always be burdened with him, and sooner or later it will bother you,' or 'You poor little white girl—look who you've ended up with.' At first these comments used to make me feel ashamed, but now I'm immune to this, and I have other worries. On the other hand, sometimes blacks also stare at us. I think black girls feel humiliated that Victor is with me."

While Yanet felt that black women were somehow wounded by her relationship with Victor, Tamara (a white woman) commented that blacks sometimes dated whites as a symbol of prestige among their black peers: "Some think that if they are going out with white girl, they have the world at their feet. So couples don't only form for love, but also for the role that it plays within their race [community]." Javier (Tamara's mulatto boyfriend) himself confessed that "people don't like to admit it, but being seen in the street with a blue-eyed blond is a point in your favor," as they are relatively uncommon in this African/Mediterranean island. Likening it to a good letter of presentation, something not available to everyone, he clearly expressed the value of whiteness and that status was gained by a man of color who was with a white woman. But Javier also recognized that this is not the only scale of values that exists. Interés can work both ways. Some whites pursued people of color (especially women) in search of the exotic or the hypersexuality of blacks—or at least some Cubans read their relationships that way.[8]

Luis, an energetic black man in his early twenties, was Lazaro's cousin and a frequent visitor in our house. He worked at a weekly newspaper doing deliveries and errands. At the time I interviewed him he had recently ended a five-year relationship with a white woman named Irena. He distinctly felt the public gaze of disapproval when they were out together, and he commented on public reactions they received as an interracial couple:

> People in the street sometimes are very indiscreet. . . . They look at you. They ask questions. . . . Irena used to wait for me after work in front of the building and my co-workers used to say, "What have you done to that little white girl, that she's tied to you like this?" . . . The people are very bold. At the beach, . . . she would be lying next to me with her head on my chest, and people would walk by and look at us strangely. They looked at us in the street, on the bus. In restaurants it was the same. . . . When I used to meet her as she was leaving school . . . I could feel the people talking about me. . . . It was something that gave the teachers complexes: "This little black guy (ese negrito) is her boyfriend?" You feel that they are talking about you. Then time goes by and these things don't worry you so much. They never bothered her. She always was very strong.

Indeed, Luis encountered public inquiries into what interés motivated and maintained the relationship he had with Irena. He was asked to somehow justify the relationship. What had he done to this white girl that she was so interested in him—"tied to him"? Luis observed: "I think that Cuban society still has not adapted to the idea of blacks and whites together as couples. They look at [interracial] couples and ask, 'Why are they together? There has to be something.' Almost always think it's something material. They don't understand that you could love a person—a black, a mulatto, a jabao, someone ugly, someone lame, or a dwarf. People don't understand that I'm with a white woman because we like each other. People think that behind it there is something material." Luis and Irena and Yanet and Victor were young couples who understood their own relationships in color-blind terms that resonated with socialist egalitarian ideology. They were together because they fell in love and were good companions to each other. However, while their personal understandings of their relationships were rooted in racial equality, others interpreted them through racist lenses. The meanings of interracial couples were never singular, but layered with personal understandings and emotions as well as a range of familial and public interpretations that could draw on both racist and non-racist frameworks.

Since Luis was poor, the popular perception of their relationship was that his supposed potent sexuality as a black man kept Irena involved with him. The racist ideology supported ample stereotypes of black males' primitive, animalistic, and uncontrollable sexuality. However, notions of potent sexuality were not exclusively associated with black and mulatto Cubans. The anthropologist David Forrest (1999) noted that perceptions of Cubanness, in general, were closely linked with sexuality, and there was a sort of national pride about Cubans' mythical sexuality and ardency.[9] Forrest argues that Cuban men and women were seen to possess an uncontrollable "latino passion," particularly in comparison to Europeans and North Americans. However, Cubans themselves often imagined that skin color determined the *fogosidad* (passion) of the person; the darker the skin, the more highly sexed the individual (Forrest 1999). This idea of a potent black sexuality was one frame used for understanding and justifying interracial couples in the public eye.

The mythic Cuban sexuality and especially black sexuality helped give rise to yet another type of interracial couple: the Afrocuban/white foreigner couple. These couples appeared with increasing frequency in 1990s Cuba. The expanding tourism industry brought with it large numbers of male and female tourists looking for sexual adventure. Some young Cubans (of all shades) mobilized the global perceptions of a racialized and sexualized Cubanness to attract foreign lovers and gain access to the ever-growing dollar economy on the island. Forrest reminds us that "Cubans often imagined themselves to be racialized and sexualized within an *international* context. It is imperative that we consider how such sexual imaginings necessarily draw heavily upon *internal* imaginings of a racialized sexuality" (1999, 75). Faye Harrison notes that some "Cubans themselves buy into the same racial and racialized gender stereotypes that drive sexual tourist behavior. They often subscribe to the belief that blacks are naturally hypersexual, athletic, and rhythmic; sexuality is more untamed, primitive, uninhibited, and exciting than white sexuality" (2008, 207).

Ever-changing racist ideology expressed in verbal and visual representations of blackness gave interracial relationships yet another patina within the context of the growing dollar economy, the increased presence of foreign tourists, and the economic hardships of the 1990s in Cuba.

5

Blackness, Whiteness, Class, and the Emergent Economy

In response to the economic crisis and material deprivations known as "the Special Period in Times of Peace" (1990–2006), precipitated by the collapse of the socialist bloc, the Cuban government actively pursued a number of reforms designed to jump-start the economy.[1] The government legalized of the possession of hard currency, expanded tourism and joint ventures with foreign corporations, liberalized remittances from abroad, and augmented the types of self-employment permitted (including some services and family restaurants known as *paladares*).[2] Since the start of the special period in 1990, tourism has grown exponentially and has replaced sugar as the country's main source of revenues. In 2008 the number of visitors reached a record 2.35 million (nearly ten times the visitors just a decade earlier), and the gross tourism revenue was $2.7 billion (a 13 percent increase over the previous year) (Adams 2009). Tourism, of course, is not new to Cuba. Pre-1959, tourism had been Cuba's second largest industry after sugar and was rife with gambling, drugs, organized crime (under U.S. Mafia leaders), and a flourishing prostitution trade (del Olmo 1979; Diaz, Fernandez, and Caram 1996; Schwartz 1997). In 1957 close to 350,000 tourists visited Cuba, most of whom were from the United States (Espino 1993). After 1959, the materialism and hedonistic consumption associated with tourism clashed with socialist ideology, and the revolutionary government touted the dismantling of the tourism industry as one of its early successes. Returning to tourism in the 1990s had been particularly painful for Cuban leaders, given that the revolution strove for equality and equal access for all to the nation's resources. Fidel Castro declared tourism "a necessary evil." These macroeconomic transformations of the 1990s had micro repercussions. As Michael Burawoy and Katherine Verdery (1999) suggest, understanding the transformation of post-socialist societies requires a close examination of the micro level of daily life as people revise, innovate, and resist the structural changes mandated from above (Burawoy and Verdery 1999).

Cubans on the island met their needs in the special period through improvisation—by *resolviendo* and *inventando*, tactics that at best bent the rules and at worst broke the laws. As one friend who worked as a construction engineer said to me, "From the time I get up in the morning until the time I go to bed, practically everything I do is illegal." In the special period, basic consumption took on political significance and each act of resolviendo became a strategy of resistance against the failing state distribution system, the controlling bureaucracy, and the state definition of material needs.

The economic reforms, the hardships and scarcities, the lack of electricity and transportation fostered what I call a "solidarity of suffering" that to some degree transcended social difference but at the same time highlighted and redefined meanings of color and class, material well-being and deprivation. Throughout the 1990s access to hard currency became critical in determining one's standard of living. All Cubans sought to get hard currency to survive the crisis. The dollar sector grew proportionally as the Cuban peso economy shrank. Cubans began to rely increasingly on the hard currency stores, locally known as *el chopin* or *aréa dólar*, to obtain needed items no longer available through the state rationing system.[3] Average Habaneros had two primary means of accessing hard currency: through employment or contact with the tourism industry and through remittances from family members living in exile.

Healthy economic growth in what Cubans call the "emergent" (hard currency) sectors of the economy did not result in many job opportunities for black and mulatto Cubans. Cuban researchers have found that blacks and mulattos were underrepresented in these sectors. Whites were more than twice as likely as blacks and mulattos to have jobs in dollar-related industries (Espina Prieto and Rodríguez Ruiz 2006).

...d mulattos who did work in tourism tended to be relegated to positions in which they did not have contact with the tourists, such as maintenance. By contrast, they comprised less than 5 percent of the managers and professionals in the tourism industry (Espina Prieto and Rodríguez Ruiz 2006). The resurgence of tourism had a racial and class component, both in terms of access to lucrative tourism and emergent-sector jobs and in terms of tourist hustling, prostitution, and black market engagements.

Remittances from Cubans living abroad were the other primary source of hard currency for the Cuban government and probably the most important source of hard currency for ordinary Cubans. Scholars estimated that annual remittances may total over $900 million dollars (Pérez-López and Díaz-Briquets 2005). Since over 80 percent of the exile community was white, blacks had limited access to dollars through family remittances. Whites in Cuba were more than twice as likely as blacks and mulattos to receive remittances from abroad (Díaz-Briquets 2008).

In Cuba new social/economic classes emerged, namely, those with hard currency and those without. The strategies available to whites and Afrocubans for acquiring hard currency differed dramatically. Everyday practices for obtaining dollars—legal, illegal, commercial, and sexual—became coded by race, class, and place. In the new tourism-infused topography of Havana, being white in black spaces and black in white spaces meant new privileges for the former and new dangers for the latter. The material scarcities, the growing presence of foreigners, and the expanding tourist zones heightened sensitivities to race and class, created new visibilities and invisibilities, new inclusions and exclusions, new interpretations of Cuban interracial couples, and even new types of interracial encounters as Cubans and tourists came together in fleeting trysts and enduring romances.

Interracial Couples: Afrocubans with Tourists

Marucha la jinetera, tiene un dolor en el alma
Le duelen las margaritas que le huyeron de la infancia,

Marucha, la jinetera, has a pain in her soul
The daisies (innocence) of her childhood that she avoids pain her,

Marucha la que se acuesta   Marucha sleeps with men for
  por un poco de esperanza   a bit of hope
No es justo que se le nombre,   It's not fair that she is given a
  como una mala palabra   bad name.
       —Pedro Luis Ferrer, "Marucha la Jinetera"

The expansion of the tourist industry birthed the *jinetero,* or "hustler/ prostitute." The term *jinetero* can be translated as "jockey/horseback rider," with obvious sexual and economic connotations involved in "riding" the tourist. Though most often *jineterismo* referred to prostitution with foreigners, in daily parlance the term described a broad range of activities related to tourist hustling. These could include selling sex, black-market cigars, rum, and coral jewelry; providing private taxi services or access to "authentic" Santería rituals; or simply serving as informal guides in return for a free meal or some token gifts from the tourist. Apart from these street-level dealings, the term could also apply outside of the tourism arena to name any dollar-generating activity or connections with foreigners. In its most inclusive sense, jineterismo referred to any activity outside of one's salaried (peso) employment that generated hard currency, dollar-store goods, or the possibility of foreign travel. In other words, *jineteando* was the uniquely Cuban attempt for individuals to integrate themselves into the global market economy at whatever level and through whatever means. Under this inclusive umbrella of jineterismo the sexual and informal commercial activities of whites and blacks were differentially coded, valorized, and visible. Blackness and Cubanidad gained new significance in juxtaposition to the large numbers of (predominately) white tourists coming from Europe and Canada and the dual dollar/peso economy.

Female *jineteras* made a living in the chaotic situation of Cuba's economic crisis. It was their creative response to gaining access to dollars—one livelihood tactic in the struggle to make ends meet (Herrera 2000, 124; Rundle 2001). Dating a foreign man was a strategy for forming instrumental alliances which could bring material benefits as well as give them access to the growing consumer economy. As Mette Rundle (2001) noted in her study of jineteras, the young women involved in these relationships did not see their behavior as morally questionable. Despite the women's own self-perceptions, the dominant sentiment continued to associate jineteras with moral corruption. Like Rundle, Pedro Luis Ferrer, a Cuban Nueva Trova artist known for his sharp critiques of the government and social issues, questions why *Marucha la jinetera* should have such a bad reputation in his song quoted above. Coupled with the perception of these women being predominantly Afrocuban, sexual jineterismo augmented the continuing negative views of blacks and moreover was evidence of the government's inability to address continuing racial and social inequality (Rundle 2001).

The interracial couples of black or mulata women and white male tourists reinforce historical construction of a sexualized Cubanidad and, in particular, Afrocuban women as exotic, erotic, sexually available, and licentious Others (Cabezas 1998; Davidson 1996; Fernandez 1999; Fusco 1998). If guapos draw on racialized masculinity, jineteras draw on racialized female sexuality. Gender, race, class, and space become the salient features in interpreting these new foreign/Cuban interracial couples and in defining those blurry boundaries between who is and who is not a jinetera. As Coco Fusco (1998) notes, in the context of growing jineterismo, even Afrocuban women married to white men (foreign or Cuban) are often taken for jineteras. In fact, young women seeking contacts with foreign men often exploit this stereotype. The continuing myth of the ardent Afrocubana contributes to their appeal for foreign tourists. Fusco notes that "to engage in sex work practically means to assume a *mulata* identity by association," despite what a women's racial designation might be in another context (1998, 155). Elsewhere (Fernandez 1999) I explore how the strength of the association between Afrocubanas and sex make sexual encounters between white Cuban women and tourists invisible while heightening the visibility of those between Afrocubanas and foreigners. White Cuban/tourist relations are more easily and more likely to be couched as "romance" than as jineterismo, even though money or goods might be exchanged for sex.

Persistent denigrations of blacks and mulattos, and particularly sexualized conceptions of Cuban women of color, make it difficult for Cubans to perceive of interracial relationships between Afrocubans and tourists as anything more than purely sexual and por interés. In the Cuban/tourist relationships, interés is not only for immediate material gains, but moreover could be parlayed into a more long-term advantage, namely, a ticket out of Cuba through marriage. In the special period and post-Soviet Cuba, mestizaje is not a means of building the nation, but a way to flee it. Interracial unions between Cubans and foreigners are not an escape hatch out of blackness, but one out of the country. These relationships do not build a nation in a geographically bounded sense, but rather create a diasporic web of familial relations across the globe that could serve as a conduit for remittances and a safety net for those left behind on the island. Ironically, by marrying out (not only up), these interracial couples extend the transnational connections of Cubans that began with the mostly white political exiles decades earlier. The impact and meanings, both personal and geopolitical, of these interracial trans-national marriages with Cubans remains a rich site for future research.[4] Cuban men also engage in sex work and romances with both male and female tourists.[5] Some scholars (Fosado 2004; Hodge 2001) have begun to explore the experiences of these *pingueros.*

Cuban Interracial Couples:
Skin Color and Cultural Level

The hardships of the special period cast a pall of "blackness" over daily life and Cubanness/Cubanidad that brought yet another level of disap-proval to whites' readings of interracial romance between Cubans. For many white Cubans, the economic crisis, scarcities, and daily struggles were both personally and collectively "denigrating," quite literally blackening them in the very racial sense of the word. As David Forrest (1999) notes, in the special period many white Cubans felt compelled to "act like blacks" in order to survive and make ends meet. For some of his white informants, this meant a new kind of aggressiveness, pub-lic rudeness, and a suspension of niceties like polite manners (Forrest 1999, 130). Lily, the white, middle-aged mother of one of my informants, also noted this in behaviors. She commented: "When I was younger we were living in difficult times (before the revolution and the early years of the revolution), but those hardships brought people together. Now we also have a lot of hardship, but now it separates people. There is no sense of helping each other, everyone is now much more selfish, more concerned with their individual needs." Rundle's (2001) research echoes s observations that the behaviors needed to survive in the special period had shaken the moral foundations of Cuba. Rundle also notes that Cubans lamented the change in interpersonal relations, the new self-centeredness, the loss of social solidarity and neighborliness, and a heightened and more exclusive focus on the well-being of one's immediate family. She suggests that this deterioration of the moral fabric evidenced in the paucity of communal courtesies and kindness, as well as in jineterismo, is further proof for many white, middle-class Cubans that "low culture" is predominating in the public domain (Rundle 2001).

"Low cultural level" (*bajo nivel cultural*) is a common and socially acceptable nomenclature for talking about a host of racially and class-coded traits and behaviors in a society that had officially abolished classes and prohibited discussions of race. The youth I interviewed had difficulty defining concretely what *nivel cultural* (cultural level) meant, but it included factors such as the level of formal education, decency and restraint especially in public settings, propriety, moderation, etiquette, and the degree of social refinement. It also referenced a spectrum of styles and tastes in music, clothing, hair, and speech (Berg 2005). The term referred to not only the person in question but also their family, their social background, the environment in which they were raised, their living conditions, and their barrio. For example, guapos and the social environment of solares epitomized "low culture." As Mette Berg noted, the term "is embedded in a moral and racial economy that devalues expressions of blackness and lower class culture" (2005, 143). Low culture was conflated with blackness.

Moreover, Berg argues, cultural level is presented as a choice for individuals regardless of social background. Likewise, Matthew Hill (2004) quotes white, middle-class Cubans who argued that blacks chose not to take advantage of the educational opportunities afforded them by the revolution. Hill's informants note that there were few blacks in their university classes—so blacks must be "less motivated" than whites, they concluded (2004). In this way, cultural level is a central vehicle for racism in Cuba, a method of making blacks themselves solely responsible for their social position and the discrimination directed at them and their culture. This racist thinking was exacerbated in the special period, as blacks struggled to gain access to hard currency through either openly or implicitly illegal acts. Alejandro de la Fuente notes: "To many whites this serves as confirmation that blacks are in fact naturally predisposed to corruption and crime. In the eyes of some of these individuals this may be one of the most important lessons of the revolutionary experience: if after several decades of social engineering blacks were unable to achieve full equality, then they must have some constitutional, genetic, deficiencies" (1998b, 5).

Nearly a century ago, the renowned Cuban ethnologist Fernando Ortiz, espousing a constructivist view of race, purported that the blacks' "backward and primitive" culture was the source of their marginalization and the resulting discrimination by whites. Ortiz, whose work spanned the first half of the twentieth century, saw culture as malleable and envisioned blacks assimilating and becoming culturally more like whites, and as they did inequalities between the races would ultimately be eliminated (Helg 1990). Ortiz believed that as blacks integrated into national (white) Cuban culture, their "atavistic" practices would disappear as part of a living culture and would rather be preserved as examples of the folklore of an extinct culture. He dedicated much of his career to documenting these folkloric practices before they suffered the demise that he predicted would happen. However, the Afrocuban culture Ortiz painstakingly documented continued to live, change, and grow. The project of whitening (cultural and physical) did not progress as nineteenth- and early twentieth-century white Cuban leaders had hoped. The special period (and for some whites the revolution itself) further derailed the process of whitening by nurturing low culture and blackening Cuba even more.

These white perceptions of black culture and lower-class culture forced some blacks in interracial couples to distance themselves from these negative associations, and in so doing they reinforced the racial hierarchy. Javier, a mulatto, and his white girlfriend, Tamara, illustrated this dynamic.

Javier and Tamara

Tamara, a young white woman with blond hair and crystal blue eyes, and her boyfriend, Javier, whose freckles seemed to crowd out the tawny skin of his face, had been dating only two months when we met, but both also had previous experiences in interracial relationships. They were both studying biology at the University of Havana. Tamara was from Matanzas, a province northeast of Havana, and lived in a student dormitory near the university. Javier, a native of Havana, lived with his family in Habana Vieja (Old Havana). They had met the previous year while attending a boarding high school in the countryside and started dating once they entered the university.

Javier's family had a history of racial mixing. He described his mother as a light-skinned mulata who has had three husbands of varying shades. The first, Javier's father, was *moro*—dark skin with "good" hair. The second, the father of his half-sister, was lighter skinned and with straighter hair than the first one, traits his sister also bears. Finally, the third husband was, in Javier's words, "*un negro tosco*" (a heavy-featured black man). As for his own relationships, he realized that his last three girlfriends had been white and with light eyes, in his words, clearly showing a personal inclination for this type of woman. He attributed this to the fact that in his social circles there are few people of his color, not only at the university but also at the selective high school he attended, which was predominantly white.

Though he exclusively dated white women, Javier often had trouble convincing their families that he was not a typical low-cultured black. Even though he was mulatto, the middle-class white families assumed he possessed the same negative traits associated with blacks. The fact that he lived in Old Havana also served to "blacken" his lighter complexion in the eyes of some whites. His experiences called into question the extent to which mulattos' situations differed from darker-skinned black Cubans. Mark Sawyer (2006) noted that many Cubans think mulattos have a higher status than blacks. However Sawyer's research showed that there was no evidence to support the idea that they benefit economically from this perceived higher position (2006). Javier's experiences confirmed this finding in the realm of social relations, as he struggled to distance himself from the devalued blackness and stereotypes whites projected onto him. His mulatto phenotype in and of itself did not differentiate him from darker-skinned Afrocubans in the views of some of the white families he encountered. He told of one successful battle to "whiten himself" in the eyes of his white girl-friend's mother:

> The girl's mother was extreme. She sent word to me that I was
> not wanted in her house. At that time I was more optimistic
> than now. Now if they tell me that, I simply won't go, but then I
> wanted to show her what kind of person I was. At that time, I was
> a student leader. I directed a theater performance. I wasn't just a
> nobody, and I wanted her to treat me for who I was. I wanted to
> break her stereotypes of me, so I would ask her to lend me a book
> or a cassette, or talk about the theater, to show the differences
> between me and the type of person she thought I was. That is, I
> tried to use these [cultural] values to get closer to her, to change
> her ideas [about blacks]. And weeks later she began to change,
> and even today I get along better with her [the mother] than
> with the daughter [who I dated]. I needed to change the criteria
> that she used to judge me. I didn't want to personify myself for
> everyone of my race [but have her accept me as an individual].
> Later, I would say to her, "You have to admit that you were
> mistaken about me . . . because one of my good points is that I
> don't go around with the gangs [of blacks] that go to the Tropi-
> cal and fight, and you feared for your daughter—you didn't want
> her to be with that type of man. But look; I'm like this; here's my
> mother's telephone number; call her [for proof]." And day-by-
> day I showed her [how I was]. I showed her! And finally she [the
> mother] treated me as an equal.

Tamara added, "Of course, the same characteristics [of blacks] are what create the rejection of them by whites. That's why you hear those argu-ments like the girl's mother presented. 'I don't want [my daughter] with [a black] because she'll just get into trouble.' And even some girls our own age will say things like 'I won't got out with blacks; they're disgust-ing.' This comes from the characteristics of blacks and the idea that whites are more refined."

Similarly, José Miguel, a white university student dating a dark-skinned mulata student (sometimes considered black), reflected on racial stereotypes that make interracial couples noticeable.[6] He commented, "Although sometimes we make comments about the negative characteristics of black people, it's really not because they are black, but rather it's their upbringing from their families and the barrio. I don't think that they have less intellectual or artistic abilities."

Javier's exchange with the white mother and Tamara's and José Miguel's comments all represented a kind of cultural racism. It was the blacks' low culture, background, problematic behaviors, and upbringing that caused the discrimination against them. In this discourse, blacks could change their *nivel cultural,* but they had (freely) chosen not to. Tamara expressed it most virulently, as she essentially blamed the blacks themselves for these characteristics and for the fact that white families would not want their daughters dating blacks. José Miguel recognized the distinction between how Cubans talk about blacks and the source of those negative associations, which he saw as the family and neighborhood environments. None of these examples supported a biological or inherent inferiority of blacks or blackness, but rather attributed problematic behaviors to their low culture. This discourse resonated with what Lawrence Bobo (2000) has called "laissez-faire racism" that places the responsibility for blacks' social and economic position on the blacks themselves, not due to their biological or inherent inferiority, but to their cultural shortcomings.

In this sense, the cultural racism couched as low culture was also a class discourse embedded within a racial one. Javier commented that he dated white women because there were few blacks in his social circles at the university or the selective high school he attended. Javier managed to convince the mother of his white girlfriend that he was different by engaging her on an intellectual and high cultural level. His project was to demonstrate who he was, his interests and activities that depicted a more middle-class habitus that belied his both phenotype and his barrio.

José Miguel also referred to the barrio as a source of the problem, affirming the spatial aspects of race and class that have contributed to keeping the poorest Cubans (of all skin colors) marginalized. Sawyer(2006) noted that Havana's housing patterns reflected the durability of the racial hierarchy and evidenced the government's failure to implement a system that would equalize both income and access to important resources such as housing. The economic crisis, the influx of tourism, and the emergent economy gave new currency to the race/space connections in the ever-changing map of Havana.

Blackness, Whiteness, and Dollarized Spaces in Havana

As black, mulatto, and white Cubans moved through the newly dollarized spaces of Havana that were increasingly colonized by foreign (mostly white) tourists, Cuban identities and activities became racialized in contradictory ways. Black spaces and barrios like Old Havana became tourist destinations and turned increasingly white and foreign. Black Cubans in these barrios struggled as the growth of tourism and the emergent economy at their doorsteps further marginalized and racialized them. In the context of global tourism, Cubanidad/Cubanness itself came to symbolize blackness when juxtaposed to the privileged, leisured consumption of the predominantly white European and Canadian tourists (Roland 2006).

The restoration of Javier's barrio, Old Havana (Habana Vieja), a UNESCO World Heritage site, was illustrative of these changing connotations of race, space, class, and culture. In their research on the restoration process in Old Havana, Berg (2005) and Hill (2004) argued that the heritage narrative being constructed in this historic zone and communicated through museum exhibits reached back into the past to establish a direct connection between the colonial period and the present (glossing over the Cuban republic). As colonial buildings were transformed into museums, they presented a colonial past that overlooked the urban slaves and their presence and contributions to the city (Berg 2005; Hill 2004). In this narrative, Afrocubans were seen as outsiders and white Cubans as insiders (Berg 2005). The Old Havana for tourist consumption valorized European cultural contributions and conjured up a time-space of exclusionary belonging and whiteness (Berg 2005; Hill 2004). This vision of history projected an image of colonial Cuba as an affluent, cosmopolitan, cultured, and primarily white nation. The restoration of Old Havana breathed new life into the failed colonial project of whitening by reinterpreting former colonial spaces as white and by emphasizing the whiteness and "Europeanness"

a.[7] Ironically, this narrative was staged in the predominantly
ind poor barrio of Old Havana. Berg (2005) argues that the heritage narrative managed to overcome this reality and to celebrate Cuba
as a white nation because it was both a "transtemporal and transloca-
tive" narrative oriented toward the past and toward Spain.

While a historical narrative may be painting Cuba as white, the
presence of mostly white tourists was painting contemporary Cuba as
black in comparison. Whiteness in the context of tourism and the dollar
economy equaled foreignness and access to hard currency. By corollary,
Cubans were racialized as nonwhite and classed as non-moneyed—what
Kaifa Roland called a "(dis)honorary 'blackening' . . . a negrification" of
Cuban identity (2006, 160). She argued that when Cuban racial understandings were considered in the context of tourism, skin color and
nationality often became conflated, such that the category of "tourist"
was recognized as white (and comparatively wealthy and included in
the emergent economy), while the category of Cuban was alternately
recognized as black (and comparatively poor and excluded from the
emergent economy). Though Roland (2004) concurred with Berg that
most Cubans would never conceive of themselves as a "black nation,"
she argued that through tourism they have rejoined the global political
economy at precisely that level.

White, middle-class Cubans tried to distance themselves from
this dynamic, in part by personally excluding themselves from the discourse of mestizaje and the national ideology that all Cubans are mixed
racially. Many proudly emphasized their Spanish ancestry and family
genealogies that attested to their European/white identity (Berg 2005;
Ryer 1998). In the context of tourism, white, middle-class Cubans could
assert a non-Cuban identity and reveled in tales of passing as foreigners, a highly privileged status in the emergent economy (Ryer 1998; Berg
2005). In doing so, they also cast Cubanness as nonwhite. By the same
token, black tourists or researchers were often mistaken for Cubans
and questioned or excluded from hard currency venues (Allen 2003;
Roland 2004; Sawyer 2006).

This new conflation of whiteness/foreignness/dollars afforded
white Cubans a certain invisibility and inclusion in dollarized areas of
Havana. Blacks, by contrast, were hypervisible and more conspicuously

"Cuban" in tourist zones such as Old Havana or La Rampa. Associations of blackness with crime colored perceptions of Afrocubans found in tourist locations. For example, throughout the 1990s the plainclothes police stationed outside all dollar stores and hotels would stop anyone they suspected of being Cuban, ask to see their identity cards, and inquire what they were doing there. It was fairly common for Cubans (but particularly black Cuban men) to be stopped going into hotels or even walking by them. Jafari Allen (2003) referred to this urban ballet between the police and black youth (particularly men) as "hailing." The usual procedure was that the police would ask to see their ID cards. All Cubans must carry their *carnét de identidad* with them at all times. In the early 1990s these small passport-like booklets included the person's picture, age, skin color, home address, and workplace. They also designated Communist Party membership. The booklets were later replaced by wallet-size laminated cards which included skin color but not employment information.

Afrocubans' presence near tourist installations read "crime" until proven otherwise. Take, for example, Antonio's experience when he went to a nearby Havana hotel to pick up a letter that a Spanish friend had sent to him via another Spaniard who had come to Cuba on vacation. He left the apartment at 6 P.M. and did not return until after 9 P.M. I assumed the Spaniard had perhaps invited Antonio for a drink or they were perhaps discussing the Spaniard's vacation plans. Antonio finally arrived home shaken and furious. He had been stopped by the guard outside the hotel and had explained to him that he was meeting someone to collect a letter. The white police officer wasn't interested in Antonio's "stories." He twisted Antonio's arm behind his back and led him at gunpoint to the detention area located in the hotel's underground garage, where he was held for several hours while they supposedly checked his documents. He was released with a perfunctory apology from the police and came home, needless to say, without the letter. Antonio's hotel encounter was particularly abusive, but certainly not the only one of its kind. According to Rundle (2001) police harassment was one of the most commonly voiced complaints of young Afrocuban men and women living or working near a tourist area. Her Afrocuban informants in Old Havana recounted stories of being asked by police to leave a public park in a tourist zone, being fined for simply being on the street, and even being detained for several days in police custody under the suspicion of sexual jineterismo (Rundle 2001). Afro-cubans faced new dangers in the dollarized geography of Havana. Old Havana, like Centro Habana, had a long-standing reputation for crime and delinquency and a deep association with blackness. Already these assumptions made residents of these zones suspect in ways that would be unlikely in the more suburban, middle-class areas of the city, where residents were also deeply involved in the black market, but often in less publicly visible ways.[8]

Jaime's involvement in black market activities also illustrates how his whiteness afforded him invisibility, even in Centro Habana. This was a luxury blacks and mulattos like Antonio did not enjoy. In Jaime's household, income came from various sources both legal and illegal. His uncle earned a monthly salary as a night watchman of approximately 180 pesos. His grandmother received a small pension from the state (less than 100 pesos per month), and Madaleis (his mulata girl-friend) contributed part of her 128 peso per month salary, which she earned working in a bookstore. This was supplemented occasionally by money and food from other family members, such as Jaime's father and mother, both of whom lived nearby. Jaime also had a paternal uncle in Miami who on rare occasions would send a package of goods to the family. Mostly these parcels contained medicines for his grandmother, but several years earlier he did receive a pair of sneakers that he wore until they were in tatters. The family did not receive any regular remittances or visits from their relatives in exile.

The household income benefited most significantly from Jaime's illegal black market activities. He was what the government termed *un joven desvinculado* (a disconnected youth), that is, he was neither enrolled in school or the military, nor had salaried employment. He was outside or disconnected from any state institution. Government agencies perceived these youth as dangerous "antisocial elements." In the 1990s the government attempted to control them with what became known as *el ley del vago* (a vagrancy law), which gave the police the right to detain anyone suspected of antisocial behavior, which included loi-tering. This law targeted disconnected young men like Jaime. However,

"disconnected" is the last word that could be used to describe Jai
He was, in fact, extremely well connected and cultivated these conr
tions as the source of his income. He often attempted to earn money as
a *jinetero*, a dollar-changing, black-market dealer in the early 1990s. At
that time, he could exchange forty pesos for one dollar and usually had
several hundred pesos in his pocket—more than a worker's monthly
wage. Jaime commented to me that he always had pesos: "That's never
a problem. I buy things and sell them." These "things" were either items
from the dollar stores that he resold at a higher price in pesos or anything else that happened to come into his possession, usually pilfered
from warehouses or workplaces where his friends were employed.[9]

This type of leakage in the state's distribution system was not new.
Cubans were adept at subverting the tightly controlled distribution system. I knew of people who for years continued receiving the rations for
family members who were deceased or had left the country but through
a bureaucratic oversight remained on the family *libreta* (ration book). If
in Chicago the dead could vote, in Cuba the dead and exiled could eat.
I asked Antonio's half-brother, who was a *bodegero* (shopkeeper), about
this practice, and he replied that it was his duty to distribute rationed
food for the people listed in the libreta. It was *not* his responsibility
to make sure that list was accurate. These instances of internal resistance and daily forms of sabotage occurred at all levels of the system
and constantly undermined state power. As Katherine Verdery argues
of Eastern Europe, socialist governments were not as all-powerful as
sometimes imagined because they were only partly successful in win-
ning support and compliance from their citizens (1996). Cuba was no
exception to Verdery's observation.

Jaime enjoyed a certain level of protection in his activities by virtue
of being white. His geographic and social location made his activities
more likely to be scrutinized by authorities due to Centro Habana's
reputation for delinquency. Jaime's jinetero activities were very much
in the public domain, however; his whiteness, while by no means making him immune to police vigilance, did make him slightly less visible
to controlling eyes. Race, class, and place were key factors in shaping
police and public perceptions of jineterismo and afforded Cubans differential access to the underground economy. Class, race, and place

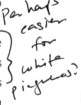

Perhaps easier for white pingueros?

could mark behaviors as illegal, immoral, and problematic or could allow for the same activities to be more easily overlooked by authorities. Most blacks and mulattos, however, were not so lucky, and their survival strategies were more dangerous, though equally discreet.

Jaime and Madaleis

For whites living in black spaces like Old Havana and Centro Habana, maintaining whiteness and avoiding the racial and class implications of low culture became even more difficult in the economic crisis of the special period. For some interracial couples, like Jaime and Madaleis, the growing sense of the "blackening" of Cuban culture and daily life in the 1990s influenced how interracial couples were treated in white homes. Interracial pairs like Jaime and Madaleis bore this new burden.

Jaime, the son of a mechanic and a nursery school teacher, dated Madaleis for several years. They met in their Centro Habana barrio. The three- or four-story apartment buildings in their area, built in the first half of the 1900s, were in various states of disrepair—some just in dire need of paint, others *apuntalada,* with layers of sagging balconies precariously supported by spindly beams like tiers on a wedding cake. Madaleis lived on the same block as Jaime—a narrow street littered with garbage and rutted with gaping potholes.

From the couples' perspective their meeting and courtship were unremarkable, an ordinary attraction between two neighbors. Race was not an issue for them, attesting to the revolution's integration and ideology of equality and also perhaps to the fact that their relationship reflected the more socially acceptable traditional pattern of white male with a mulata female (more on this in the following chapter). The generational differences are noteworthy, and Jaime had little to say about his decision to become involved romantically with Madaleis. He took it for granted that they were attracted to each other and started dating. However, it certainly was an issue for Jaime's family. His interracial relationship with Madaleis brought the racialization of the special period home in a powerful way.

Madaleis lived with Jaime in his grandmother's crowded one-bedroom, ground-floor apartment that housed seven people spanning four generations of his family. Extended kin relations became even more important in the post-Soviet era as the family became a key resource for survival in the austere times (Safa 2009). Jaime's household illustrated not only the chronic housing shortage in the city but also the fluid marital relations (and remarriages) and the web of extended kin, step-relatives, and fictive kin that formed the family's closest associations.[10] Jaime shared the *barbacoa* (loft) above the living room with Madaleis, and sometimes also her four-year-old daughter (by another man). The bedroom was for his grandmother, his five-year-old nephew (his sister's son by her first husband), and sometimes his sister.[11] His unmarried uncle (his grandmother's son) slept in the barbacoa over the bedroom. These cramped conditions and extended family arrangements were prevalent throughout the city, though in the more middle-class neighborhoods the larger apartments and houses often could accommodate extended families more comfortably.

Jaime's tiny living room was crammed with well-worn and half broken furniture: a stained plywood table and stools, a small sofa, and a one-armed rocking chair. One wall was occupied by a home-made plywood wall unit that housed several shelves of knickknacks and glasses, as well as the large black-and-white TV (the same model found in virtually all Cuban homes in the 1990s). The radio was usually tuned to the anti-Castro, U.S.-funded Radio Martí that his grandmother enjoyed for the *novelas* (soap operas) and his disgruntled uncle for its antirevolutionary propaganda. The other wall, under the staircase to the barbacoa, was filled by a hulking but reliable 1950s American-made refrigerator, the appliance which during the special period people jokingly referred to as *el coco* (the coconut)—white on the outside and containing only water on the inside. Off to one side of the living room was a narrow kitchen and beside that a door leading out to the floor of the building's airshaft, which now served as a pen for several of the family's chickens.[12]

In his household, Jaime felt his grandmother was most bothered by his relationship with Madaleis, but he mainly attributed that to her old age. Then, pausing a moment, he added with a laugh: "She really never likes any of my girlfriends. She doesn't think anyone is good enough for me. [Although Madaleis is living with me,] my grandmother still doesn't accept her—she deals with her but doesn't 'swallow' her (*la trata, pero no la traga*)."

Despite Jaime's claim, his grandmother was not the only family member bothered by Jaime's relationship with Madaleis. His uncle also was quick to show his disfavor in his own way. He saw Madaleis as the bearer of lower culture that he perceived as inferior. On one visit to Jaime's house, I arrived as Jaime was just waking up. He came down from the barbacoa and began to look for something to eat. After opening and closing the refrigerator several times and finding nothing, he poured himself a glass of water and mixed in several large spoonfuls of sugar. Watching this, Jaime's uncle made the following comments in a very agitated voice:

> Here whites never drank sugar water. Never. That was always a thing of blacks. It is a black thing from slavery or something. A white would never drink it. I cannot drink it. It makes me vomit. Just the thought of it makes me vomit. I don't know how Jaime can drink it—he must have some mixture (racial mixture) in him. It's a thing blacks do, and look, Jaime is drinking it. He picked it up from the blacks. You know his girlfriend is . . . [the uncle rubbed his index finger on his forearm, a common gesture used to indicate a person is black]. That's where he got it from. It's not something whites do, but now look what we've come to here. There's nothing else for people to drink, no soda, no juice, and nothing to eat. Nothing. So they drink sugar water. They even sell it in the streets now. People call it "sopa de gallo" (rooster soup). Whites never used to drink that here.

Jaime's sister, who was also sitting in the living room, took on the role of the diplomat and tried to soften her uncle's often stormy racist rhetoric with the comment, "He says that because he just doesn't like sweet things." But there was no stopping him. The uncle turned to me and asked, "What did you have for breakfast?" I replied, "Coffee, bread, juice, and a banana." The uncle countered: "Coffee! [with disgust]. I don't drink coffee. I don't like it. I like tea. But in this country there's no tea, but I always manage to get some." I tried to counter his negativity by saying, "You can always get fresh mint and other herbs to make

very good teas." My comment only served to launch him on anoth[er]
antiblack diatribe: "No, no, no! That's not tea. Those herbal things the[y]
sell in the street as tea—that's not tea. That's something the blacks
drink. That's what the black witches (*brujos*) use in their spells. Those
are things of blacks. I don't drink those herbs. No, no, no! [To me:] Do
you know what witches (*brujos*) are? [I nod yes.] They use those herbs in
black magic. They are things of blacks and witches. I don't touch those
herbs." I commented that herbal teas are very popular in the United
States. He chose to ignore this comment.

The uncle's racist rantings were delivered with a frightening mix of
vehemence and bitterness. His comments gave voice to popular racist
sentiments. The uncle's disgust over what he saw as low culture (sugar
water, herbal cures, and spells) was clearly racialized. He perceived these
traits as inferior cultural practices attributed to blacks. Furthermore,
blackness brought with it danger. He rejected Santería not only for being
black but also for possessing threatening powers and primitive magic.
Despite the virtual explosion in Santería practice in the post-Soviet era,
for some whites, Afrocuban religions were undesirable expressions of
low cultural level (Berg 2005; Sawyer 2006). In sharp contrast to the
tourist gaze, which sought out exotic black Cuban culture, among some
whites these cultural elements still epitomized black primitivism.[13]

Jaime's uncle also offered a sharp critique of socialism and consumption. His comments showed his frustration with the homogenization of taste under socialism that insisted on a homogenous dominant
culture—where people drank coffee, ate pork, and danced *casino* (salsa).
The state made no effort to encourage individuality or diversity in its
promotion of "Cuban" culture. As Verdery (1996) noted, socialism's
neglect of consumption made it in turn deeply political. It allowed
people to dispute the state's definition of "needs." The state sought
to meet only "basic needs": edible food and adequate clothing. The
centralized economy did not attempt to determine what kind of goods
people wanted or to supply an array of products to meet diverse or
expanding consumer appetites. Jaime's uncle was an extreme example
of an individual whose personal tastes and habits could not be accom-
modated by the centralized planning and distribution system and the
state-controlled consumption and prescription of needs.

[handwritten margin notes: "my respondents talked about brujería far from religious"; "Interesting way to think about commodity cultures popularity"; "Efforts against decades of homogenization"]

Explicitly his comments critiqued Madaleis's bad influence on Jaime, but implicitly he also critiqued the intense level of integration fostered by the revolution, particularly among the youth. For Jaime's uncle, no good was to come from these close interracial associations—associations that overstepped the social norms and boundaries of cordial relations between neighbors or amorous trysts with women of color. Living with Madaleis brought the low/black culture into his poor but respectable white home, and that level of integration was not welcomed from the family's perspective.

Finally, his comments revealed that his racism was closely intertwined with his critiques of the socialist state. The fact that the government was now selling sugar water in the street during the special period reflected, from the uncle's perspective, a degeneration of national culture. The special period had thrust many Cubans into austere conditions of poverty, and poverty was equated with blackness. The necessities of the special period (and for Jaime's uncle socialism in general) had degraded Cuban culture, turning it black and primitive. Customs and habits of the white working class or middle class could not be maintained materially, so those of the poor and blacks were taking over. It was this cultural "darkening" that seemed to cause Jaime's uncle the greatest despair. Only the worst, the lowest cultural habits, tastes, customs, and practices were flourishing. For Jaime's uncle, as socialism advanced and then floundered, "civilization" (whiteness) receded further and further away. To be powerless and in miserable material conditions was to be black. Class was, indeed, lived through race in the special period. Jaime's relationship with Madaleis brought these issues home in the most intimate way.

6

Interracial Couples and Racism at Home

Among other social actors, the family plays a preponderant role . . . as the primary place which socializes and enculturates individuals, [and] during these processes racial prejudices, stereotypes, and other patterns of behaviors and conducts are formed.

—Rodrigo Espina Prieto and Pablo Rodríguez Ruiz,
"Raza y Desigualdad en la Cuba Actual"

One day when I was visiting Jaime's house his five-year-old nephew, Albertico (his sister's son), had just returned from school, and Jaime's grandmother was preparing the child a glass of warm milk with sugar. As is common in many extended families, child care becomes the responsibility of the elder family members; in this case, Jaime's grandmother was the primary caretaker of her great grandson, Albertico. Jaime's uncle looked at the little boy and asked him to explain to me how he got the scratches on his face. The boy answered that he got them fighting with another boy who wanted to steal his girlfriend away from him. Then the grandmother chimed in teasingly from the kitchen, "Oh, and his little girlfriend is so black! She's very, very black (*negrita prieta*)." "No!" the little blond boy protested. His great-grandmother continued, "Yes, that's the truth. She's a black, black little girl (*negrita prietecita*). But blaaaack, black!" she said, stretching out the words for extra emphasis. Albertico, becoming very angry, responded indignantly, "No, No, No! I'm not with a black girl. Never! My little girlfriend is white!" Jaime's grandmother smiled triumphantly and handed the boy his milk. Jaime's uncle turned to me and with a sigh of resignation

'That changes when they grow up," casting a glance at Jaime in a [...] -subtle reference to Jaime's mulata girlfriend, Madaleis.

An interview with a mulato informant confirmed the commonality of this scene I described above with Jaime's nephew. As he recounted: "When [a boy] is five or six, the parents and grandparents start to inculcate these ideas in him, 'Who are you going to marry? A little black girl, no? A black girl with big red lips?' The child protests and is bothered by the taunts, but the parents continue to tease him." There is no doubt that "learning is embedded in living" (Hannerz 1992, 172), and in these encounters in Jaime's household what is learned is the racial hierarchy, which types of interracial relations are acceptable and which are not. Albertico is teased about having a black girlfriend, a romantic courtship that could lead to a reproductive relationship—not a desirable outcome from the white family's perspective. So he is taunted until he proclaims his commitment to dating only white girls.

What is evident in these encounters is that within the family children learn to navigate among a variety of contradictory meanings and messages about race. Within the white family, the interracial sexual relationship can become simultaneously a joke, a means for expressing white anxiety about racial mixing, and a way of manifesting and teaching (through taunting) the racial hierarchy. While neighborly interracial interdependence and friendships are common and fostered, sexual interracial encounters should be more closely controlled—encouraged for white male pleasure, discouraged for serious relationships—and should be unthinkable for white women (particularly middle-class women). Racial mixing is a process that must be carefully managed, despite national rhetoric of mestizaje. In fact, in over eighty interviews conducted on racial attitudes in Santiago de Cuba by sociologist Rafael Duharte Jiménez, the most commonly articulated theme by both black and white informants was an aversion to interracial couples (Duharte Jiménez and García 1998). Racism is not only reproduced in media representations, structural patterns of housing, and popular discourse, but also found in the intimate sphere of the family. Alejandro de la Fuente notes that "racist culture seems to have been reproduced in the safety of private spaces, where it remained hidden for many years" (2008, 714).

When the topic of race made a tentative return to the state-controlled media in the early 1990s, it did so first in the context of family conflicts over interracial romance.[1] Several articles appeared in popular magazines recounting the trials of interracial couples as they struggled to maintain relationships in the face of parental disapproval and social censure. In the 1992 and 1993 Valentine's Day issues of *Bohemia*, the widely circulated weekly magazine, articles followed the development and then demise of an interracial courtship between a young white woman and a black man. The couple, first introduced in the 1992 article, lamented in the 1993 article that under increasing pressure from the white parents, their relationship had become "more tragedy than happiness," so they separated. A 1990 article on high school students in interracial romances published in the youth magazine *Somos Jóvenes* posed the question, "How can we be surrounded by these daily tragedies [of interracial couples] and we pretend to ignore them?" Until the 1990s these tragedies may have been ignored in the press, but they sprang immediately to the lips of my informants when I asked them about interracial dating.

As Robin Sheriff notes of racism in Brazil, "It is the concrete, structural association between blackness and poverty, between color and oppression, between the history of enslavement and the contemporary, quotidian manifestations of political and economic marginalization upon which internalized racism and racist discourse most fully rest, rather than upon individualized consciousness. . . . [I]ndividual selves, families, and subaltern communities [are] permeable sites (rather than sources) into which racism, as both a structural and ideological force, penetrates" (2001, 129). The interracial couples I spoke with did confront racism at home in the reactions of their parents and grandparents. Research conducted in the 1990s by the Cuban Institute of Anthropology in Havana also drew our attention to the family as one site where racism and racial stereotypes were learned (Pérez Alvarez 1996). But that was not the only place couples met with racism. The family was one site, among many, where couples encountered the structural and ideological aspects of the racial hierarchy. Other Cuban researchers, such as Rodrigo Espina Prieto and Pablo Rodríguez Ruiz (2006), highlight some of the structural inequalities that the revolution has not been able to overcome that also contribute to racism in Cuba, such as housing patterns and unequal access to jobs in the dollar sector (Espina Prieto and Rodríguez Ruiz 2006). Interracial couples also met both the structural and ideological manifestations of the racist culture in language, in media representations, and in the racial/class overlay of Havana's barrios.

The question then is not whether the family is the only or most important factor in perpetuating racism. Rather, recognizing the complexity of racism and the diffuse nature of power, we can consider the family as one site among many where racism emerges. Within the family racism articulates with gendered discourses of family belonging and loyalty. With that lens, the questions become these: How do families communicate racist views within their households, and how do the young people involved in interracial relationships respond? How do interracial couples negotiate among national ideologies and discourses of racial harmony and race mixture/mestizaje and families' attempts to control interracial mixing through discourses of family loyalty, gendered obligations and roles within households, and visions of family genealogies?

Expectations and Hesitancy

A friend of mine insisted I interview a twenty-two-year-old white university student named Yanet, as her story was a real "tragedy," in my friend's words. After speaking with Yanet, I also found her story to be one of triumph and a determination to pursue her love at all costs. Of the interviews I conducted on this topic, hers seemed to communicate the most personal pain, but also a deep sense of commitment to her partner and fiancé, Victor. I interviewed Yanet in the courtyard of the University of Havana. Victor, a twenty-three-year-old dark-skinned black man, sat several hundred yards away reading a book on the other side of the courtyard. He didn't want to talk about their relationship or discuss racial issues, as Yanet explained during our interview.

Yanet lived with her maternal grandparents (a working-class couple originally from the central province of Camagüey) and her married older sister and her husband in Cayo Hueso. Yanet was studying psychology, and Victor recently graduated with a degree in history. He lived with his brother and mother in the comfortably middle-class section of Havana called Playa. Victor was a rather unique among men his age, as he already owned a car, a major status symbol that few adults achieve in their lifetime. His privileged position was the result of both his mother's middle-class background and professional position as a doctor and his father's tragic history. His father was a military officer who died in the war in Angola. To compensate for a family's loss, the Cuban government often gave some material benefits (like a car) to high-ranking veterans' families.

As with other interracial couples I interviewed, Yanet embarked on this relationship with trepidation. Hers was not the first interracial relationship in the family, so she knew how her grandparents would react. After divorcing her father, Yanet's mother had married a black man. She recounts: "They have been together for years now, and I have a little four-year-old sister from this relationship. But it has been the biggest tragedy in the family; my grandparents have not spoken to my mother for years. It [the marriage] divided the family. . . . Knowing this precedent, to bring Victor home to my house would just repeat this difficult history—I knew this. I didn't say anything to him, but I thought that at any moment I would end the relationship. I told him he should go back to his old girlfriend [a black woman]." It was not only her grandparents' reaction she feared: "I was very afraid about going back to the university [after vacation]—I was afraid of people's reactions—all of my previous boyfriends had been the complete opposite [of Victor]. I was very afraid of what people would think, and I recognized that deep inside me I had this prejudice too." According to Yanet, Victor also harbored some hesitation of his own as they began their relationship: "He tells me now that he was interested in me for a long time before we actually started dating, but he was afraid [to approach me] because many people are prejudiced [and he wasn't sure how I could react]."

Sometimes fear and the energy and effort required to maintain an interracial relationship become overwhelming. Even before they take flight, some of these relationships crash under their own weight. Eladio, my neighbor, a twenty-five-year-old dark-skinned black man from a poor family, told of an experience he had while he was studying nursing several years earlier. He was dating a white woman whose father was a colonel in the Ministry of the Interior and whose mother was an important union leader. Her race and her class status immediately became a source of conflict. Though he didn't articulate any specific incidents, Eladio recounted that her parents were horrified to see him with their daughter. Shortly after the relationship started, he broke it off. He told her: "I'm a student. I have good social conduct, but I'm black, and I live in a *solar* in a [bad] neighborhood. I don't have anything to do with the social circles in which you were raised, and [this relationship] is going to cause problems." Eladio said that at first she didn't want to accept it, but he insisted on ending the relationship, "because at that point in my life I didn't want to look for trouble." He had dated other white women before and afterward, but he said, "It's always the same problem." His race, but also his class and barrio, would continually be something he would have to justify, explain, or overcome in relationships with white women and their families. By referring to his "good social conduct" (*buena conducta social*), Eladio was attempting to distance himself from the "low culture" associated with blacks living in solares in Cayo Hueso. Conscious of the social boundaries he was crossing by dating a middle-class white woman, he instead retreated to avoid the inevitable conflicts that he knew would ensue with her family.

Despite the national ideal of racial mixing and harmony, interracial couples (particularly when also interclass) can be thought of as radical actors breaking more narrowly prescribed race relations and the norm of acceptable interracial encounters. Many people involved in these relationships stressed how much they had broken with tradition and how many obstacles they had crossed to pursue or maintain these relationships. Yanet expressed the transgressive nature of her relationship quite directly. As she had anticipated, she encountered vehement protests from her grandparents when she began dating Victor. She recounted:

> The conflict started with my [grandparents] when [Victor] started to pick me up at my house. [At first] he was one friend among many, but then they began to notice because before he came

with a group of friends, now it was him alone. They never directly asked me about him, but I began to feel the friction develop in my relations with [my grandparents]. They always compared me to my mother. We are the type of people—path breaking (*emprendedora*)—that go against everything. My mother when she was very young joined the literacy campaign, although her parents didn't want her to go. I'm the same way, but not my sister. She never gets into trouble. When I had my first boyfriend and started having sex, [my grandparents] had to cope with it, but this [relationship with Victor] was much more difficult. I began to notice the tension. . . . My case is a reflection of many cases—of a latent prejudice—sometimes with extreme reactions like in my case or sometimes just underlying prejudice, but I think it is a problem among many people. There have been some people who have said nothing to me directly, but they don't like the idea (of interracial couples) and that's a form of prejudice too. Even I hadn't considered an [interracial relationship] before I met Victor. Marisela, a good friend of mine, said to me, "Think about it; if I had shown up in the same situation, what would you have thought? Maybe you would have understood because we are so close, but you would have been shocked in the beginning. Maybe you would have gotten over it, but you wouldn't have taken it as natural, because it is still not something natural."

Marisela's comment that interracial relationships are "not something natural" complements Pablo Rodríguez Ruiz's findings that the majority of couples in Cuba are intraracial (Espina Prieto and Rodríguez Ruiz 2006). However, these findings belie the prevailing discourse in Cuba that these types of relationships are common and that they, in fact, prove that there is no racism on the island and challenge the revolution's color-blind stance on race relations. Young interracial couples find themselves navigating through a mine field of mixed messages—of contradictory desires, fears, and assumptions about race and color that emerge in the context of interracial dating and marriage. As we see with Yanet, there is also a generational aspect to the conflicts, with older relatives expressing more racist views than younger generations.

However, the generational tendencies are not necessarily clear-cut divisions. There are members of older generations, such as Yanet's mother, who welcomed interracial unions, while there are some in the younger generations, such Yanet's sister, who did not.

In some families, as Sheriff (2001) also notes in Brazil, family bonds and interdependence surmount concerns over skin color. Not all people entering interracial relationships with fear have their nightmares become reality. For some, their worries evaporate as the families of both partners embrace and support the relationship. Zulema, a black university student who was married to a white man, represents a pattern I encountered many times with other interracial couples. Often it seems that race is a central issue for the families when the couple first starts dating, but its significance seems to dissolve as the families get to know the new partner better or simply resign themselves to the fact that their adult children must be allowed to make their own choices. Zulema was together with her ex-husband for six years. She recounted: "Luckily, they were families without prejudices in this sense. My mother took it as normal, and so did his family. Of course, in the beginning, I was a little afraid because I didn't know what kind of family he had. . . . I hadn't gone to his house yet. I hadn't met his parents, and here in Cuba there still are generations that don't accept [these relationships]. I didn't know if his family would accept it or not, but as the relationship developed, they accepted me. Maybe they had some objections, but I never knew it. I never felt any sign of this type, and they treated me normally, as if I were white, normal, without problems." A mulato friend, Chicho, recounted that his three brothers (also mulatos) were happily married to white women. When I asked if any of them had encountered problems with the white families, he responded: "I don't think there were these [negative] reactions. Because my brothers are not so black. They are mulatos with pretty good hair and features. So with mulatos [the interracial issue] is not so blunt, not so strained."

In some white families interracial relations with mulatos may not have been initially welcomed, but the white family may quickly have been won over by the individual their child was dating. Adela, a middle-class white women in her mid-fifties, told me about her white son's relationship with their mulata neighbor, Yaseli. Adela was very committed to the revolution and was married to a high-ranking military officer. I think because of her political identity, she was embarrassed to describe her reaction to her son's interracial romance. Yaseli was a very attractive light-skinned mulata—her mother was mulata and her father white. Adela began: "I have to be honest with you; at first I was not happy about the relationship. I had known Yaseli since she lived next door. . . . But honestly I wasn't happy with the news." "Because she was mulata?" I asked. Adela continued:

> Yes, I have to admit that was the reason. But I didn't say anything to my son. You know, I try not to get involved like that in my kids' lives, and sometimes it's best not to say anything because you might influence them or they might react against you—so it's just best to stay out of it. Anyway, as time went on, Yaseli spent a lot of time in our house, and I began to see that she was really a wonderful person, and I became very fond of her. She was very well mannered and educated . . . a very fine person. As time passed they spoke of getting married and I was thrilled. . . . But after two years together, they started drifting apart . . . and decided to break up. I was sad, but that's what happens.

Adela told me that within a year after the breakup Yaseli married a "very handsome and fine-featured" mulato man. When Yaseli came to invite Adela and her family to the wedding, Adela recounted that they both burst into tears: "Not that I wasn't happy for her, or that she wasn't happy with her soon-to-be husband, but we both missed the relationship she had with our family." Though at first she was hesitant about her son's relationship with Yaseli, it was, in fact, Adela who was more upset when they broke up. She had come to completely accept and cherish Yaseli's presence in their home. Yaseli's race was no longer an issue at all.

In some instances the racial/phenotypical differences between mulatos and whites were minimal or could be overlooked by some white families. Jaime (white), who was dating Madaleis (mulata), summarized this point quite directly: "You see mulatos and whites together on the street and no one really notices. [Madaleis] is light-skinned and her hair isn't bad, so her race was never really an issue for me. But you see a black [man] with a blond [woman] and everyone notices. It looks bad. Even I don't like to see it. A pretty blond with an ugly black. It's ugly. I wouldn't want to be with that blond after she was with a black. I don't like it. It's ugly." So for Jaime, who was involved in an interracial relationship himself, there were parameters or limits on what types of mixing he condoned and what types he viewed as unacceptable. In his case, Adela's and Chicho's *mulato* was a significantly distinct category from *negro* (black) when it came to interracial unions. The combination of lighter skin tone and more European features helped to make these interracial couples more acceptable to the white families or the partners themselves. As the Cuban researchers noted, most interracial relationships occur with mulatos and whites or mulatos and blacks. The least common pattern of couple is between whites and blacks, and that is the combination that provokes the most family conflict—as in Yanet's situation (Rodríguez Ruiz 2008).

From the extremes of Yanet's and Zulema's experiences to those of mulato/white couples that faced few adverse reactions, we see the panorama of the possible familial responses to interracial relationships. All of the types of responses are deeply rooted in culturally significant racial discourses that can support both racist and antiracist ideologies—historical tendencies of integration and mixing as well as preferences for patterns of couples. Some families can draw on national ideals of mestizaje and revolutionary values of egalitarianism to welcome and justify racial mixture in the family, while other families tap into the deeply ambivalent feelings about race and blackness that continue to permeate daily life in contemporary Cuba and respond, as Yanet experienced, in ways that demonstrate that these relationships are not always thought of as "normal" or "natural."

Family Protests, Tactics, and Subversions

Many couples I spoke with, particularly if one partner was black and the other white, found that their relationships provoked the ire of their families. In most cases, this type of interracial encounter was welcomed in neither the white nor black family. Parents and relatives manifested their disapproval in numerous ways—some subtle, some explosive. The couples' stories are of sorrow, humiliation, disappointment, and resignation, but also of love, resilience, perseverance, and hope.

White Families and Friends

Yanet continued our interview describing the hurt and degradation she experienced with her grandparents and her sister as they demonstrated, in no uncertain terms, their racism and their disapproval of her relationship with Victor. She recounted:

> There have been days when I've arrived home to find my clothes bundled up and they've told me I have to choose between one thing or the other [them or Victor]. Other days they've told me that if I'm not home by 7:00 P.M. I can't eat, or if I don't come home before midnight, I'll be locked out to the house, and that happened to me one day. So I've had to become very strong. . . . With my grandparents I can understand [their rejection], but I have a sister with whom I was very close, but she has not been able to deal with [my relationship]. She's young, twenty-six years old. She . . . and her husband won't even speak to me. I live in the house, but I come and go, and I spend most of my time in my friend's houses or in Victor's house. . . . My grandparents talk about him disrespectfully as a dirty, disgusting black (*Negro sucio, asqueroso*). It's shameful! When he walks me home, he has to leave me on the corner [as if I were] a little girl [hiding something]. . . . These things make me ashamed. For example, one day Victor came to pick me up at my house early in the morning—it was so early he decided to go directly to the door, but at that moment my grandfather came out of the door and created a tremendous scene in the middle of the street. He even said to Victor, "Don't even touch the door, because you'll stain it (black)." This broke my heart. Nevertheless, Victor didn't even raise his voice. He just lowered his head. I began to cry, and he [Victor] told me he wouldn't lower himself to my grandfather's level. He's above these things. Now we can talk freely about these incidents, but in the beginning he didn't even want to touch the topic. . . . I am going to marry because I have left everyone else behind. I had

to break with many things for this [relationship]. But time will tell. So we decided to get married. . . . [W]e've already arranged the papers, but no one in my house knows about this. I won't leave my house, as everyone dreams, dressed as a bride. That will be impossible. . . . I have suffered tremendously. I've been caught between the sword and the wall with no one to help me.

Yanet felt forced to choose between pursing her relationship with Victor and staying with her family. In front of their Cayo Hueso home, her white grandfather caused a public scandal on the street. In the barrio, where this type of "low-culture" behavior was attributed to blacks, Victor, by contrast, refused to lower himself and engage with her grandfather's outburst. Her grandparents' palpably racist invectives were painful and shameful for Yanet. She was not only offended by her family but also empathized with how this must have felt for Victor. She felt deeply betrayed by her family, particularly her sister. She justified her grandparents' racism as a feature of their generation and origin in Camagüey, an eastern province known for its racial segregation in prerevolutionary Cuba. Her sister's racism, however, she could not dismiss so easily. Despite growing up in revolutionary Cuba in the same integrated social spaces as Yanet, her sister adhered to racial views more akin to those of her grandparents. The generational changes in racial views that occurred over the course of the revolution were at times uneven. Youth in and of itself could not be a sure-fire predictor of racially progressive attitudes.

Despite the difficulty of Yanet's situation, she and Victor actually were in a much better position than many of the couples I met. They planned to marry and move into an apartment carved out of Victor's mother's house. While this solution still may seem very close to family, it is actually a luxury few can afford. Yanet and Victor's marriage was in part made possible by the fact that his mother was willing (and able) to subdivide her house so that the young couple could have a relatively independent living space.

While racist ideology was most often expressed in jokes and embedded in popular expressions, white daughters involved in inter-racial relationships sometimes sparked racist confrontations that were rarely seen in other contexts. While Yanet attributed her grandparents' reaction to their lack of formal education, their class, and their regional origin, other parents from a range of class and social backgrounds responded similarly when they found their teenager, particularly their white daughter, in an interracial relationship. The most violent encounter I heard was the story of Luis, a dark-skinned black man, and Irena, his white girlfriend. They were neighbors in Centro Habana and met when he was seventeen and she fifteen. They were together for five years. Luis recounts: "Everything wasn't perfect, but we liked each other. We hung out together; we made love; we had a relationship. She never told me that her father was prejudiced (*que tenía prejuicios de color*). Her mother more or less accepted me; well, '*me masticaba pero no me tragaba*' (she chewed me but didn't swallow me)."

Luis characterizes Irena's mother's feelings for him with the popular aphorism "*me masticaba pero no me tragaba*" (literally, "she chewed me but didn't swallow me"). The metaphor of food and eating is significant. Physical consumption that assimilates food into the body becomes a metaphor for assimilating a new member into the family. Irena's mother could never corporally make him part of the family, which is what a potentially reproductive relationship would do. The reproductive potential of these relationships is often at the core of white family protest. Blacks cannot be accepted into the white family and "not into the bodies of family members via sex or procreation" (Frankenberg 1993, 96).

Luis continued to recount his courtship with Irena:

I began to visit her house and met her parents after we'd been together for more than a year and a half. All that time I was meeting her on the corner. When her father found out that I had come between the family and his daughter, he became furious. I tried to explain to him that I had good intentions. She told me what her father was like. He had a car [a major status/class symbol] and a bad temper.

Once I had a fight with him over Irena. Irena had told her parents that she was going to a friend's house but instead came to spend a weekend in my house. Her father found out and hit her. Gave her a black eye. Her mother had tried to stop him but couldn't. I went to talk with him about what had happened, and he got really angry. He grabbed me by the shirt collar and I pushed him off me, and that got him really mad. He ran into another room and came back with a 38 revolver to threaten me. He said, "Not with my daughter because I'll kill you. I don't understand this (relationship), you black shit (*negro de mierda*). You don't know who I am. I have done a lot for the Revolution." Then he told me all these things that had nothing to do with Irena and me. I was nervous with the revolver in between us, but I tried to explain that I didn't want to fight with him; I just wanted to clarify my relationship with Irena. He told me, "My daughter doesn't have to get involved with any black man. My daughter has to study. She has to think about studying."

I kept going to her house, but it wasn't the same after that. I told her she had to decide if we should continue. Our relationship had gotten bad, and we didn't enjoy anything together. The relationship with her parents really affected us as a couple. She said there was no decision to be made. Her father was like this, and it would get better with time. We stayed together three more years [after the gun incident]. Her parents knew but never accepted it. Her father wouldn't even greet me—not even "good afternoon."

After five years Luis and Irena also broke up by mutual agreement. Of their breakup, he said:

What affected us most were her parents. Not her mother so much, but her father. A real S.O.B. The thing that really bothers me about it is that he's a [Communist] Party member, someone well respected. He fought in the Bay of Pigs. But nevertheless he can't tolerate blacks. I really suffered because of him. I suffered, but I was in love, so I tried to overlook the pain. . . . This relationship was really difficult for me. I've had other white girlfriends and it wasn't like this, but they also weren't as serious as this relationship. I really liked her, but it just couldn't continue. In the end I got tired.

The father's revolutionary credentials and ideals did not extend into the private sphere of the family. The revolution's hope for a color-blind and egalitarian society was not something Irena's father could support in his home. In his fight with Luis, he conjured up images of his revolutionary commitment to vouch for his character and integrity, which his behaviors seemed to be simultaneously undermining, given revolutionary rhetoric and ideals of equality. His tirade to Luis about his revolutionary work was more of a soliloquy that expressed the extent of his sacrifices and contributions to the revolution. From his perspective, he had given enough for this revolutionary project and he would not "sacrifice" his white daughter to the cause of racial equality. The boundary of racial integration stopped at his front door. Instead, Irena was to occupy herself with her studies and enjoy the benefits of other aspects of the revolution for which her father had fought. Luis pondered the possibilities of future interracial relationships for himself and Irena:

> I think Irena can't have another relationship with a black man until she's independent from her family. Because she's still depending on her family materially, and they impose a certain pattern of behavior on her that she has to adapt to so she can live in that house. After we broke up she starting seeing a white guy, and her father lent him his car and invited him over to eat [after being together a little while]. He never lent me the car even though I know how to drive, and I never ate in her house, and we were together five years. . . . I could date another white woman. I know of another [interracial] couple that has no problems. The mother [of the white woman] is a doctor with a high cultural level—she hasn't said anything to her daughter [about her relationship].

Like Yanet, material dependence on her family (especially for housing) made Irena vulnerable to their demands and pressures. Irena was unable to become independent from her family and the restrictions they impose on her. Even if Irena lived alone, it is uncertain that family pressure would not continue to bear on her relationships. Particularly for daughters, gendered family relations and obligations can operate even when they are living under separate roofs.

While Yanet's and Luis's experiences were dramatic for their violence and directly racist harangues, more typical were the subtle, indirect manipulations and subversions of parents attempting to control and shape their teenagers' activities. It was particularly the mothers of the white young women who tried to undermine these relationships with psychological pressure and guilt, cajoling their daughters to remain loyal to family responsibilities, household duties, and their proper role as obedient children with the family well-being and particularly their mothers' happiness in mind.

Irena's and Aliana's mothers were typical of this strategy. Irena's mother used subtle subversions to obstruct her relationship with Luis, make them late for events, or delay their dates—each time calling on Irena's family allegiance and her obligations to the household. Luis described the following examples of this:

> If we were going out at 7:00 P.M., why would her mother send her at 7:00 P.M. to run an errand or clean the rice or iron? Once we were going to Karl Marx Theater to see a comedian, and the show started at 8:00 P.M. I came to pick her up and we were in a hurry because the buses were always so delayed, and just then her mother breaks a jar of tomato sauce and makes Irena stay and help her clean it up. A jar of tomato sauce! I don't know if she did it on purpose or not. These were her tricks and schemes. . . . Irena never argued with her mother; she just did whatever she asked her to do. Little by little this started to build up. Everybody's patience has a limit.

These situations required Irena to choose between going out with Luis and completing whatever task her mother had set before her. Like Yanet, she was forced into an either/or situation where she had to decide where her loyalty lay and whether or not she was strong enough to follow her own desires, despite possible risks and dangers entailed in alienating her family. It was a serious burden for the young woman herself and for the couple. For many couples like Irena and Luis, the daily dramas soon drained away the joy, and the relationships ended out of sheer exhaustion.

Aliana, a white woman, met her black boyfriend, Rafael, in high school. About six months after they had broken up, I interviewed her about her two-year romance with Rafael. Aliana recounted her experiences with a kind of adolescent melodrama. Unlike the couples I interviewed in their early-to-mid-twenties, at nineteen, marriage and children were not an immediate concern for her. Aliana's story was less about them as a couple as it was about how their relationship affected her friendship group and most importantly her family. She had an extremely close relationship with her mother. Even in later romances with white men, Aliana's mother was her confidant. She would share letters her boyfriends wrote to her with her mother, and on several occasions she had her mother listen in on phone conversations with her boyfriends to help her figure out how to handle certain relationship issues. While her dependence on her mother may seem extreme, it was not uncommon for parents to be directly involved in the intimate lives of their teenage and young adult children, particularly their daughters. This was due in part to the mere fact that they lived together in often very crowded conditions where privacy was not possible—nor valued— and the family for many was, and continued to be, their main social as well as material support well into adulthood. This supportive role of the family only intensified during the austere years of the special period.

In high school, Aliana and Rafael were part of a racially mixed group of friends who studied together, socialized together, and hung out together. Despite this integrated friendship group, her romance with Rafael was a surprise to the others in the group, rather than a natural or predictable outgrowth of their integrated social life. Aliana recounts: "We were a very close group . . . maybe too close. We were all very involved in each other's lives, and Rafael helped me a lot, and this started to create closeness between us. My mother let me go out with this group because she never imagined it [a relationship with Rafael]. No? When we started dating it was like an explosion. She [her mother] could never have imagined it." A few days after they started dating, they went out together with their group of friends, and here too Aliana felt that their friends did not welcome her relationship with Rafael. With this new couple, the group dynamics had changed. Eventually the friendship group split up, some staying with Aliana and Rafael, and others distancing themselves from them.

Aliana continued to date Rafael, but secretly, that is, without telling her family, particularly her mother. However, her mother began to suspect something when she started to arrive home late. Keeping the relationship secret from her mother was painful and stressful for Aliana. She recounts:

> I swear I couldn't sleep, because I had always told Mami everything—even the fly that flew by me—and now I had made a decision without consulting her even though I knew that I shouldn't do it, knowing how she thinks. She always wanted me to have this type of friends, people of color, but only up to there. She always made sure I understood that. . . . Finally, I couldn't take it anymore, so I sat down with her one day and started to cry. . . . I couldn't take it anymore. We had gone a week almost without talking. When I told her, she said, "Ay Aliana try, make an effort. You have barely been together with him. . . . [M]ake an effort to distance yourself from him. Don't you realize that you're going to suffer? And you've already suffered lying to me. You're going to suffer more because this society says there's no racial discrimination, but there is. In school you've already realized it. For everything, for your own good, for the good of the family." Well, I broke up with him, but that only lasted a few days. Then we started seeing each other again, but secretly because I knew how she thought and I didn't want to make her suffer. . . . I told her I wouldn't get back together with him, but I did, even though I had promised her I wouldn't . . . but the temptation was too great.

Although Aliana had not told Rafael about it, he had already guessed what was happening. Her friends, however, were not willing to participate in her secret. She recounts: "Well, my other friends (from the group) told me they wouldn't lie to my mother; they didn't like to lie, so they wouldn't go out with us as a group anymore. They wouldn't help me. They were my friends and they should have helped me, but no, they turned their backs on me." Again, betrayal becomes a theme, not only from family, but also from friends. Aliana found herself without the help of her closest group of associates—her peers whom she thought would have been in the best position to understand and support her relationship with Rafael. Like Yanet's sister, even members of their own generation could not be counted on to support the interracial courtship.

First Lily (Aliana's mother) had tried to reason with Aliana to end her relationship, and then Lily tried to enlist the aid of Aliana's father, Oswaldo. When these two tactics failed to produce results, she then resorted to another distinctly female strategy: she internalized the conflict and became physically ill. Lily began to suffer from *enfermidad de los nervios* (sick nerves). Aliana continued:

> When I started coming home late again, she said to my father, "Oswaldo why don't you watch her? Why is she getting home so late?" . . . My mother grew ill. She started to take pills, to have nerve illness (*enfermar de los nervios*). . . . [E]veryone started saying to her on the street, "Ay, but Lily have you seen your daughter?" . . . My mother looked terrible with her nervous problems—she had been operated on before for stomach ulcers. I felt awful because I could see that the bleeding ulcers had returned. I was happy because I was with Rafael, but I also felt bad to see my mother suffer. . . . She even talked to Rafael. They argued, but later they became friends when she realized what kind of person he was—exactly the opposite of what she imagined. She use to say, "If only Rafael wasn't black." She almost accepted him, but his color was a barrier. She said to me, "If you had a daughter that you raised, that you gave her everything, and you wanted her to have all the best, everything you didn't have, and now you see her being criticized by everyone, that people look at her in the street . . ."

Aliana's interracial courtship not only came between her and her mother but also threatened the family reputation and made them the subject of local gossip and comments. One aunt told Aliana she would be the family's damnation. Her interracial relationship not only was about her, but encompassed her extended family's reputation and their relationships in the neighborhood as well.

For the white women the sorrow and anguish in these relationships came from family stress and tension, from being put in the position of having to choose between one love and another, one loyalty
and another, one future and another. For the black men, the pain was
caused by the racial assaults and indignities they suffered, the public
degradations, and from the deep disillusionment that came with the
realization that racism was undermining their intimate relations. For
the white families, the injury was from a sense of perfidy—a sense that
the families' sphere had been violated and could be potentially pol-
luted by this interracial relationship. Suffering and love were frequent
bedfellows in interracial courtships between blacks and whites, and
black families felt that as well.

Afrocuban Families and Friends

Given the often explosive encounters some interracial couples confronted with white families, it was not surprising that some black and
mulatto families were hesitant for their children to become involved
with white partners, despite the centuries-old rhetoric about "advancing the race" and whitening. The protests of black families mostly
centered on themes of fear of humiliation and betrayal of allegiance to
black family and friends.

Olga and José Miguel met in the university dormitory in Havana,
where they both were living. Olga, a black or dark-skinned mulata
woman, is the daughter of two mulatos. Despite the history of racial
mixing in their family, her parents (and, in particular, her father) were
initially displeased with their relationship. José Miguel is a twenty-
eight-year-old white man, also a student at the university. Both are
from working-class families, and both came to Havana from other
provinces to study. At the time of the interview they had been together
three years and were living in student dormitories.

José Miguel stated:

> We were best friends for a year and it was I who suggested we start
> dating. It was my idea, but she agreed. The start of the relation-
> ship was difficult. I think because of her upbringing. She's too
> pampered and dependent on her parents—mainly because she

had been involved in a bad relationship before that affected her studies. She failed some classes and her parents didn't want her to get involved with another boyfriend, and I could understand that. . . . Her father used to say to me, "*El blanquito ese* (that little white guy)." It didn't bother me; well, yes it did. No, it didn't bother me. I always thought that it was a way to shield Olga—so she wouldn't have another boyfriend. . . . But once they knew me and saw that I wouldn't interfere with her studies, in fact I helped her, . . . then they accepted me. So I came to the conclusion that they raised the racial problem for that reason.

In a separate interview Olga recounted the same story of their meeting, stressing that it was José Miguel who first fell in love with her and really initiated the relationship. Regarding her parents' reaction to José Miguel, she reiterated his account of her parents' hesitation for her to have a boyfriend and said: "I think they rejected him a bit for his color, a bit for being different. They're very protective of me and would like to have me at home where no one can get close to me. . . . My father told me that I was changing my way of being—influenced by José Miguel. I told him no, and we began to argue and then he said to me, 'You should see yourself—so in love with that, that abnormal little white guy (*abnormal el blanquito ese*).' . . . At that point my sister intervened and said, 'We're adults now, and white, Chinese, black, you're going to have to accept whoever we choose or you'll have spinster daughters.'"

José Miguel waffled as he pondered his feelings about the racialized comments he was subjected to by Olga's father. Ultimately, he decided in this interview that when he contextualized the comments within Olga's previous experiences, he could understand her family's trepidations. Whether protesting José Miguel's race or simply Olga's dating, her family drew on a racial idiom to voice their disapproval. As with all interracial couples, racial stereotypes provide a deeply wounding but ready-made vocabulary to employ in disagreements or disputes that may have very different roots. The racial barbs can come from families of all colors.

Luis also reflected on how his family reacted to his relationship with Irena, his white girlfriend. At first Luis said that his family had

accepted Irena without any problem, but as our conversation continued, he commented:

> At first my mother wasn't completely happy that I was dating
> Irena. She said that when black men are with white women they
> make fools of themselves and are very jealous and are always
> running after the white girl. The black man lowers himself to
> be with her. For example, if his family says something bad about
> the white girl, he'll fight with his family to defend her. Even
> my siblings said, "Since you've been with Irena you've changed.
> When black men are with white women they act differently." For
> example when she was at my house I would try to give her the
> best seat to watch TV. If she came over to eat I tried to give her
> the best food or serve her extra. Not because she was white, but
> because she was my girlfriend. I think anybody would have done
> same thing. . . . OK, this used to happen. Before, a black man with
> a white woman would buy her things and bring all sorts of gifts
> to her house—he would live only for her and forget all about his
> family. I've known cases like this, but not everybody is the same,
> and it's another era now.

The family problems that Aliana experienced in her relationship
with Rafael came not only from her parents, but from Rafael's mother as
well: "I wasn't treated well by his family [his mother]. They said I would
humiliate Rafael and that my family humiliated him . . . even after my
family accepted him. His mother said I would always humiliate him. . . .
She didn't understand that I was different, that I loved him and would
fight for her son. It's a bit like my mother said—I'll always suffer with
him. His mother didn't want me in his house. She said he should look
for someone his own color, and that's what he did in the end." Given the
response of Aliana's family, it seems Rafael's mother was justified in her
stance against the relationship. Indeed, it would prove to be a difficult
one, despite Aliana's affections. Families' responses, explosive or subtle,
were often couched in the discourse of protection—safeguarding their
children's best interests, their futures, their careers, their dignity, and,
in the case of women (especially white women), protecting the family's
virtue by controlling their sexuality. If families, both black and white,

sensed this need to shield their children from the emotic
material, fallout involved in interracial relationships, it
they feared or perceived that racial discrimination in Cuba
a real threat to their children. Aliana's mother expressed
but other families hinted that the wounding would continue, whether
it came from the white family or neighbors or workmates or strangers
on the street. The interracial relationship—particularly between blacks
and whites—more than any other type of interracial encounter, could
raise the racist wrath of others. Protest to interracial relationships from
the white family was also about protecting the family genealogy. The
reproductive potential of these relationships would simultaneously
give birth to mestizaje as well as white families' angst.

Genealogical Dreams and Realities:
Reproducing the Future and Unmaking the Past

> Discourses on libidinal desires were invariably shaped by how
> those desires were seen in relationship to their reproductive
> consequences.
>
> —Ann Laura Stoler, *Race and the Education of Desire*

Even in the best-case scenarios with little or no objection from the families, there was great concern over the reproductive future of the couples. White families' anxiety centered on the color of future offspring,
since the relationship would bring blackness directly into the family.
The actual practice of mestizaje was problematic for most white families, despite the national ideology embracing the concept as central to
Cuban identity. Other anthropologists have also noted the hesitancy of
white families, particularly the middle class, to partake in this supposedly national project. Paul Ryer (1998) and Mette Berg (2005) document
the ease with which the national ideal of racial mixture is articulated by
their white informants, who in the next breath proceed to detail with
pride their purely Spanish/white ancestry. The valuation of whiteness
and European ancestry has grown in the context of international tourism and the dollarized economy. In this framework being able not only
to claim but also to document Spanish ancestry could be parlayed into
a Spanish passport and the opportunity to travel abroad, thus making

European descent a very material asset. By contrast the "genealogical embarrassment" (Ryer 1998) that actually having black blood in the family would cause is evident in the responses of even supportive white parents to their children's interracial relationships.

For many white families the reproductive prospects of these couplings were threatening. Even for couples that encountered few, if any, problems with their families, the color of the potential offspring always warranted commentary, again undermining the "naturalness" of mestizaje in actual practice.

Speaking of how his mother reacted to his relationship with Olga (a black woman), José Miguel (a white man) recounts: "My mother found out through a friend—who was a bit fearful when he told her that [Olga] was black. But my mother told him that she didn't care what color she was as long as we got along well. . . . My mother joked with her neighbors. 'Now you'll see me with a little black baby in the street. And this little black kid? No, it's my grandchild!' . . . I'm going to tell you the phrase she always uses, *'No son negros de casta.'* Because they are black by color but are very good people. . . . I don't think that my family is at all racist." Despite his claim that his family welcomed Olga without any trouble, the color of the would-be grandchildren was worthy of speculation by his mother. The reproductive possibilities of this couple demand remark. The potential grandchildren are not just descendents but are racially marked as black grandchildren.

Zulema, a black university student, had a similar experience. Although she felt the relationship was welcomed and supported by both her family and her white husband's family, she stated: "[Everything was] normal without any problems. . . . Not even in his family, but there always was the distinction. His mother used to say [referring to her other sons who had white girlfriends], 'From you I expect blondes, but from you [referring to us] *jabaitos.*' But this was just kidding around. Really [the racial difference] didn't influence anything." As in the case of José Miguel's mother, the white family accepted the mulata girlfriend without much commotion. However, the offspring, who would be the embodiment of this mestizaje, were at issue. What will these mulato children mean for the white family as a whole? It seems that such grandchildren would be met with a mixture of pride—about having a grandchild—and shame that it is not white. The location of the concern in these relations is lodged in the future still unborn generation, not in the present relationship with the couple. Nonwhite offspring disrupt and upset the white family's line of descent and, indeed, become a "genealogical embarrassment," as Ryer (1998) describes.

From the black family's perspective the prospect of whitening was also not always welcomed. Despite both families' acceptance of Sofia's (a mulata) marriage to Fernando (a white man), racial issues were never completely absent from their relationship. Racial observations and discussion often centered on the couple's two young daughters. Sofia recounts, for example, incidents when her mother, who is a very dark-skinned Haitian immigrant, was out with one of their two daughters, both of whom are very light-skinned and show only the slightest traces of their mixed blood: "When my mother was carrying our baby who was rosy skinned and had lots of blond hair, and people would stop her in the street and say, 'Look at that. How white the baby is! Oh you must be so happy that she turned out so advanced (*adelantada*).' It makes me so angry. Why should I want to deny my color? Why should I be happy that she is lighter than me?" Sofia's comments reflect a racial conscious-ness not often associated with blacks in Cuba. Her interracial marriage was not prompted by an interest in whitening as a means of securing a better future for her children. Her pride in her blackness resonates with views from Luis's family, who worried that he will belittle himself to maintain his relationship with his white girlfriend, Irena. Racial dignity and identity as well as family solidarity could be disrupted by whitening—or at least that is what some black families feared.

Sofia and Fernando's daughters, then five and seven years old, encountered the need to define their racial identity when they arrived at school and classmates tried to locate them in Cuba's racial/color continuum. Were they white? Were they mulata? And why were they so different, since they were sisters? One of the girls was a *jaba*, while the other, though brunette, was less apparently of mixed race. The elder daughter came home from school one day and asked her parents if she was mulata or white, and Sofia said, "You tell your friends you're mulata and very proud of it." Even in cases where race mixing is accepted by the families, it is never a nonissue, and at very early ages the children themselves learn that in Cuba today their social identity relies in a fundamental way on their racial identity.

Ultimately, many courtships and potentially reproductive couplings are about the future, about producing the next generation. In the context of Cuba in the post-Soviet period, what will that next generation be? Will it be a generation of revolutionaries? A generation intent on maintaining the racial hierarchy? Or one willing to embrace racial equality in all arenas of life? What hopes, worries, or maybe miracles await the children of these young interracial couples I interviewed?

Epilogue

Sex can be properly understood only in its social context. . . . It is not so much that love breaks down barriers and unites human beings as that racial ideologies extend their conflicts even into love's embraces.

–Roger Bastide, "Dusky Venus, Black Apollo"

Probably the most fool-proof index of qualitative change in the color-class system is the incidence of "mixed" marriages, of formal unions between persons of markedly different physical appearances, and moreover, roughly equal socio-economic standing.

–David Booth, "Cuba, Color, and the Revolution"

The Cuban revolution turned fifty in January of 2009, and the global context in which Cuba now positions itself has shifted dramatically since the band of bearded rebels took power half a century ago. This important anniversary has been a time for reflecting on the past as well as looking forward to the future. Academic journals both on and off the island have published special issues and a variety of institutions have organized conferences to assess and discuss the revolution.[1] Scholars have been weighing the successes and limitations of the revolution's social, political, and economic agendas with a level of scrutiny unparalleled in recent years. Much of this recent attention has focused on Cuba since 1990, when the Cold War ended and the socialist bloc collapsed. The post-Soviet era, if nothing else, has been a time of profound change. In this period, the family has assumed a greater role as a social safety net as the state's ability to deliver goods and services has wavered. The socialist and egalitarian ideologies and symbols of the revolution now coexist with growing foreign tourism; billboards for

Benetton stand next to those bearing revolutionary slogans. Tourism is racializing spaces in new ways and creating new meanings of whiteness, blackness, and mixedness and new zones of inclusion and exclusion. It is forcing Cubans to ponder their own and others' visions of Cubanidad as their "national culture" is packaged and marketed abroad. Amid all of this, interracial couples continue to populate the island.

Interracial unions have been imbued with many meanings. For Roger Bastide, writing on race relations in Brazil, such unions could be nothing but expressions of the society's racial hierarchy. In contrast, David Booth, writing on Cuba, looked to them as the litmus test of the island's racial climate. Both approaches, however, take the meanings of blackness, whiteness, and these unions as somehow fixed rather than in flux. In the previous chapters, I have explored the shifting racial context and meanings that surround contemporary interracial couples in Cuba in order to problematize facile understandings of mixed-race unions in a country that has ensconced mestizaje (racial mixing) as a national ideal for centuries. To conclude, then, I wish to revisit the ever-changing ideological milieu of race in post-Soviet Cuba.

Anthropologist Heather Settle posed the provocative question, "What new conceptions of time and progress are being put forward in the wake of socialism's collapse—not as institution, or regime, but as dream, aspiration" (2008, 4). I would add this: What hope is there for progress in terms of racial equality and for reimagining whiteness, blackness, and mestizaje? How will tourism and the new spaces for public discourse on race opening in art and music percolate through the family and everyday interracial encounters? While I cannot predict what racial mixing and interracial couples will mean in Cuba's future, I hope here to sketch some features of the symbolic terrain on which they will move. Some trends bring hope, while others give pause. The landscape begins with the enduring centrality of mestizaje as embodied in the Virgen de la Caridad del Cobre, Cuba's patron saint.

In the Church of Carmen in Centro Habana, on the transept's vaulted ceiling, the painted image of La Virgen de la Caridad del Cobre soars over the pews like a giant blue bird with outspread wings. Her bronze-hued countenance is topped by a golden crown. She stands on a downturned crescent moon hovering above a tormented sea in which a small wooden rowboat is tossed about like a toy. The boat's occupants, three strapping young men, one black between two whites, look up at her with beseeching eyes as they struggle to steady the violently pitching craft.[2]

Images of La Caridad, who was declared the patron saint of Cuba by papal decree in 1916, were and continue to be ubiquitous. Every church and many households have a statue, painting, or altar dedicated to Cachita, as she is popularly known. She is, even today, referred to as the "mulata virgin," and references are made to her coppery skin (Kutzinski 1993), but in actuality she is more often depicted as a light-skinned brunette with European features. Her mulata persona comes from her syncretic counterpart, Ochún, in the Yoruba-based pantheon of Santería.[3] The syncretic nature of La Caridad also includes the Taíno mother of the waters and childbirth, Atabey. She is thus the melding of Spanish Catholic, indigenous Taíno, and African Yoruba deities.[4] Antonio Benítez-Rojo points out that La Caridad first emerged as an important figure in colonial Cuba amid a nation-building process fraught with conflict and exploitation. In this turmoil, "the Virgen de la Caridad represented a magical or transcendental space to which the European, African, and American Indian origins of the region's people were connected" (Benítez-Rojo 1992, 52). In the social imagination of early Cubans, La Caridad was both the pure and holy virgin mother of Jesus and the mulata goddess of love, sensual pleasure, and fertility. It is no insignificant fact that Cuba encoded its national identity in this mythic figure of a sacred mulata—the product of an interracial union.

Likewise, the three men floundering in their faltering vessel symbolized much more than just divine intervention and salvation from the storm: they offered the budding nation a blueprint for race relations. Again, Benítez-Rojo writes: "The fact that the three men carried the name Juan—they are known as the Three Juans—that they were together in the same boat, and that all were saved by the Virgen conveys mythologically the desire to reach a sphere of effective equality where the racial, social and cultural differences that conquest, colonization, and slavery created would coexist without violence" (1992, 52). As in the Christian trilogy of Father, Son, and Holy Spirit, the three Juans formed "one Juan" of three parts; the "*indoafrohispano*" Cuban nation (Arrom

1990, 306) . The Juans and the Virgin constituted one of the earliest (1830s) symbolic representations of the creoles' integrationist desires for Cuba (Benítez-Rojo 1992, 52). The rowboat with the three Juans encapsulated the hopes for social relationships in an independent Cuba, or at least held out the promise and ideal of racial peace, while racial mixing became symbolically, but not unambivalently, encoded on the mulata virgin herself.

The Virgen de la Caridad del Cobre illustrated the centrality of mestizaje in the symbolic imagination of the new mestizo nation. The Virgin embodied the abstract principles and ideals of the nation and subsumed racial complexity and heterogeneity under what Eric Wolf would call a "unifying master symbol" (1958, 34). The Virgin in colonial Cuba, as Benítez-Rojo notes, "defuse[d] . . . the blind violence with which Caribbean social dynamics collide, the violence organized by slavery, despotic colonialism and the plantation" (1992, 23). She was an omnipresent reminder of the mestizo nature of Cuba and of the nation's hopes for racial accord. As Cuba's patron saint and national icon, Cachita still fulfills that need, but now, of course, the context has changed.

Since the 1990s there has been a religious revival on the island that can be attributed to a combination of factors, including a new political tolerance for believers; a sense of disorientation after the collapse of the socialist bloc, pushing more people to turn to religion; and the appeal of religion as a vehicle for expressing nonconformity, especially among youth (Ayorinde 2004). With the explosion of religiosity on the island, and particularly of Afrocuban religions, Cachita's image is more present and visible than ever. The widespread practice of Santería and the racial message encoded in the omnipresent Virgin may now be contributing to reshaping ideas of blackness and race relations on the island. The collapse of socialism left an ideological void which Cubans sought to fill with a reassessment and reassertion of Cubanidad that involved looking inward to the island's cultural roots, such as those embodied in syncretic religious practices (Ayorinde 2004). For many, Santería answered that need for identity, and it also offered Cubans a way to help ameliorate the hardships of daily life. They turned to the *orishas* (deities) not for miracles or eternal salvation but for solutions to the storm of everyday problems brought on by the special period. It is a religion of efficacy, focused on here-and-now results. Historically, Santería was primarily practiced by lower-class blacks and therefore considered unacceptable by many other Cubans, but the current surge of Santería practice is now more than ever a multiracial phenomenon, with many whites among both followers and even religious leaders (Ayorinde 2004). Though some prominent Cubans, such as Minister of Culture Abel Prieto, proclaimed that this multiracial aspect of Afrocuban religions made them central in combating racism, Christine Ayorinde (2004) cautions that this new movement will not in and of itself alter race relations or racist structures in the wider society. This growing religious trend, however, is reason for optimism on several levels. Santería itself is tolerant of diversity and is an open religion characterized by inclusiveness and a cooperative tradition that can be used to promote social change (Ayorinde 2004). While it might not exactly be Cachita's message of racial harmony and integration, the spread of Santería and other African-derived religions on the island across racial groups does represent a validation of these once-marginalized traditions and a source of racial pride for many black Cubans. With national identity in a perpetual state of flux, the current prominence of Santería as a symbol of the nation may bode well for keeping the racial synthesis embodied in the iconic Virgen del Cobre at the heart of the nation (Ayorinde 2004).

The long-standing and historical silence inhibiting public discourse on race is now also being uprooted. While I have argued that racially discriminatory commentary permeated interpersonal communications and stereotypes populated media images of blacks, since the late 1990s artists, musicians, and academics have started a more public debate about Cuba's racist culture and the discriminatory practices that have surfaced with the expansion of the so-called emergent economy.[5]

Young Afrocuban rappers have used their music to contest racial hierarchies and stereotypes, demand social justice, and appeal to the state to uphold the promise of socialist egalitarianism (Fernandes 2006). Emblematic of the hip-hop response to racial discrimination is the Hermanos de Causa song "Tengo" (I Have), which rewrites the famous Nicolás Guillén poem of the same name. While the 1964 Guillén

poem praises the nascent revolution for providing blacks with education, jobs, and basic needs, the hip-hop version recognizes continuing
discrimination against blacks, the lack of freedom of expression, and
critiques the new lines of exclusion and inclusion that have emerged
with the growth of tourism. Other hip-hop lyrics counter stereotypes
of blacks as delinquents and criminals and highlight the police harassment and racial profiling experienced by so many young black Cuban
men. Rappers have also used Afrocuban religious symbols to affirm African contributions to Cubanidad. Their music has validated Afrocuban
historical figures and celebrated heroes of struggles for racial justice
elsewhere in the world (such as Malcolm X and Nelson Mandela) (de la
Fuente 2008). Though female rappers struggle for space in the largely
male-dominated genre, female groups, such as Las Krudas, have used
their music to contest Eurocentric notions of beauty and have endorsed
and promoted more Afrocentric styles in their own hairstyles and dress
(Fernandes 2006). Women rappers have also critiqued the eroticization
of the mulata as presented in tourism. As Sujatha Fernandes notes,
female rappers "reclaim for women the capacity to think, make rhymes,
and produce the best hip hop" (2006, 117). Overall, the genre has been
an outlet for the frustrations and concerns of young Afrocubans and a
way for them to publically raise and discuss racial issues.

A number of visual artists have also been engaging with similar
racial issues in their works since the mid-1990s (de la Fuente 2008;
Fernandes 2006). Through paintings, prints, installations, and performance art, young artists such as Alexis Esquivel, Manuel Arenas, Elio
Rodríguez, and Roberto Diago have been countering racial stereotypes,
racial discrimination, and the continued marginalization of blacks in
Cuban society. Like the rappers, "the artists are concerned with the
social conditions of race as a lived reality" (Fernandes 2006, 165). The
works of Roberto Diago, for example, engage with black history and
draw attention to topics often overlooked in Cuban schools. Some of
the artists parody the racist images embedded in the tourism industry and the folkloric vision of Afrocuban culture. Artists such as Elio
Rodríguez also address the notions of gender, sexuality, and nation
that are marketed to tourists, alluding to the tourists' desires for sexual
encounters with Cubans as well as stereotypes of a predatory black male

sexuality. In Rodríguez's prints, the mulata is less a symbol of national reconciliation, but rather the embodiment of "the conflictive relationship between race, gender and nation" (de la Fuente 2008, 703).

Paralleling and to some extent predating this burgeoning artistic production has been the work of intellectuals and civic leaders to bring racial issues to the forefront. In addition to scholarly works I outlined in chapter 1, Teresa de Cárdenas has published children's books which unravel racial prejudice and stereotypes and draw connections between the past and present social conditions for black Cubans (de la Fuente 2008). Although membership is very small and is still largely drawn from black intellectuals, budding Afrocuban civic groups such as Confradía de la Negritud and Movimiento de Integración Racial (MIR) have contributed to raising public consciousness of continuing racial discrimination and have engaged state officials in dialogues on these issues (de la Fuente 2008). The Confradía's platform includes a call to narrow the income gap between white and black Cubans, to showcase Afrocuban achievements, and to respect the rights of Afrocubans (Gross 2008). These new race-based groups are creating agendas similar to those of the former *sociedades de color,* the black social clubs that the revolutionary government dismantled in the early 1960s. Even Fidel Castro has stated since the late 1990s that racial differences and inequalities require additional attention, particularly in terms of representation within government and Communist Party leadership (de la Fuente 2008). Now for the first time in decades the government is allowing nongovernmental clubs and groups to provide some of this extra attention to the issue of racial inequality.

Alejandro de la Fuente concludes that "given the actions and efforts of all these intellectuals, artists and activists it is increasingly difficult to sustain . . . that race continues to be a taboo in public discourses" (2008, 712). This may be true, but both Fernandes and de la Fuente also recognize that the struggles are far from over for ideological terrain, a public voice, and actual on-the-ground changes. Visual artists were less optimistic than the rappers about sustaining black voices in the arts given the state's resistance and lack of support for their work (Fernandes 2006). Both the visual artists and some rappers have difficulty in promoting their art on the national level, and likewise many writers face obstacles and a lack of state support to get their work published (de la Fuente 2008, 719). Furthermore, there is no coordinated voice among all of these cultural actors and activists; there is, says de la Fuente, no "Afrocuban cultural movement in a programmatic sense" (2008, 719). He asserts that the educational successes of the revolution have created an "unusually large black intelligentsia . . . who are now demanding concrete government actions to turn official rhetoric of equality into a reality" (720). He concludes on a sanguine note that the deeply rooted ideologies of racial fraternity and the revolution's touted commitment to equality will in a sense force the state to respond to these now-public concerns.

Clearly, this new possibility for dialogue still rests on contested ideological terrain; multiple meanings and symbolic connotations of blackness, whiteness, and mestizaje still circulate. While intellectuals may decry racism and artists parody the images of black Cubans and Afrocuban culture marketed to tourists, some rappers such as the Orishas seek to exploit local and international markets by reproducing representations of blackness that sell (Fernandes 2006). The burgeoning tourism market thus offers both possibilities and challenges for remaking the symbolic landscape of color. Adrian Hearn's (2008) research on community development initiatives based in local Afrocuban religious groups demonstrates how the "folkore-development complex" can cut both ways. Some of the organizations he studied were able to stage Afrocuban cultural performances for tourists and in turn use that money to finance local community improvement projects. Local civic groups that successfully harnessed earnings from tourism while validating Afrocuban traditions and educating others about them offer examples of the tremendous potential in tapping into tourists' interests in Afrocuban performances. Well-organized efforts linked to tourism can serve as the basis for true community revitalization. However, Hearn also described groups whose original community-based goals were derailed as the groups became overly focused on the commercialization of the performances. There is a well-documented tendency to distort Afrocuban practices in tourism spectacles. If Santería, for example, is truly becoming a national religion that transcends race, why is it marketed to tourists as an exotic practice of blacks rather than represented in its multiracial reality? If the religion is losing the stigma it once had from being associated with lower-class blacks, why do some Afrocuban cultural productions continue to root and market their "authenticity" through their spatial location in marginalized, run-down barrios such as Centro Habana? Global images of blackness can reinforce local representations in ways that may undermine more progressive racial re-imaginings. Tourism offers tremendous opportunities for positive change, but also tremendous potential for entrenching racialized notions that denigrate rather than elevate blackness and Afrocuban culture.

There may now be more whites among Santería believers, more public voices speaking out on racial issues, and some artists and intellectuals may have gotten the ear of government officials, but are white Cuban families ready to listen to these concerns? The racist culture, which did not wither away after fifty years of socialism, may be even harder to uproot now, given the weakened power of the state since the special period. Artists and intellectuals may have successfully raised public awareness of racial issues, but they have done so just at a moment when the state has lost much of its credibility and the moral mandate for social justice needed to deracinate racism. The optimism and euphoria of building a new society that the state fostered and harnessed to mobilize projects in 1959 are not present in 2009. By giving racial issues visibility, the special period may have forced this conversation on the Cuban people, as de la Fuente asserts, but the special period also caused many to retreat to the family for support. As the state's ability to deliver services declined, many Cubans were engulfed by a sense of hopelessness and disillusionment. Heather Settle suggests that the "revolution no longer provides the template for discourse and dreaming . . . [nor] the possibility of transcendence through sacrifice, solidarity and socialist values" (2008, 4).

An encounter with Jaime captures some of these tensions. One day in late January, Jaime and I were walking along Prado, the broad promenade that divides Centro Habana from Habana Vieja. As usual the Parque Central was bustling with people, some sitting, but many passing through. That day the park was elaborately decorated for the annual commemoration of José Martí's birthday. At sundown, the *antorcha* (torchlight march) would begin on the steps of the University of Havana and end at the Parque Central, where a stage had been erected for the closing speeches and concert. As we passed the stage the large speakers started blaring the Cuban national anthem—surely as a test run for the events that evening. The people in the park, and in fact everyone within earshot of the anthem, froze in their tracks while the anthem played, and those who had been seated stood up in patriotic respect. Jaime, however, continued walking. I asked if he wanted to stop, thinking maybe he was continuing for my benefit, but he replied with a tone of disgust, "Oh, patriotism. My patriotism is for my family. For my mother, my father, my grandmother. Not for this country. Not for anything else." So we wove our way through the park, past the statue of José Martí and all of the statuelike Cubans—more than black, more than white, more than mulatto—who stood at attention for the anthem.

The interracial couples, the engines of mestizaje, I have presented in this book are embedded in families. Jaime, coming of age in the 1990s, poignantly expressed where his loyalty lies—as was true for many of his generation. During the special period and the post-Soviet era, the family has consistently borne the brunt of the economic hardship and changes (Safa 2009). Survival strategies have been rooted in family, more so than in individual responses. Extended families, either sharing a household or spread over various households, allowed for a diversification of income sources and a broader potential for emigration or remittances (Safa 2009). In interviews Helen Safa (2009) conducted with a large extended family she has known since 1987, family members now claim that everyone wants to emigrate because they see little possibility for improvement and are tired of struggling.

Settle echoes this pessimism in her recent interactions with informants on the island. One woman, for example, is convinced the revolution can't be "fixed" but now expresses her faith in the future and in progress through her offerings to the orishas. She hopes first for help with a legal title for her *solar* apartment, then maybe her own business or a chance to emigrate. Settle observes that "[this woman's] faith, hope and the future are no longer tied to the advance or arrest of teleological revolutionary time" (2008, 5). Settle cites other informants who expressed a loss of faith in the expansive social projects of the revolution. She suggests that "the revolutionary template for thinking about the future—as a place of fulfillment, or as a process of working through historical stages—has lost the power to define both progress and exception" (Settle 2008, 7). The return to the family, the increasing desire for emigration, and the disillusionment with the revolutionary project may temper the more optimistic trends and assessments of the future of race relations on the island.

In the postmodern world, we are beyond easy beliefs in master narratives, whether they come in the form of virgins or doctrines. The new public conversations about race and continuing racial inequalities on the island, the growing visibility and popularity of African-derived religions, and the potential for validating Afrocuban culture through tourism are indeed hopeful signs for the future. These movements may contribute to creating a climate where interracial couples may not only symbolize but enact racial transcendence. However, the persisting material hardships, the loss of faith in the revolutionary project and the efficacy of the state, and the potentially racially and spatially polarizing effects of tourism may hinder attempts to uproot Cuba's racist culture and recast meanings of blackness, whiteness, and mestizaje.

Moreover, racial endogamy remains the norm on the island and is strongest among educated whites, particularly those working in the emergent sectors of the economy, where the goal is not collective progress but individual social mobility (Rodríguez Ruiz 2008). Rodrigo Espina Prieto and Pablo Rodríguez Ruiz (2006) note that within racially endogamous families there may be a tendency for children to be exposed and absorb racial stereotypes and prejudice. So the centrality of the family in the post-Soviet period may also present obstacles in furthering the struggle toward racial equality. Most interracial unions still continue to "come from below," that is, they are more prevalent among the poor and working classes (Espina Prieto and Rodríguez Ruiz 2006). When racial mixing is most prominent among only certain (and especially socially marginal) populations, we cannot assume that the society's racist culture is dissolving through interracial embraces. Donna Goldstein (1999) observes the often practical and pragmatic nature of interracial relationships in Brazilian shantytowns between poor black women and wealthier white men and notes that interracial sex may be consensual but it is not egalitarian.

When anthropologists from the Instituto de Antropología interviewed a racially diverse sample of people from across the island about race relations, 90 percent thought racism existed on the island (Espina Prieto and Rodríguez Ruiz 2006). However, when asked about the future of race relations, nearly two-thirds believed race relations would improve. The respondents cited the presence of racial mixing (mestizaje) and the government's stance on social equality in supporting their views. This optimistic outlook is surely a positive sign. Interestingly, the majority of those who felt race relations would get worse were those involved in interracial unions. The researchers suggested that their pessimism might be based on the difficulties they experienced as interracial couples. In conclusion, the authors state that the racial question in Cuba is expressed in a framework of contradictions (Espina Prieto and Rodríguez Ruiz 2006). Indeed, this has always been the case.

The Virgen de la Caridad del Cobre and the three Juans represented racial harmony in juxtaposition to the racial violence and oppression in colonial Cuba. Now her image proliferates through the burgeoning practice of Santería, where she symbolizes not only racial unity but also love and passion—forces with which to be reckoned. Verena Martínez-Alier observes that among the justifications for interracial marriages, even in the colonial period, "love, by overriding social restraints, meant the assertion of individual freedom of choice over social conventions. . . . Love and passion are unpredictable and render people insensitive to their duties to family and society" (1989, 66). For now, a racially transcendent mestizaje lingers as an iconic hope, and interracial couples remain commonplace, but by no means simple in their meanings or connotations. Contradictions still abound, but we should not underestimate Cachita's/Ochún's emblematic powers and the audacity of love.

NOTES

INTRODUCTION

1. Although Christopher Columbus actually arrived in Cuba first in 1492, Diego Velázquez is known as the conqueror of the island.

2. It is estimated that in 1510 the island had 112,000 indigenous inhabitants of three groups, Taínos, Subtainos, and Guanahatabeyes (Guanche 1977).

3. The first wave of Chinese immigration began in 1848 and continued until 1861. A second wave of immigration (1860–1875) came in the aftermath of the California gold rush, when Chinese made their way to Cuba via Mexico. Chinese immigration continued through the early decades of the twentieth century.

4. Irish were brought in as contract labor along with men from the Canary Islands to build the railroad to carry the sugar from the mills in Güines to Havana. As sugar was made with blood, so too was the railroad; for every kilometer of track laid, thirteen men died (Moreno Fraginals 1978).

5. The idea of race-based initiatives is not unknown in Cuba. Afrocuban intellectuals like Juan René Betancourt argued for race-based organizations in the 1950s, and more recently Cuban sociologist María del Carmen Caño Secade (1996), exposed to North American scholars and racial paradigms, called for more affirmative-action measures in Cuba.

6. Some anthropological fieldwork was conducted by Helen Safa on women and work in the mid-1980s, and brief visits were made in the early 1990s by Nancy Scheper-Hughes, who wrote comparatively on AIDS in Cuba and Brazil (Safa 1995; Scheper-Hughes 1993).

7. Ariana Hernandez-Reguant (2005) provides an excellent overview of the fate of the discipline of anthropology under the revolution. Heavily influenced by the approach of Soviet ethnography and ethnology, Cuban anthropology from the 1960s through the 1980s focused largely on the recovery and preservation of Afrocuban and other ethnic cultural expressions. Only in the 1990s did Cuban anthropologists begin to conduct research on social issues (such as youth and race relations).

8. Phone service began to improve in the late 1990s, when the Cuban government joined with Mexican and Italian phone companies to revamp Cuba's

antiquated phone system. By the early 2000s many Cubans who never had phones were able to get service, and the quality and reliability also improved.

9. Later in the summer, when the energy shortage reached even greater crisis proportions and the blackouts were endless, this window and all the windows in the museum were covered with plywood to guard against their becoming targets of the frustrated rock-throwing youth who took to the streets that hot August of 1993.

CHAPTER 1   INTERRACIAL COUPLES
FROM COLONY TO REVOLUTION

1. For more on race and Afrocuban participation in the independence war, see Aline Helg (1995) and Ada Ferrer (1999).

2. In Argentina miscegenation became a partial explanation for the apparent disappearance of blacks as a separate group; and, as a result, Argentineans discounted miscegenation as a major factor in the formation of their modern society, which they attribute to massive European immigration after 1880, and thus constructed an national image of themselves as white Europeans (W. Wright 1990). Brazilians, by contrast, thought of miscegenation as an essential contributor to formation of their national image, which was exalted in the mid-1900s by cultural nationalists such as Gilberto Freyre, a student of Franz Boas (W. Wright 1990). Citing Boas to disprove biological theories of race, Freyre stressed instead environmental factors, which, of course, discounted the belief that the inferior races could not advance (Skidmore 1990). During the 1890s, Venezuelan elites lamented the lack of whites in their country and attributed political and economic stagnation to the presence of a predominantly mixed-race population and so supported white immigration as a panacea for their problems. However, they soon shifted to more moderate views of race and an acceptance of a tricolor population and, along with Brazil, adopted the idea of a "racial democracy." Recently, the idea of racial democracy in Latin America has been challenged. See Amalia Simpson (1993), Robin Sheriff (2001), and France Twine (1998) on Brazil, Peter Wade (1993) on Colombia, and Winthrop Wright (1990) on Venezuela.

3. See Everett Stonequist (1937) for early twentieth-century views on social position and marginality of mixed-race individuals in various societies. Also see William Provine (1973) for history of scientific theories of racial mixing.

4. Even during the colonial period some free blacks and mulattos were able to attain a certain social status and wealth as skilled craftsman or sometimes as landowners.

5. The United States joined the Cuban independence war when victory for Cuba was imminent and then occupied Cuba from 1899 to 1902. In 1901 the

United States agreed to withdraw its troops on condition that Cuba append the Platt Amendment to its constitution. The U.S. military occupied Cuba again from 1906 to 1909. The Platt Amendment granted the United States the right to intervene militarily in Cuba; it remained in effect until 1934.

6. The first discoverer is Christopher Columbus and the second is the German naturalist Alexander von Humboldt. Interestingly, Fernando Ortiz is the only Cuban in this trilogy. According to Paul Ryer (2006), the "third discoverer" title was coined by Cuban scholar Juan Marinello in his 1969 essay on Ortiz, published in the journal *Casa de las Américas.*

7. See Alejandra Bronfman (2004) for a discussion of Ortiz's work on the Cuban Penal Code as well as his engagement with and subsequent distancing from penitentiary anthropology and Lombrosian criminology.

8. This critique is not true for historical accounts of race in Cuba, which have offered sophisticated and nuanced analyses of racial dynamics in nineteenth- and twentieth-century Cuba (See Bronfman 2004; de la Fuente 2001; Helg 1995; Kutzinski 1993; Martínez-Alier 1989; and R. Moore 1997).

9. Helen Safa (2005) notes that in revolutionary Cuba legal marriage has lost much of its importance as the symbol of status and religious respectability, due in part to the decline in the influence of the Catholic Church and to a more liberal conceptualization of sexuality, in which virginity is no longer the mark of virtue.

10. Analyzing 1981 census data, researchers find that 93.1 percent of all white heads of households are married to whites, 70.1 percent of black heads of households are married to blacks, and 68.7 percent of mestizo heads of households are married to mestizos (Reca Moreira et al. 1990, 50–51).

11. The researchers reported the racial breakdown in the Barrio Chino as 42 percent white, 21 percent black, 34 percent mestizo, and 3 percent other. In Carraguao the racial breakdown was 43 percent white, 22 percent black, and 35 percent mestizo (Rodríguez Ruiz 2004).

CHAPTER 2   SOCIALIST EQUALITY AND
THE COLOR-BLIND REVOLUTION

Alan Dundes defines *piropos* as publicly made verbal comments by men toward women. The comments, ostensibly complimentary, can often be insulting or crude and usually focus on the woman's physical features (Dundes and Suárez-Orozco 1987).

1. This is not to imply that race was not a political issue before the revolution. See Alejandro de la Fuente's (2001) book for a detailed account of race and politics under the Cuba republic and the Cuban revolution.

2. Jafari Allen (2003), writing on black masculinities in Cuba, documents how black masculine sexuality is characterized as dangerous and aggressive in Cuban literature and popular culture.

3. Many (Booth 1976; Casal 1979; de la Fuente 2001; Hoffman and Hoffman 1993; C. Moore 1988; Sawyer 2006; Taylor 1988) have noted that despite this effort, Afrocubans continue to be scarce in leadership positions.

4. Housing, however, has remained a severe problem. The current housing short-age and the deteriorated state of much housing, especially in Havana, is more acute than before the revolution in 1959 (Díaz-Briquets and Pérez 1987).

5. In Marxist-Leninist doctrine nationalism itself is perceived as epiphenom-enal, despite this fact it has been used as a unifying force by every socialist government (Verdery 1996).

6. During the years of the Cuban republic, the Afrocuban societies, such as Atenas, were mutual support groups and civic organizations. They served as a political voice for blacks and mulattos and as public platforms for black and mulatto intellectuals (de la Fuente 1998a, 2001). See de la Fuente 2001, 280–282, for a more complete history of the closure of the Afrocuban societ-ies in the early 1960s.

7. Carlos Moore's interpretation, while thought provoking, has also been criticized (Brock and Cunningham 1991; de la Fuente 2001). Lisa Brock finds Moore's argument weakened by his use of hearsay, his overgeneralizations, his lack of solid references and historical context, and his use of a narrow racialized framework (Brock and Cunningham 1991).

8. See Mark Sawyer (2006) for a more detailed discussion of African American activists' views on Cuba.

CHAPTER 3   MAPPING INTERRACIAL COUPLES:
RACE AND SPACE IN HAVANA

1. Habana Vieja is currently undergoing massive restoration and has been designed a UNESCO World Heritage Site. Some of the residents have been removed from historic buildings and relocated—sometimes out of the city center. See Mette Berg (2005) and Matthew Hill (2004) for more details on this process and its effects on the populations in Habana Vieja.

2. Housing was a hot-button public issue even in the 1950s before the revolu-tion came to power. In the 1970s the government mobilized construction microbrigades, mostly in Havana, to accelerate housing construction, but even this effort was insufficient to meet growing demand (J. Domínguez 1978). By the end of 1989, the housing crisis, especially in Havana, had deepened to the degree that only half of the 528,000 dwellings in Havana were classified to be in good condition, 23 percent in fair condition, and 23 percent in bad condition.

3. Urban planner Jill Hamberg notes that without the revolution many of these barrios may have been demolished or gentrified, as there were plans in the 1950s to develop high rises in Old Havana and along the Malecón in Centro Habana (personal communication, October 12, 2007).

4. The Cuban tendency toward a diffuse and unothodox religiosity was noted by Fernando Ortiz and still continues today, according to more recent research (see Ayorinde 2004).

5. Before the 1990s the city parks had been well maintained; however, the city no longer had the resources to maintain all of the parks, and many, such as Parque Trillo, quickly fell into disrepair.

6. The artist Florencio Gelabert, unhappy with the first version of *Quintín Bandera,* later replaced the statue with a superior rendition on August 23, 1953, the forty-seventh anniversary of Bandera's death.

7. Allan Pred (2000) found a similar pattern in Sweden, where segregated immigrant suburbs perceived to be problematic areas, in fact, had a lower-than-average crime rate for youth, compared to low-income public housing areas without a high density of immigrants. He argued that inaccurate images of immigrant areas played on widespread fears and uncertainties caused by various economic and political crises in Sweden in the 1990s.

8. In the introduction to his book, *Los Negros Curros,* Fernando Ortiz expresses shame and asks the reader to pardon him for describing such an unsavory segment of black urban life that "un siglo después . . . en nuestra tierra no ha muerto del todo el halito de la currería [a century later . . . in our land all traces of *currería* have not died]" (1986, 2). Thus, Ortiz acknowledges the thread of continuity between the eighteenth-century *negros curros* and their contemporaries, the guapos. Negros curros were known for their delinquency and their dangerousness, which, along with their economic position and their free status, clearly made them a threat to the existing order of the colonial slave society. Thus, in paradoxical ways the free curros were both socially marginal and high status in the context of colonial Cuban society.

9. The Tropical is a legendary outdoor beer/dance garden on the outskirts of Havana where many of the popular salsa bands perform. When I went to the Tropical in the early 1990s, there was an enormous line to enter and an even more impressive police presence. Men were practically frisked before entering, and people in line were struck with billyclubs to force them into a single file. The audience was predominately black—with the exception of some elderly white men going there to buy beer, not to hear the music. The Tropical was one of the many venues where Afrocubans experienced police control. It was also notorious for violent fights that sometimes erupted during the concerts. Photographer David Turnley made an insightful documentary titled *La Tropical* in 2002. *Casino* refers to both salsa music and salsa dancing. Carlos Paz Pérez defined *casino* as a Cuban dance and then added the following quote, "*El casino es baile de guapos*" (1994, 144).

10. Gisela Arandia Covarrubias is a black researcher and independent scholar living in Havana. Her comment was in response to a paper I pre-

sented on interracial couples and divisions among youth at the annual U.S.-Cuba Philosophy Conference held at the University of Havana, June 23–25, 1993.

11. The CD was named after a painteresque homeless man who wandered the streets in Havana and called himself El Ilustrado Caballero de Paris (the Illustrious Gentleman from Paris). He is now memorialized in a bronze statue in Old Havana. As Havana had so few homeless people on the streets—a testament to the success of the socialist safety net—they were often neighborhood fixtures and known to all. Cayo Hueso also had one mentally ill man who regularly paraded through the barrio with a makeshift military uniform and toy sword. He was called "the General." Lyrics used with permission of the author.

12. Other religious systems include the all-male secret Abakuá society, originating in the Epke society of the Cross River region of southeastern Nigeria; Palo Monte–Bantu religious cults from the Congo region; and, to a lesser extent, Arará and Vodu (Barnet 2001).

13. However, learning about Afrocuban traditions is not so easy. As Robin Moore (2006) discusses, the opportunities to study Afrocuban performative culture in music conservatories are still marginal, at best. The situation is even grimmer at the universities, where even today Afrocuban subjects are largely absent from the curricula (R. Moore 2006). Extracurricular lectures or summer workshops are often the only options for instruction on Afrocuban subjects, and, according to Moore (2006), these are often poorly attended.

CHAPTER 4   THE EVERYDAY PRESENCE OF RACE

1. Here Alejandro de la Fuente (2008) is drawing on Edward Telles's concept of "racist culture" that naturalizes the subordination of nonwhites and therefore curtails the analysis of racial inequality (see Telles 2004).

2. Stuart Hall (1986) notes that although Antonio Gramsci (1971) was not writing specifically about race, a number of his emphases can greatly enhance the analysis of race and ethnicity: the focus on historical particularity, regional and national characteristics, the dismissal of economic reductionism, and the centrality Gramsci gave to the cultural factor in social development.

3. Tomás Fernández Robaina is referring to the serial *La Guerra de los Palmares* (1991, 38).

4. Cirilo Villaverde himself had a reputation as a "*mulatero*" (a man who loved mulatas) (R. González 1993).

5. The prevalence of the love triangle theme is not only about representations of reality on stage. It was through the unequal power dynamics of the interracial couple that blackface *teatro bufo* performances were able to depict colonial exploitation under Spanish rule, and this made the genre a unique

expression of national Cuban, not Spanish, culture. The oppression of the Afrocubans as portrayed in the shows was conflated with the experience of the entire nation under colonial rule. Spanish authorities censored and at times banned the productions, forcing shows to rely increasingly on allusion and allegory to voice political critique (R. Moore 1997).

6. *Gallegos* refers to people from the Galicia region in northwestern Spain. Many Spanish migrants in Cuba originated from this region.

7. Gisela Fosado (2004) examines the concept of relations *"por interés"* in her work on *pingueros* (male sex workers) in contemporary Cuba.

8. Stereotypical images of blacks were also shared by blacks themselves. Iris, a black university student dating a white man, proudly spoke of the sexual prowess of blacks and the sensuality of black women that white men found attractive.

9. The 2002 novel *Dirty Havana Trilogy,* by Cuban author Pedro Juan Gutiérrez, certainly supports David Forrest's (1999) claim.

CHAPTER 5   BLACKNESS, WHITENESS, CLASS, AND THE EMERGENT ECONOMY

1. Scholars question whether or not the special period has ended and, if so, when. The Cuban minister of Economy and Planning told journalists in September 2006 that the Cuban GDP had returned to 1989 levels, marking the end of the special period (hence the end date I note here). Jorge Pérez-López (2006) argues, however, that the special period can be defined two ways: (1) by levels of production and consumption and (2) by policies of experimentation and reform. According to the first definition, by 2006 some sectors of the Cuban economy surpassed 1989 levels of production, but many other sectors remained depressed, so Pérez-Lópcz argues that by this measure the special period continues. From the second definition, he concludes that the special period has ended since the economic recovery (however uneven) has meant that the government no longer needs liberalizing reforms and thus returned to centralization in 2005 (Pérez-López 2006).

2. *Paladares* were named after a catering business in a Brazilian soap opera, *Vale Todo,* that was broadcast in Cuba in 1992 and 1993. In the soap opera, Raquel, a poor woman, goes from selling homemade sandwiches on the beach to running her own highly successful catering company named Paladar. This rags-to-riches story was, of course, the dream of every Cuban *paladar* operator.

3. U.S. dollars were used as legal tender in these stores until 2004, when the Cuban government introduced the Cuban Convertible Peso, or CUC, as it is commonly known.

4. Anthropologists have begun to explore this phenomenon in other parts of the world. See Nicole Constable (2003, 2005).

5. Nueva Trova artist Gerardo Alfonso sings of one such long-distance international romance in his song "Espacio de Mar" on his 2001 album *El Ilustrado Caballero de París.*

6. Both live and met in a university dormitory, as Olga comes from La Isla de Juventud and José Miguel from the central province of Santi Espiritus. They had been together over three years at the time of our interview.

7. This is not the first time Cuba has drawn on its Spanish roots to emphasize a white national identity. Juan Martínez (2000) documents the *origenista* movement in art in the 1940s, which promoted a white-criollo national identity in part in response to the Afrocubanismo movement of the previous decade. In the 1990s the revival of the Spanish cultural societies in Havana is another example of Cubans reclaiming their Spanish/white roots.

8. White, middle-class households also relied on the dollar black market but sometimes had more direct connections and access to desired goods. For example, one friend often gave dollars received as remittances to a neighbor who worked for the Cuban/foreign joint venture and traveled abroad frequently. She would purchase cases of soap, detergent, or cooking oil at wholesale prices much lower than those in the dollar stores in Havana. Like all black-market activities, these exchanges took place through personal networks, but the family's race and class position and their constant access to dollars provided them contacts with a broader and more well-positioned set of people.

9. These included anything from spare parts to light bulbs to plastic cutlery. He checked these warehouses almost daily in his search of items to ply his trade. The functioning of the black market depended on networks of *socios* (friends), like Jaime's warehouse connections. The importance of personal connections has long been part of life in Cuba. Oscar Lewis's team of anthropologists noted this trend in the late 1960s. Almost everything had to be done through the proper channels, a process involving a good deal of bureaucratic red tape. To speed up action, many Cubans rely on informal personal contacts with friends, relatives, associates, or anyone willing to help them. These strategically placed persons are known as socios, and the use of them exists to such a degree that some Cubans jokingly call their system *socioismo* instead of *socialismo* (Lewis, Lewis, and Rigdon 1977, xiii).

10. The 1981 census found that nuclear families comprise 60 percent of households in Cuba. In urban areas, the percentage of nuclear families is slightly lower at 57 percent (Reca Moreira et al. 1990, 41). Marguerite Rosenthal suggests that the sharing of housing and other material resources among extended families may result not solely from the shortage of housing but from traditional patterns of mutual aid found in Latin America and among economically disadvantaged people in general (1992, 168).

11. Jaime's grandmother raised both him and his sister. The grandmother had been so strict in guarding his sister's virginity that she basically was not

allowed out as an adolescent. The sister's response was to marry while she was still a virgin at seventeen (grandmother's triumph, in Jaime's words), give birth to her son at eighteen, and divorce at nineteen, leaving the child with the grandmother to raise. Later during my fieldwork, his sister moved in with and then married her boyfriend, a man twenty-five years her senior (who himself had a daughter around her age) and had her second child with him. Her first son, however, continued to live with her grandmother and Jaime.

12. For several months in 1992, the government sold baby chicks to the people. Many Habaneros saw this as an opportunity to supplement their families' meat and egg consumption and quickly built makeshift cages on their balconies or in windows to house the tiny, fluffy chicks. However, the task of raising chickens bred to survive on a specialized diet of processed feed in urban conditions, where they received only meager table scraps and vitamin pills meant for human consumption, proved extremely difficult. Most of the chicks died, and the few who survived grew into scrawny, unsightly creatures that rarely laid eggs and were usually far more bone than meat. Some people, like Jaime's family, bought hardier and less finicky *criollo* chicks from *campesinos* and were, indeed, able to increase the family meat/egg consumption a bit.

13. It should be noted, however, that there are also many whites who are believers and practitioners of Afrocuban religions. Some scholars have recently argued that, in fact, Santería has become the country's national religion and is widely practiced and accepted by Cubans of all skin colors and social groups (Ayorinde 2004).

CHAPTER 6   INTERRACIAL COUPLES AND RACISM AT HOME

1. Elsewhere I explore the reemergence of race in the public domain (Fernandez 2001).

EPILOGUE

1. Among the special issues on the revolution, see the two *Latin American Perspectives* 2009 issues (vol. 36, no. 5 and 6). The Cuban journal *Temas* is also planning a commemorative issue to be published in 2009, and an international conference titled "The Measure of a Revolution: Cuba, 1959–2009" was held at Queen's University in Kingston, Canada, in May of 2009.

2. There are various versions of the myth which set the time of the apparition anywhere between 1604 and 1628 (Arrom 1990). Cuban historian Olga Portuondo Zúñiga carefully documents the emergence of this icon of the nation and the evolution of the original story. The names and number of the boats' occupants, their occupations, and their races can vary. Portuondo Zúñiga (2001) cites the Indians' names as Rodrigo and Diego, not Juan, de Hoyos and notes that over the centuries the boats' occupants have been described

as one white, one black, and one mulatto or Indian, or as all white or all black. Some versions present them as fishermen, while others claim they were mining salt.

3. Ochún, wife of Orula (San Francisco de Asisi), is the beautiful and flirtatious mistress of one of the major deities, Changó, whom she lured with her honey-drenched lips. Legend has it that vanity made the impoverished Ochún wash her only dress so often that it yellowed, the color which now represents her (Rosete Silva 1993). She is the patroness of rivers, love, and fertility. She is symbolized by pumpkins, mirrors, fans, seashells, and yellow metals and is said to rule over the abdominal region of the body.

4. She is also thought by some (I. Wright 1928) to be associated with the Spanish Virgin de la Caridad de Illescas, although the similarities and connections between the two virgins have been disputed (González y Arocha 1928; Portuondo Zúñiga 2001).

5. Recent publications provide an excellent and detailed analysis of the trends within the musical genre of rap and the visual art world (see de la Fuente 2008; Fernandes 2006).

REFERENCES

Adams, David. 2009. Cuba's aim: Tourist magnet. *St. Petersburg Times,* January 26, 2009.

Alfonso Wells, Shawn. 2004. Cuban color classification and identity negotiation: Old terms in a new world. PhD diss., University of Pittsburgh.

Allen, Jafari Sinclaire. 2003. Counterpoints: Black masculinities, sexuality, and self-making in contemporary Cuba. PhD diss., Columbia University.

Alvarado Ramos, Juan Antonio. 1996. Relaciones raciales en Cuba: Notas de investigación. *Temas* 7:37–43.

———. 1998. Estereotipos y prejuicios raciales en tres barrios habaneros. *América Negra* 15: 89–115.

Ames, David W. 1950. Negro family types in a Cuban solar. *Phylon* 11(2):159–163.

Arandia Covarrubias, Gisela. 1994. Strengthening nationality: Blacks in Cuba. *Contributions in Black Studies* 12:62–69.

Arrom, José Juan. 1990. La Virgen del Cobre: Historia, leyenda y símbolo sincrético. In *Estudios Afro-Cubanos: Selección de lecturas*, vol. 2, ed. L. Menéndez, 269–310. Havana: Facultad de Artes y Letras Universidad de la Habana.

Ayorinde, Christine. 2004. *Afro-Cuban religiosity, revolution, and national identity.* Gainesville: University of Florida Press.

Bair, Barbara. 1999. Remapping the black/white body: Sexuality, nationalism, and biracial antimiscegenation activism in 1920s Virginia. In *Sex, love, race: Crossing boundaries in North American history*, ed. M. Hodes, 399–422. New York: New York University Press.

Bardaglio, Peter. 1999. "Shameful matches": The regulation of interracial sex and marriage in the South before 1900. In *Sex, love, race: Crossing boundaries in North American history*, ed. M. Hodes, 112–138. New York: New York University Press.

Barnet, Miguel. 2001. *Afro-Cuban religions.* Princeton, NJ: Markus Wiener Publishers.

Bastide, Roger. 1961. Dusky Venus, Black Apollo. *Race* 3(1):10–18.

Beatriz, Mayra. 1990. Sencillamente amor: En blanco y negro. *Somos Jóvenes* 123:2–9.

Bell, Diane, Pat Caplan, and Wazir Jahan Karim. 1993. *Gendered fields: Women, men, and ethnography.* New York: Routledge.

Benítez-Rojo, Antonio. 1992. *The repeating island: The Caribbean and the postmodern perspective.* Trans. J. E. Maraniss. Durham: Duke University Press.

Berg, Mette Louise. 2005. Localising Cubanness: Social exclusion and narratives of belonging in Old Havana. In *Caribbean narratives of belonging: Fields of relations, sites of identity*, ed. Jean Besson and Karen Fog Olwig, 133–148. Warwick University Caribbean Studies. Oxford: Macmillan Caribbean.

Bobo, Lawrence. 2000. Race and beliefs about affirmative action: Assessing the effects of interest group threat, ideology, and racism. In *Racialized politics: The debate about racism in America,* ed. David Sears, Jim Sidanius, and Lawrence Bobo, 137–164. Chicago: University of Chicago Press.

Booth, David. 1976. Cuba, color and the revolution. *Science and Society* 11(2):129–172.

Brock, Lisa, and Otis Cunningham. 1991. Race and the Cuban revolution: A critique of Carlos Moore's *Castro, the blacks and Africa. Cuban Studies* 21:171–185.

Bronfman, Alejandra Marina. 2004. *Measures of equality: Social science, citizenship, and race in Cuba, 1902–1940.* Chapel Hill: University of North Carolina Press.

Burawoy, Michael, and Katherine Verdery. 1999. *Uncertain transition: Ethnographies of change in the postsocialist world.* Lanham, MD: Rowman and Littlefield.

Burke, Nancy Jean. 2001. Creating islands in the desert: Place, space, and ritual among Santería practioners in Albuquerque, New Mexico. PhD diss., University of New Mexico.

Butterworth, Douglas. 1980. *The people of Buena Ventura: Relocation of slum dwellers in postrevolutionary Cuba.* Urbana: University of Illinois Press.

Cabezas, Amalia. 1998. Discourses of prostitution: The case of Cuba. In *Global sex workers: Rights, resistance and redefinition,* ed. Kamala Kempadoo and Jo Doezema. New York: Routledge.

Calderon, Mirta, Félix Contreras, Ariel Terrero, P. Juan Gutiérrez, and Claribel Terre. 1993. Pasiones y prejuicios. *Bohemia* 85:4–9.

Caño Secade, María del Carmen. 1996. Relaciones raciales, proceso de ajuste y politica social. *Temas* 7:58–66.

Carbonell, Walterio. 1961. *Crítica, cómo surgió la cultura nacional.* Havana: Editorial Yaka.

Carneado, José Felipe. 1962. La discriminación racial en Cuba no volverá jamás. *Cuba Socialista* 2(5):54–67.

Casal, Lourdes. 1979. Race relations in contemporary Cuba: The position of blacks in Brazilian and Cuban society. *Minority Rights Group Report* 7:11–27.

Castillo Bueno, María de los Reyes. 2000. *Reyita: The life of a black Cuban woman in the twentieth century, as told to her daughter Daisy Rubiera Castillo.* Trans. A. McLean. Durham, NC: Duke University Press.

Castro, Fidel. 1959a. Discurso. *Revolución,* March 23, 1959, 24+.

———. 1959b. El espiritu renovador va a superar al tradicionalista. *Revolución,* March 26, 1959, 1+.

———. 1963. Castro defines the theory of the Cuban revolution. *El Sol,* May 10, 1963, 4+.

Cervera, Elvira. 2000. Todo en sepia: An all-black theater project. In *Afro-Cuban voices: On race and identity in contemporary Cuba,* ed. Pedro Pérez Sarduy and Jean Stubbs. Contemporary Cuba. Gainesville: University of Florida Press.

Clytus, John. 1970. *Black man in red Cuba.* Coral Gables: University of Miami Press.

Colantonio, Andrea, and Robert B. Potter. 2006. *Urban tourism and development in the socialist state: Havana during the "Special Period."* Burlington: Ashgate.

Cole, Johnetta. 1986. *Race toward equality.* Havana: José Martí.

Cole, Sally. 2003. *Ruth Landes: A life in anthropology.* Lincoln: University of Nebraska Press.

Comité Estatal de Estadísticas. 1981. *Censo de la población y viviendas: Provincia de Ciudad de la Habana.* Havana: Comité Estatal de Estadísticas.

Constable, Nicole. 2003. *Romance on a global stage: Pen pals, virtual ethnography, and "mail-order" marriages.* Berkeley: University of California Press.

———. 2005. *Cross-border marriages: Gender and mobility in transnational Asia.* Philadelphia: University of Pennsylvania Press.

Coyula, Mario, and Jill Hamberg. 2003. Understanding slums: The case of Havana, Cuba. In *Working Papers on Latin America.* Cambridge: Harvard University, David Rockefeller Center for Latin American Studies.

Coyula, Mario, Rosa Oliveras, and Miguel Coyula. 2002. *Towards a new kind of community in Havana: The Workshops for Integrated Neighborhood Transformations.* Havana: Group for the Integrated Development of the Capital.

Crabb, Mary Katherine. 2001. Socialism, health, and medicine in Cuba: A critical re-appraisal. PhD diss., Emory University.

Daniel, Yvonne. 1994. Race, gender, and class embodied in Cuban dance. *Contributions in Black Studies* 12:70–87.

———. 1995. *Rumba: Dance and social change in contemporary Cuba.* Bloomington: Indiana University Press.

Davidson, Julia O'Connell. 1996. Sex tourism in Cuba. *Race and Class* 38(1):39–48.

Davis, Kingsley. 1941. Intermarriage in caste societies. *American Anthropologist* 43(3):376–395.

de la Fuente, Alejandro. 1995. Race and inequality in Cuba, 1899–1981. *Journal of Contemporary History* 30:131–167.

———. 1998a. Race, national discourse, and politics in Cuba: An overview. *Latin American Perspectives* 25(3):43–69.

———. 1998b. Recreating racism: Race and discrimination in Cuba's Special Period. In *Cuba Briefing Paper Series,* no. 18, ed. Gillian Gunn Clissold. Washington, DC: Georgetown University.

———. 2001. *A nation for all.* Chapel Hill: University of North Carolina Press.

———. 2008. The new Afro-Cuban cultural movement and the debate on race in contemporary Cuba. *Journal of Latin American Studies* 40:697–720.

del Olmo, Rosa. 1979. The Cuban Revolution and the struggle against prostitution. *Crime and Social Justice* (winter): 34–39.

Depestre, René. 1965. Lettre de Cuba. *Presense Africaine* 65:102–142.

Díaz, Elena, Esperanza Fernández, and Tania Caram. 1996. *Report: Turismo y prostitución en Cuba.* Habana: Facultad Latinoamericana de Ciencias Sociales.

Díaz-Briquets, Sergio. 2008. Remittances to Cuba: An update. *Annual Meetings of the Association for the Study of the Cuban Economy* (ASCE), Miami, Florida, 2008. 18:154–159.

Díaz-Briquets, Sergio, and Lisandro Pérez. 1987. The demography of revolution. In *Cuban Communism,* ed. I. Horowitz, 409–436. New Brunswick, NJ: Transaction.

Domínguez, Jorge. 1978. *Cuba: Order and revolution.* Cambridge: Harvard University Press.

Domínguez, María Isabel. 1989. *Parte 1: Estructura generacional de la población cubana actual.* Habana: Centro de Investigaciones Psicologicas y Sociologicas, Academia de Ciencias de Cuba.

Domínguez, María Isabel, María Elena Ferrer, and María Victoria Valdés. 1989. *Parte 2: Diferencias y relaciones intergeneracionales en la clase obrera y los trabajadores intelectuales.* Habana: Centro de Investigaciones Psicologicas y Sociologicas, Academia de Ciencias de Cuba.

————. 1990. *Parte 4: Características generacionales de los estudiantes y los desvinculados del estudio y el trabajo*. Havana: Centro de Investigaciones Psicologicas y Sociologicas, Academia de Ciencias de Cuba.

Dubisch, Jill. 1995. Lovers in the field: Sex, dominance and the female anthropologist. In *Taboo: Sex, identity and erotic subjectivity in anthropological fieldwork*, ed. Don Kulick and Margaret Willson, 29–50. New York: Routledge.

Duharte Jiménez, Rafael. 1993. The nineteenth-century black fear. In *Afrocuba: An anthology of Cuban writing on race, politics and culture*, ed. Pedro Pérez Sarduy and Jean Stubbs, 37–46. Melbourne: Ocean Press.

Duharte Jiménez, Rafael, and Elsa Santos García. 1998. *El fantasma de la esclavitud: Prejuicios raciales en Cuba y America Latina*. Bonn: Pahl-Rugenstein Verlag.

Dundes, Alan, with Marcelo M. Suárez-Orozco. 1987. The piropo and the dual image of women in the Spanish-speaking world. In *Parsing through customs: Essays by a Freudian folklorist*. Madison: University of Wisconsin Press.

Eckert, Penelope. 1989. *Jocks and burnouts: Social categories and identity in high school*. New York: Teachers College Press.

Espina Prieto, Rodrigo, and Pablo Rodríguez Ruiz. 2006. Raza y desigualdad en la Cuba actual. *Temas* 45:44–54.

Espino, Maria Dolores. 1993. Tourism in Cuba: A development strategy for the 1990s? *Cuban Studies* 23:49–69.

Essed, Philomena. 1991. *Understanding everyday racism*. Newbury Park, CA: Sage.

Estroff, Sue E. 1981. *Making it crazy: An ethnography of psychiatric clients in an American community*. Berkeley: University of California Press.

Fernandes, Sujatha. 2006. *Cuba represent! Cuban arts, state power and the making of new revolutionary cultures*. Durham, NC: Duke University Press.

Fernandez, Nadine. 1999. Back to the future? Women, race, and tourism in Cuba. In *Sex, sun, and gold: Tourism and sex work in the Caribbean*, ed. Kamala Kempadoo, 81–92. Boulder: Rowman and Littlefield.

————. 2001. The changing discourse on race in contemporary Cuba. *International Journal of Qualitative Studies in Education* 14(2):117–132.

Fernández Robaina, Tomás. 1991. *La lucha contra la discriminación racial y el prejuicio en Cuba, 1959–1991*. Havana.

————. 1993. The twentieth-century black question. In *Afrocuba: An anthology of Cuban writing on race, politics and culture*, ed. Pedro Pérez Sarduy and Jean Stubbs, 92–108. Melbourne: Ocean Press.

————. 1998. Marcus Garvey in Cuba: Urrutia, Cubans and black nationalism. In *Between race and empire: African-Americans and Cubans before the Cuban Revolution*, ed. Lisa Brock and Digna Castañeda Fuertes, 120–128. Philadelphia: Temple University Press.

Ferrer, Ada. 1998. The silence of patriots: Race and nationalism in Martí's Cuba. In *José Martí "Our America,"* ed. Jeffrey Belnap and Raul Fernandez, 228–249. New Americanists. Durham: Duke University Press.

————. 1999. *Insurgent Cuba: Race, nationalism, and revolution, 1868–1898*. Chapel Hill: University of North Carolina Press.

Foner, Philip S. 1977. *"Our America" by José Martí: Writings on Latin America and the struggle for Cuban independence*. New York: Monthly Review Press.

Forrest, David Peter. 1999. Bichos, maricones and pingueros: An ethnographic study of maleness and scarcity in contemporary socialist Cuba. PhD diss., University of London.

Fosado, Gisela C. 2004. The exchange of sex for money in contemporary Cuba: Masculinity, ambiguity, and love. PhD diss., University of Michigan.

Foucault, Michel. 1980. *Power/knowledge: Selected interviews and other writings.* New York: Pantheon.

Frankenberg, Ruth. 1993. *The social construction of whiteness: White women, race matters.* Minneapolis: University of Minnesota Press.

Fusco, Coco. 1998. Hustling for dollars: Jineterismo in Cuba. In *Global sex workers: Rights, resistance and redefinition,* ed. Kamala Kempadoo and Jo Doezema, 151–166. New York: Routledge.

Geertz, Clifford. 1975. Common sense as a cultural system. *Antioch Review* 33(1):5–26.

Goldstein, Donna. 1999. Interracial sex and racial democracy in Brazil: Twin concepts? *American Anthropologist* 101(3):563–578.

González, Gilberto. 2008. El Callejón de Hamel. In *Radio Coco Cuba.* http://www.radiococo.cu/miciudad/ciudad06.htm (accessed September 18, 2008).

González, Reynaldo. 1993. A white problem: Reinterpreting Cecilia Valdés. In *Afrocuba: An anthology of Cuban writing on race, politics and culture,* ed. Pedro Pérez Sarduy and Jean Stubbs, 204–213. Melbourne: Ocean Press.

González y Arocha, Guillermo. 1928. La piadosa tradición de la Caridad del Cobre. *Archivos del Folklore Cubano* 3(2):97–114.

Gould, Stephen Jay. 1981. *The mismeasure of man.* New York: W. W. Norton.

Graham, Richard. 1990. *The idea of race in Latin America, 1870–1940.* Austin: University of Texas Press.

Gramsci, Antonio. 1971. *Selections from the prison notebooks.* New York: International Publishers.

Gross, Liza. 2008. Race-based clubs see revival in Cuba. *Miami Herald,* December 28, 2008.

Guanche, Jesus. 1977. *Etnología: Cuba panorama etnografico.* Habana: Ministerio de Cultura.

Guillén, Nicolás. 1959. Una revisión entre otras. *Hoy,* March 29, 1959, 1,3.

Guimeras, Gilda. 2004. Un parque con el sabor de lo propio. http//: www.lacalle.cubaweb.cu/ cuadra/trillo.htm (accessed February 23, 2004).

Gutiérrez, Pedro Juan. 1992. Hablar de amor: Blancos y Negros, obstaculos? *Bohemia* 84:4–7.

Hall, Stuart. 1981. The whites of their eyes: Racist ideologies and the media. In *Silver linings: Some strategies for the eighties,* ed. George Bridges and Rosalind Brunt, 28–52. London: Lawrence and Wishart.

———. 1986. Gramsci's relevance for the study of race and ethnicity. *Journal of Communication Inquiry* 10(2):5–27.

———. 1992. Race, culture, and communications: Looking backward and forward at cultural studies. *Rethinking Marxism* 5(1):11–18.

Hamilton, Douglas. 2002. Whither Cuban socialism? The changing political economy of the Cuban Revolution. *Latin American Perspectives* 29(3):18–39.

Harris, Marvin. 1970. Referential ambiguity in the calculus of Brazilian racial identity. *Southwestern Journal of Anthropology* 26(1):1–14.

Hannerz, Ulf. 1992. *Cultural complexity: Studies in the social organization of meaning.* New York: Columbia University Press.

Harrison, Faye V. 1998. Introduction: Expanding the discourse on "race." *American Anthropologist* 100(3):609–631.

———. 2008. *Outsider within: Reworking anthropology in the global age.* Urbana: University of Illinois Press.

Hearn, Adrian H. 2004. Afro-Cuban religions and social welfare: Consequences of commercial development in Havana. *Human Organization: Journal of the Society for Applied Anthropology* 63(1):78–87.

———. 2008. *Cuba: Religion, social capital, and development.* Durham, NC: Duke University Press.

Helg, Aline. 1990. Race in Argentina and Cuba, 1880–1930: Theory, policies, and popular reaction. In *The idea of race in Latin America, 1870–1940*, ed. Richard Graham, 37–70. Austin: University of Texas Press.

———. 1995. *Our rightful share: The Afro-Cuban struggle for equality, 1886–1912.* Chapel Hill: University of North Carolina Press.

Hernandez-Reguant, Ariana. 2002. Radio Taino and the globalization of the Cuban culture industries. PhD diss., University of Chicago.

———. 2005. Cuba's alternative geographies. *Journal of Latin American Anthropology* 10(2):275–313.

Herrera, Georgina. 2000. Poetry, prostitution, and gender esteem. In *Afro-Cuban voices: On race and identity in contemporary Cuba,* ed. Pedro Pérez Sarduy and Jean Stubbs, 118–126. Gainesville: University of Florida Press.

Hill, Matthew. 2004. Globalizing Havana: World heritage and urban redevelopment in late socialist Cuba. PhD, University of Chicago.

———. 2007. Reimagining Old Havana: World heritage and the production of scale in late socialist Cuba. In *Deciphering the global: Its spaces, scales, and subjects,* ed. Saskia Sassen, 59–78. New York: Routledge.

Hodge, G. Derrick. 2001. Colonization of the Cuban body: The growth of male sex work in Havana. *North American Congress on Latin America Report on the Americas* 34(1):20–28.

———. 2006. Pragmatic socialism or neoliberal capitalism? Tourism and sustainable development in Special Period Cuba. Unpublished paper.

Hoffman, Edwin, and Jo Ann Hoffman. 1993. Race relating in Cuba. *Crossroads* 35:25–28.

Jones, Hettie. 1990. *How I became Hettie Jones.* New York: E. P. Dutton.

Kapcia, Antoni. 2005. *Havana: The making of Cuban culture.* New York: Berg.

———. 2009. Lessons of the Special Period: Learning to march again. *Latin American Perspectives* 36(1):30–41.

Karol, K. S. 1970. *Guerrillas in power.* New York: Hill and Wang.

Klor de Alva, J. Jorge. 1995. The postcolonization of the (Latin) American experience: A reconsideration of "colonialism," "postcolonialism," and "mestizaje." In *After colonialism: Imperial histories and postcolonial displacements*, ed. Gyan Prakash, 241–275. Princeton, NJ: Princeton University Press.

Knight, Alden. 2000. Tackling racism in performing arts and media. In *Afro-Cuban voices: On race and identity in contemporary Cuba,* ed. Pedro Pérez Sarduy and Jean Stubbs, 108–117. Gainesville: University of Florida Press.

Knight, Franklin. 1978. *The Caribbean: The genesis of a fragmented nationalism.* New York: Oxford University Press.

Kulick, Don, and Margaret Willson. 1995. *Taboo: Sex, identity, and erotic subjectivity in anthropological fieldwork.* New York: Routledge.

Kutzinski, Vera M. 1993. *Sugar's secrets: Race and the erotics of Cuban nationalism.* Charlottesville: University Press of Virginia.

Lancaster, Roger N. 1992. *Life is hard: Machismo, danger, and the intimacy of power in Nicaragua*. Berkeley: University of California Press.

Lewis, Oscar, Ruth Lewis, and Susan Rigdon. 1977. *Four men: Living the revolution, an oral history of contemporary Cuba*. Urbana: University of Illinois Press.

Logan, Enid Lynette. 2005. Holy sacraments and illicit encounters: Marriage, race, religion, and the transformation of status hierarchies in Cuba, 1899–1940. PhD diss., University of Michigan.

López Valdés, Rafael. 1973. Discrimination in Cuba. *Cuba Resource Center Newsletter* 11(6):6–14.

Low, Setha, and Denise Lawrence-Zúñiga. 2003. *The anthropology of space and place: Locating culture*. Malden: Blackwell.

Lumsden, Ian. 1996. *Machos, maricones, and gays: Cuba and homosexuality*. Philadelphia: Temple University Press.

Martín Chávez, Juan Luis. 1990. La juventud en la revolución Cubana: Notas sobre el camino recorrido y sus perspectivas. *Cuadernos de Nuestra América* 8(15):137–143.

Martínez, Juan A. 2000. Lo blanco-criollo as lo cubano: The symbolization of a Cuban national identity in modernist painting of the 1940s. In *Cuba, the elusive nation*, ed. Damian Fernandez and Madeline Betancourt, 277–291. Gainesville: University of Florida Press.

Martínez-Alier, Verena. 1989. *Marriage, class, and colour in nineteenth-century Cuba: A study of racial attitudes and sexual values in a slave society*. Ann Arbor: University of Michigan Press.

Martínez-Echazábal, Lourdes. 1998. Mestizaje and the discourse of national/cultural identity in Latin America. *Latin American Perspectives* 25(3)21–42.

Martínez Furé, Rogelio. 1993. Imaginary dialogue on folklore. In *Afrocuba: An anthology of Cuban writing on race, politics and culture*, ed. Pedro Pérez Sarduy and Jean Stubbs, 109–116. Melbourne: Ocean Press.

———. 2000. Homogenizing monomania and the plural heritage. In *Afro-Cuban voices: On race and identity in contemporary Cuba*, ed. Pedro Pérez Sarduy and Jean Stubbs, 154–161. Gainesville: University of Florida Press.

Masferrer, Marianne, and Carmelo Mesa-Lago. 1974. The gradual integration of the black in Cuba: Under the colony, the republic, and the revolution. In *Slavery and race relations in Latin America*, ed. R. B. Toplin, 348–384. Westport, CT: Greenwood.

McGarrity, Gayle. 1992. Race, culture, and social change in contemporary Cuba." In *Cuba in Transition*, ed. S. Halebsky and J. Kirk, 193–205. Boulder, CO: Westview.

Mealy, Rosemari. 1993. *Fidel and Malcolm X: Memories of a meeting*. Melbourne: Ocean Press.

Meethan, Kevin. 2001. *Tourism in global society: Place, culture, consumption*. New York: Palgrave.

Menéndez, Lázara y Raquel Mendieta. 1985. Cayo Hueso: Una experiencia cultural. *Temas* 7:41–56.

Miles, Robert. 1989. *Racism*. London: Routledge.

Minority Rights Group. 1995. *No longer invisible: Afro-Latin Americans today*. London: Minority Rights Group.

Montane Valdés, Estrella. 1986. Elementos causales influyentes en el elevado número de menores con trastornos de conductas y desviaciones socio-morales en la Barriada. Camagüey: Federación de Mujeres Cubanas. Unpublished report.

Moore, Carlos. 1988. *Castro, the blacks, and Africa.* Los Angeles: Center for Afro-American Studies, University of California, Los Angeles.

Moore, Robin. 1997. *Nationalizing blackness: Afrocubanismo and artistic revolution in Havana, 1920–40.* Pittsburgh: University of Pittsburgh Press.

———. 2006. *Music and revolution: Cultural change in socialist Cuba.* Berkeley: University of California Press.

Morales Domínguez, Esteban. 2008. *Challenges of the racial problem in Cuba.* Habana: Fundación Don Fernando Ortiz.

Moreno Fraginals, Manuel. 1978. *El Ingenio.* 3 vols. Havana: Editorial de Ciencias Sociales.

Morúa, Martín. 1975. *La Familia Unzúazu.* Havana: Editorial Arte y Literatura.

Mullings, Leith M. 2004. Race and globalization: Racialization from below. *Souls* 6(2):1–9.

———. 2005. Interrogating racism: Toward an antiracist anthropology. *Annual Review of Anthropology* 34:667–693.

Newton, Ester. 1993. My best informant's dress: The erotic equation in fieldwork. *Cultural Anthropology* 8(1):3–23.

Nodal, Roberto. 1986. The black man in Cuban society: From colonial times to the revolution. *Journal of Black Studies* 16(3):251–267.

Ortiz, Fernando. 1959. Cuba puede y debe dar el ejemplo en cuanto al desvanecimiento de los funestos racismos. *Hoy*, April 4, 1959.

———. 1975. *El engaño de las razas.* Habana: Editorial de Ciencias Sociales.

———. 1986. *Los Negros curros.* Habana: Editorial de Ciencias Sociales.

———. 1993a. *Etnia y sociedad.* Habana: Editorial de Ciencias Sociales.

———. 1993b. For a Cuban integration of whites and blacks. In *Afrocuba: An anthology of Cuban writing on race, politics and culture*, ed. Pedro Peréz Sarduy and Jean Stubbs, 27–36. Melbourne: Ocean Press.

———. 1995. *Cuban counterpoint: Tobacco and sugar.* Durham, NC: Duke University Press.

Palmié, Stephan. 2002. *Wizards and scientists: Explorations in Afro-Cuban modernity and tradition.* Durham, NC: Duke University Press.

Patterson, Enrique. 1996. Cuba: Discursos sobre la identidad. *Revista Encuentro de la Cultura Cubana* 2:49–67.

Paz Pérez, Carlos. 1994. *Diccionario Cubano de términos populares y vulgares.* Havana: Editorial de Ciencias Sociales.

Pérez Alvarez, Magdalena. 1996. Los prejuicios raciales: Sus mecanismos de reprodución. *Temas* 7:44–50.

Pérez-López, Jorge. 2006. The Cuban economy, 2005–2006: The end of the Special Period? *Annual Meetings of the Association for the Study of the Cuban Economy (ASCE), Miami, Florida, 2006* 15: 1–13.

Pérez-López, Jorge, and Sergio Díaz-Briquets. 2005. Remittances to Cuba: A survey of methods and estimates. *Annual Meeting of the Association for the Study of the Cuban Economy (ASCE), Miami, Florida, 2005* 15: 396–409.

Pérez Sarduy, Pedro. 1998. Interview with Salvador González. http://www.afro cubaweb.com/salvadorgonzalez/salvadgonz.htm (accessed: September 18, 2008).

———. 2001. Callejón de Hamel. http://www.afrocubaweb.com/pedroperezsarduy/perezsarduy2001.htm (accessed: September 18, 2008).

Pérez Sarduy, Pedro, and Jean Stubbs. 1993. Introduction: The rite of social communion. In *Afrocuba: An anthology of Cuban writing on race, politics and culture*, ed. Pedro Pérez Sarduy and Jean Stubbs, 3–26. Melbourne: Ocean Press.

Perry, Marc David. 2004. Los raperos: Rap, race, and social transformation in contemporary Cuba. PhD diss., University of Texas at Austin.

Pertierra, Anna Cristina. 2007. Anthropology that warms your heart: On being a bride in the field. *Anthropology Matters* 9(1):1–14.

Pichardo, Hortensia. 1992. Las esclavas blancas. *Bohemia* 84: 4–8.

Portuondo Zúñiga, Olga. 2001. *La Virgen de la Caridad: Símbolo de Cubanía*. Santiago de Cuba: Editorial de Oriente.

Pred, Allan. 2000. *Even in Sweden: Racisms, racialized spaces, and the popular geographical imagination*. Berkeley: University of California Press.

Provine, William. 1973. Geneticists and the biology of race crossing: Geneticists changed their minds about the biological effects of race crossings. *Science* 182:790–796.

Ramos Cruz, Guillermina. 2000. Grupo Antillano and the marginalization of black artists. In *Afro-Cuban voices: On race and identity in contemporary Cuba*, ed. Pedro Pérez Sarduy and Jean Stubbs, 147–153. Gainesville: University of Florida Press.

Reca Moreira, Inés, Mayda Alvarez Suárez, María del Carmen Caño Secade, Gilda Castilla García, Maritza García Alonso, Orlando García Pino, Consuelo Martín Fernández, Alicia Puñales Sosa, and Maysú Ystokazu Morales. 1990. *Análisis de las investigactiones sobre la familia cubana*. Habana: Editorial de Ciencias Sociales.

Rodríguez Ruiz, Pablo. 1997. Clases y razas en el contexto cubano actual. *Revista de la Universidad Autónoma de Yucatan* 12(203):16–34.

———. 2000. Relaciones interétnicas e interraciales en el barrio Chino de la Habana. *Catauro: Revista Cubana de Antropología* 2(2):103–126.

———. 2004. Raza y estructuras familiares en el escenario residencial popular urbano. Centro de Antropología, 1–33. Unpublished report.

———. 2008. Espacios y contextos del debate racial actual en Cuba. *Temas* 53:86–96.

Rodríguez Ruiz, Pablo, and Claudio Estévez Mezquía. 2006. Familia, uniones matrimoniales y sexualidad en la pobreza y la marginalidad: El llega y pon, un estudio de caso. *Catauro* 8(14):5–31.

Rodríguez Ruiz, Pablo, Ana Julia García Dally, Lourdes Serrano Peralta, Lazara Carrazana Fuentes, Martín Chiong Aboy, and Rebeca Camhi Guillén. 1994. Estructuras y Relaciones Raciales en un Barrio Popular de Ciudad de la Habana, Carraguao. Habana: Centro de Antropología, Academia de Ciencias de Cuba. Unpublished report.

Roland, L. Kaifa. 2004. El color no importa: Tourism and race in contemporary Cuba. PhD diss., Duke University.

———. 2006. Tourism and the negrification of Cuban identity. *Transforming Anthropology* 14(2):151–162.

Rosendahl, Mona. 1997. *Inside the revolution: Everyday life in socialist Cuba*. Ithaca, NY: Cornell University Press.

Rosenthal, Marguerite. 1992. The problems of single motherhood in Cuba. In *Cuba in transition*, ed. S. Halebsky and J. Kirk, 161–175. Boulder, CO: Westview.

Rosete Silva, Hilario. 1993. Nuestra Señora de la Caridad: Madre y patrona de Cuba. *Somos Jóvenes* 126:12–13.

———. 1994. La Memoria es una piedra negra. *El Caiman Barbudo* 27:28.

Rundle, Mette Louise Berg. 2001. Tourism, social change, and *jineterismo* in contemporary Cuba. *Society for Caribbean Studies Annual Conference*, University of Nottingham, UK, 2001. Vol. 2.

Ryer, Paul. 1998. Passing for Cuban, passing for foreign: National papers and classificatory embarrassment in the Special Period. Conference paper. American Anthropological Association Annual Meetings, Washington, DC.

———. 2006. Between La Yuma and África: Locating the color of contemporary Cuba. PhD diss., University of Chicago.

Safa, Helen. 1995. *The myth of the male breadwinner: Women and Industrialization in the Caribbean*. Boulder, CO: Westview.

———. 2005. The matrifocal family and patriarchal ideology in Cuba and the Caribbean. *Journal of Latin American Anthropology* 10(2):314–337.

———. 2009. Hierarchies and household change in postrevolutionary Cuba. *Latin American Perspectives* 36(1):42–52.

Sanjek, Roger. 1971. Brazilian racial terms: Some aspects of meaning and learning. *American Anthropologist* 73:1126–1144.

Santiago, Roberto. 1990. Unlike Utopia: Racial realities in Cuba. *Emerge* 1(10):56.

Santiesteban, Argelio. 1985. *El habla popular Cubana de hoy*. Habana: Editorial de Ciencias Sociales.

Sawyer, Mark Q. 2006. *Racial politics in post-revolutionary Cuba*. New York: Cambridge University Press.

Scheper-Hughes, Nancy. 1979. *Saints, scholars, and schizophrenics*. Berkeley: University of California Press.

———. 1993. AIDS, public health, and human rights in Cuba. *Lancet* 342:965–967.

Schwartz, Rosalie. 1997. *Pleasure island: Tourism and temptation in Cuba*. Lincoln: University of Nebraska Press.

———. 1998. Cuba's roaring twenties: Race consciousness and the column "Ideales de una Raza." In *Between race and empire: African-Americans and Cubans before the Cuban Revolution*, ed. L. Brock and D. Castañeda Fuertes, 104–119. Philadelphia: Temple University Press.

Serrano Peralta, Lourdes. 1998. Mujer, instrucción, ocupación, y color de la piel: Estructura y relaciones raciales en un barrio popular de la Habana." *América Negra* 15:119–136.

Serviat, Pedro. 1986. *El problema Negro en Cuba y su solución definitiva*. Havana: Editora Política.

———. 1993. Solutions to the black problem. In *Afrocuba: An anthology of Cuban writing on race, politics and culture*, ed. Pedro Pérez Sarduy and Jean Stubbs, 77–90. Melbourne: Ocean Press.

Settle, Heather. 2008. Revolutionary end-times in a post-Castro age. Conference paper. American Anthropological Association Annual Meeting, San Francisco, CA.

Sheriff, Robin E. 2000. Exposing silence as cultural censorship: A Brazilian case. *American Anthropologist* 102(1):114–132.

———. 2001. *Dreaming equality: Color, race, and racism in urban Brazil*. New Brunswick, NJ: Rutgers University Press.

Simpson, Amalia. 1993. *Xuxa: The mega-marketing of gender, race, and modernity*. Philadelphia: Temple University Press.

Skidmore, Thomas. 1990. Racial ideas and social policy in Brazil, 1870–1940. In *The idea of race in Latin America, 1870–1940*, ed. R. Graham, 7–36. Austin: University of Texas Press.

Smart, Ian Isadore. 1990. *Nicolás Guillén: Popular poet of the Caribbean*. Columbia: University of Missouri Press.

Stallybrass, Peter, and Allon White. 1986. *The politics and poetics of transgression*. Ithaca, NY: Cornell University Press.

Stoler, Ann Laura. 1995. *Race and the education of desire: Foucault's "History of sexuality" and the colonial order of things*. Durham, NC: Duke University Press.

Stonequist, Everett. 1937. *The marginal man: A study in personality and culture conflict*. New York: Charles Scribner's Sons.

Sutherland, Elizabeth. 1969. *The youngest revolution*. New York: Dial Press.

Taylor, Frank. 1988. Revolution, race, and some aspects of foreign relations in Cuba since 1959. *Cuban Studies* 18:19–44.

Telles, Edward E. 2004. *Race in another America: The significance of skin color in Brazil*. Princeton, NJ: Princeton University Press.

Twine, France W. 1998. *Racism in a racial democracy: The maintenance of white supremacy in Brazil*. New Brunswick, NJ: Rutgers University Press.

Verdery, Katherine. 1996. *What was socialism and what comes next?* Princeton, NJ: Princeton University Press.

Wacquant, Loic. 1993. Urban outcasts: Stigma and division in the black American ghettos and the French urban periphery. *International Journal of Urban and Regional Research* 17:366–383.

Wade, Peter. 1993. *Blackness and race mixture: The dynamics of racial identity in Columbia*. Baltimore: The Johns Hopkins University Press.

———. 1997. *Race and Ethnicity in Latin America*. London: Pluto Press.

Whitten, Norman, and Arlene Torres. 1998. *Blackness in Latin America and the Caribbean: Social dynamics and cultural transformations*. Bloomington: Indiana University Press.

Williams, Brackette. 1989. A class act: Anthropology and the race to nation across ethnic terrain. *Annual Review of Anthropology* 18:401–444.

Willis, Paul. 1981. *Learning to labor: How working class kids get working class jobs*. New York: Columbia University Press.

Wolf, Eric. 1958. The Virgin of Guadalupe: A Mexican national symbol. *Journal of American Folklore* 71:34–39.

Wolfe, Lisa Reynolds. 2000. Contesting the global: Restoration and neighborhood identity in Old Havana. Conference paper. Latin American Studies Association Conference, Miami, Florida.

Wright, Irene Alice. 1928. Nuestra Señora de la Caridad del Cobre, Nuestra Señora de la Caridad de Illescas. *Archivos del Folklore Cubano* 3(1):5–15.

———. 2002. Cuban home life, 1910. In *Travelers' tales of old Cuba*, ed. John Jenkins. Melbourne: Ocean Press.

Wright, Winthrop. 1990. *Café con leche: Race, class, and national image in Venezuela*. Austin: University of Texas Press.

Yáñez, Mirta. 1989. We blacks all drink coffee. In *Her true-true name*, ed. P. Mordecai and B. Wilson, 37–43. Oxford: Heinemann International.

INDEX

ABOUT THE AUTHOR

NADINE T. FERNANDEZ is a cultural anthropologist and an associate professor at SUNY/Empire State College in Syracuse, New York. Her research and writing focus on race and gender relations and tourism in contemporary Cuba.